Coloni
the making o

MANCHESTER

To the memory
of my father

Colonial India and the making of empire cinema

Image, ideology and identity

Prem Chowdhry

Manchester University Press

Manchester and New York
distributed exclusively in the USA by St. Martin's Press

Published by Manchester University Press
Oxford Road, Manchester M13 9NR, UK
and Room 400, 175 Fifth Avenue, New York, NY 10010, USA
http://www.man.ac.uk/mup

Distributed exclusively in the USA by
St. Martin's Press, Inc., 175 Fifth Avenue, New York,
NY 10010, USA

Distributed exclusively in Canada by
UBC Press, University of British Columbia, 6344 Memorial Road,
Vancouver, BC, Canada V6T 1Z2

British Library Cataloguing-in-Publication Data
A catalogue record for this book is available from the British Library

Library of Congress Cataloging-in-Publication Data applied for

ISBN 0 7190 5725 6 *hardback*
     0 7190 5792 2 *paperback*

First published 2000

06 05 04 03 02 01 00   10 9 8 7 6 5 4 3 2

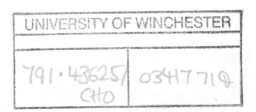
Typeset in Sabon with Gill Sans,
by Action Publishing Technology Ltd, Gloucester
Printed in Great Britain
by Bookcraft (Bath) Ltd, Midsomer Norton

Contents

Acknowledgements

This work is the result of an unexpected beginning: while collecting archival material for a monograph on gender studies I came across a freak reference regarding the outbreak of a riot in Bombay in 1938 in the wake of the screening of a British film. What began as a tentative exploration, borne out of intellectual curiosity, has evolved into a full length study. Many institutions have supported this project and I am grateful to them all: the British Council and the Charles Wallace Trust for the offer of a short-term fellowship; the University Grants Commission, New Delhi, whose travelling grant enabled me to collect very valuable source material housed in London at the India Office Library and Records and the British Film Institute; the faculty and staff of the Film and Television Institute of India, and the National Film Archives of India, Pune, for extensive discussions and for locating source material; the staff of the Maharashtra State Archives, Mumbai; the National Archives of India, New Delhi; and the director and staff of the Nehru Memorial Museum and Library, New Delhi, for providing me with space and unlimited freedom to pursue my line of interest and inquiry.

This work has gone through various stages. At each stage friends and fellow scholars have stepped in to discuss, criticise, substantiate and, above all, to encourage my second foray into what is essentially an interdisciplinary work. Special thanks to Ranjani Majumadar for providing me with indispensable reference material from her vast collection; to Ravi Vasudevan for discussions, clarifications and suggestions regarding reference material; to Biswamoy Patti for reading through and commenting upon my first draft; to Sudesh Vaid and Amit Kumar Gupta for reading parts of the same; and to Patricia Uberoi and Radhika Singha for responding to and giving extended critical comments on the entire manuscript and a refreshing new way to look at the arguments.

I wish to extend special thanks to two of my friends, Uma Chakravarti and Ramya Sreenivasan, for their extremely generous and enthusiastic involvement with my work. Uma has been closely associated with this project from inception to fruition, reading various drafts, and often lifting my sagging spirits through provocative and challenging queries and astute and perceptive comments and criticism. Ramya stepped in during the final stages. Her intervention at a crucial stage of this project has contributed immensely to a greater clarity and sharpening of my arguments and in highlighting their finer nuances. I also express my gratitude to Lola Chatterjee for an incisive editing of the text. However, I alone remain responsible for any errors in the work.

I dedicate this work to my late father. A noted political scientist, he was a purist in academic discipline. I would like to think that his unarticulated scepticism regarding the validity of a study of cinema, especially in the hands of a social historian, would have been laid to rest. He certainly would have enjoyed being proved wrong. I shall miss his laughter and pleasurable affirmation of this.

List of illustrations

Stills from British Film Institute. Every effort has been made to trace the copyright owners of these illustrations; any person claiming copyright should contact the publisher.

List of abbreviations

AICC	All India Congress Committee
BBFC	British Board of Film Censors
BFI	British Film Institute, London
CLAD	Central Legislative Assembly Debates, New Delhi
FTII	Film and Television Institute of India, Pune
ICC	Indian Cinematograph Committee
IOR	India Office Records, London
NAI	National Archives of India, New Delhi
NFAI	National Film Archives of India, Pune
NMML	Nehru Memorial Museum and Library, New Delhi
NWFP	North-West Frontier Province
MSA	Maharashtra State Archives, Mumbai
P&J Dept	Public and Judicial Department

1

Introduction

Despite the presence of hybridity in what are theoretically considered by orientalists to be homogeneous sets, the binary opposition colonial self/colonised Other is encoded in colonialist discourse[1] as a dichotomy necessary to domination. Hence the contrasting images of the racially superior white, masculinised British imperialist and its Other, the racially inferior, dark, subjugated, emasculated Indian found expression in its various disciplines, institutions and cultural practices.[2] This image emanated within disciplinary formations through the publications of histories and gazetteers, for example, and from institutions such as the colonial armed forces. Its most potent visual manifestation in the cultural domain came through the so-called 'empire cinema'. Empire cinema is a term now accepted for both the British as well as Hollywood cinema made mainly during the 1930s and 1940s, which projected a certain vision of the empire in relation to its subjects. Britain and Hollywood shared a common viewpoint and the acceptance of certain ideological concerns and images in keeping with this imperial vision. The latter emphasised the unique imperial status, cultural and racial superiority and patriotic pride not only of the British but of the entire white western world. Such a vision typified imperial perceptions not only in the nineteenth century (as argued by John Mackenzie and others),[3] for such core assumptions about British empire were common to the entire colonial period.

A great deal of work has already been done on what went into the making of this vision and how it was aggressively propagated in England from 1880 onwards through exhibitions, parades, music hall entertainment, advertising, postcards, popular literature and school books, as well as the cinema.[4] Out of all these popular cultural manifestations, it was cinema which emerged by the 1930s as the most influential propaganda vehicle. The ideological and political forces and the cultural roots of this vision in Britain have been well researched. It has been suggested that the empire cinema was successful, first, in encouraging British audiences, especially the working class and the unemployed, to identify with the empire and feel patriotic pride in its achievements, and, second, in diverting their attention from the class contradictions of their own society in order to validate the repressive machinery of law and order which was maintaining the status quo in Britain and its colonies.

A series of such empire films were made in the 1930s with India as their central theme. These films reached the height of their popularity during the decade 1929–39. Those rated among the fifteen top grossing films during the year of their release included *The Lives of a Bengal Lancer* (1935), *The Charge of the Light Brigade* (1936), *Wee Willie Winkie* (1937), *The Drum* (1938), and *Gunga Din* (1939). With the exception of *The Drum*, which was made in England, these films were Hollywood productions. They shared certain common features: the defence of India as the pivot on which the plot revolved; the North-West Frontier Province (NWFP) as location; the late nineteenth century (again, with the exception of *The Drum*) as the historical period of reference and, as the motivation behind military confrontation, the unbridled ambition of some tribal chief instigated, trained and supplied with modern fighting weapons by outsiders like the Afghans, Russians or Germans. These films paid a rousing tribute to the British Indian army and their message was that the British were in the colonies for the protection of the native inhabitants.

The present study is an empirico-historical inquiry into the empire cinema. I approach this problem as a social historian and attempt to equate the on-screen narrative with wider social and historical forces. This establishes the crucial interconnection of colonial politics and popular culture, not only as it shaped mass opinion in the imperial centre, but also in its quite different impact on the popular consciousness of the colonised.

Awareness of the historical importance of the vast moving picture material has been rapidly growing in the west since the 1960s. Historians now realise that cinema provides a very important addition to the range of sources available for the study of the twentieth century. In India, a few recent works have utilised Indian cinema as an important source of history.[5] However, no work has so far utilised the British and American films set in India in the colonial period in a similar way. Although empire cinema has been subjected to academic scrutiny by scholars outside India, such studies have located the films almost wholly within the colonising country rather than exploring their reception among the colonised. By shifting the emphasis to the historical reception of imperial popular culture among the colonised, this work seeks to fill out a certain terrain between the current Indian writing on national cinema and non-Indian writing on empire cinema.

Films, as popular culture, need to be considered as one of the repositories of twentieth-century consciousness in that they reflect and articulate, as well as shape, much of the awareness of the men and women who form that consciousness. Films are both part of and reflect their historical contexts. Cinema therefore needs to be recognised as a valid historical archive for the writing of political, social and cultural history, in addition to being a primary object of study in its own right.

By focusing on empire films as a site for understanding the social history of colonial India, I do not confine my analysis simply to the cinema itself, but use it to get at the variegated nuclei of colonial power in India. I also suggest a different way of envisioning colonial enterprise and gaining fresh insight into the voiced and unvoiced apprehensions of the British regarding India during the turbulent 1930s and 1940s. This work points to a way both of reading history on the screen as well as reading screen projections in their historical context. The study also seeks to offer fresh insights in the field of cultural and film studies from a different and multi-focal perspective. It endeavours to understand how the empire films constructed the colonial world, their reasons for doing so, and what that construction meant to the colonised people. As such, the focus of my study is at the level of the production of culture as well as its consumption.

Such an analysis goes beyond the text to suggest new insights into the socio-political pressures that underlay cinematic production specially during the interwar period, which coincided not only with greatly heightened nationalist activity in India – when the British prestige and legitimacy had reached its lowest ebb and they were forced to make substantial political concessions – but also with the aftermath of the depression, the build-up to the next world war, the rise of fascism and the outbreak of World War II. It attempts to explore the diverse processes of manipulation and control that went into the cinema acquiring and transmuting certain images and ideologies, in relation to its vast and varied consumers, both white/western and coloured/colonised. It also analyses the historical context in which these films were consumed and meanings produced.

This work argues that, as constructs within and appropriating a dominant colonial discourse, empire films were imaginatively reconstructing political practice, colonial knowledge and subjectivities.[6] Colonial discourse had itself gone through a series of shifts accommodating itself to different stages in imperialist expansion and administration. First, there was the period of individual exploitation of a mercantile agency under the East India Company and an aggressive expansive phase; second, a phase of governing institution in the late eighteenth century; third, a period of pax-Britannia consolidation; and, finally, the nationalist phase, itself divided into a series of multilayered phases, indicating a shift in power equations between the colonisers and the colonised. Such shifts offered the colonised a space in which to operate in opposition to the imperialist-capitalist interests. The construction of colonial knowledge consequently went through different historical phases and was shaped as much by the rapidly transforming colonial realities as by political and intellectual discourse, or, indeed, by historical events in Europe. In their prolonged and severely contested rule, the British devised a system of knowledge about India and themselves intended to justify and legitimise their rule over India. And yet, as Thomas R. Metcalf points out, 'at no time was the British vision of India ever informed by a single coherent set of ideas. To the contrary, the ideals sustaining the imperial enterprise in India were always shot through with contradiction and inconsistency.'[7]

The empire films emerge as a mediation on this complex socioideological formation, comprising multifarious and multivalent elements. Like other literary and cultural texts, the empire films reveal the contradictions of the social formation in which they were located and produced. Governed by several inhibiting factors, these films also accommodate sentiments important to the audience in colonial India, which did not necessarily subscribe to the dominant ideology of imperialism. Such a contradiction highlights what Tytti Soila, in her study of Swedish cinema, has described as the need for the dominant ideology to argue against other competing ideologies in order to legitimise itself.[8]

The nature of representation in the empire films highlights the contradiction between colonial ideology and cinematic practice, articulating as it does a conflict between the ideological effects of cinema and the economic pressure exercised by the market. As an ideological apparatus cinema, especially as compared to other forms of cultural production, has to realise its position as a large-scale commercial enterprise within a capitalistic system where market forces are paramount. Because of its prohibitive costs, film production and its ideological thrust need to negotiate with the economics and ideologies of the market. Clearly, in relation to the empire cinema, the needs of imperialism and capitalism did not necessarily collide, but they did not necessarily work harmoniously either. This work argues that the market reception, even under a colonial set-up with its well-defined structures of domination and subordination, created the possibility of accommodating a subversive even oppositional point of view as well as the ability to reshape the dominant ideological thrust of the visual production.

Colonial India and the making of empire cinema investigates the colonial market's reaction against certain ideological formations and its impact on production processes as well as British policy formation in relation to empire films. Such an investigation highlights the shifts within empire ideology as it responded to the needs of the empire at different historical periods.[9]

It is now accepted that the high-adventure genre films of empire demonstrated the moral, social and physical domination of the colonised by the colonisers. In the opinion of Ella Shohat and Robert Stam, 'The imperial thrust of many of these films, requires no subtle deciphering.'[10] The present work argues that such films, produced in the period between the wars, went beyond merely reiterating Rudyard Kipling's 'white man's burden', which was composed of concepts of duty, destiny and self-sacrifice. The ingenuous portrayal of the 'Great Game' in empire films can be seen to encompass a complex weave of ideologies. The coherence of the explicit message of colonialism, imperialism and racism in these films is buttressed by their depiction of ideological structures of communalism, casteism and gender. Their aim is to demolish the nationalist rhetoric of one India and unity in diversity, to emphasise instead its heterogeneity and disparity. They also strive to indicate potential social and political disruptions in India, which can be controlled only by the British presence.

However, it was the representation of precisely these latter tensions in the empire films that proved contestable, evoking protest and agitation. Significantly, these protests themselves point to a crisis of the values and ideologies that provide the context for the cinematic texts. The implications of such projections screened in the India of the 1930s, with its highly active nationalist consciousness, were not lost on the Indian audience. In fact, their readings surpassed the overt and covert intent of the films enough to provoke a political reaction, questioning the very ethics of imperialism, and challenging its justification. The moral and ideological opposition of such a varied audience – composed of diverse class, caste and community identities – to these projections assumed the form of direct political intervention, with telling effects upon the politics and cultural policy of both nationalists and colonial masters.

In this context, I take up for detailed discussion three significant films which were released in India in the successive years 1938, 1939 and 1940. Their release coincided with a special historical moment: the implementation of far-reaching political and administrative changes under the government of India act of 1935. The act created for the first time a legally accepted public space for democratic participation and protest. As the political climate altered so did the reaction of the audience. Consequently, the impact of the empire cinema, which was not noticed earlier, could now be sharply registered. The realisation that something vital was at stake consequently demanded and elicited equally sharp responses from both nationalists and the British government with far-reaching consequences. Thus, an analysis of the films released during these crucial years has special significance. It brings emerging oppositions to the fore: between imperialism and the nationalist agenda; within imperialism; and within nationalism. Centring around issues of culture, identity and self-representation the reaction to the empire cinema became fraught with the social and political tensions of the immediate historical moment of reception.

The first film, *The Drum* (1938), proved catalytic in the Indian colonial situation in more than one way. Confronted with prolonged agitation, screening of the film had to be banned. The popular reaction to this film was to influence the reception of the other films as well. *Gunga Din*, which followed in 1939, was banned before it could be screened. Made to a formula which had produced blockbusters, these two films were not particularly different from other films which had preceded them. Yet, none of the earlier films had provoked such strong reactions. The present work links the reception of *The Drum* and *Gunga Din* to specific aspects of their intended message, to their delineation of characters and recall of historical events, and to the parallels they drew with the contemporary situation.

The cognition of messages conveyed by the medium of film does not depend on the reception of any single film alone, but on the cumulative effect of regular exposure to certain stereotypes and viewpoints. This analysis demonstrates how a different set of meanings was ignited by the changing colonial situation – a significant point that has not merited attention so far. My attempt to historicise and contextualise the empire films in relation to colonised Indians helps reconceive the process of meaning production by underscoring the impact historical context has not only on production but on reception as well.

The third empire film, *The Rains Came* (1940), which attempted to reconcile some of these contradictory political and cultural pressures and contradictions, involved complex ideological negotiations. This resulted in a reframing of the colonial discourse to introduce images that were both recognisably familiar and yet innovative. Emphasising 'native' collusion rather than resistance, this film sought to mediate to a subject population firmly committed to achieving national independence an alternative imperial vision and conception of the colonial world based on modern western developmental ideals. This film sought to project princely India as a counterfoil to the rising demands for democracy in a bid to consolidate conservative opinion. At the heart of this politico-cultural negotiation lay a representation of gender, which seemingly undermined fixed categories of identity and highlighted the ambivalence that both coloniser and colonised felt towards themselves and each other. Questioning the earlier representations of difference as 'fixed', the popular stereotypical images of both now underwent a dynamic reinvention as well as renewal.

The Rains Came dramatically altered certain stereotypes while retaining and reinforcing others to suit the colonists' changed purpose. The empire films' contradictory mode of address could now be seen on the screen articulated as an ambivalently positioned colonial presence, which emerged as a site of competing voices and contradiction. For the colonisers, 'the strength of white representation', unlike that of black, already lay, as Richard Dyer suggests, 'in the apparent absence altogether of the typical, the sense that being white is coterminous with the endless plenitude of human diversity.'[11] This potential diversity was now expressly useful in reframing the hitherto projected white image. For example, the substitution of the white female in place of the white male as the imperial protagonist had a range of ideological consequences, such as adding to the essence of 'whiteness'. The emphasis on the non-threatening white woman and therefore feminine nature of imperialism opened up possibilities for negotiating a different agenda within the colonial setting.

My detailed analysis of these three films highlights the nuances of the contemporary context as they affected the production of these films. Questions of contemporaneity verge on those of realism and authenticity and become relevant especially in cases where there are real life prototypes for characters (as in *Gunga Din*) and situations (as in *The Drum*), and where the film implicitly makes and is received as making historical-realist claims. Film adaptations of popular novels and poems by authors well-reputed for their knowledge of India, heightened the feeling that these representations were 'reliable'.

Moreover, these cinematic representations brought forth real life assumptions not only about space and time but also about social and political relationships. Historical incidents and personalities took shape and contour through the medium of what was being thought and felt at the time and were interpreted on such grounds. Admittedly questions of such interpretation are complex. Yet, as Janet Staiger points out, it is not the 'correct reading' of films that is important, but the range of possible readings and reading processes at historical moments and their relation, or lack of relation, to groups of historical spectators that is important.[12] Such questions arise out of the crucial connection forged by Indian audiences between these films and their socio-political location and experience. A self-identified, self-conscious community now recovered possible subversive readings already embedded in these films, or constructed alternative readings afresh.

This emphasis on questions of the contemporaneity of reception and its impact upon subsequent productions has so far not been investigated by film and social historians. This in-depth analysis uncovers in the empire films, set in the late Victorian period, their contemporary relevance in the eyes of both imperial and Indian audiences of the 1930s and 1940s.

The study highlights the difference between cultural space, which legitimised the projection of these films in Britain and the western world, and the cultural space of India and its empire market, where the films met with resistance that invalidated their message. Because this vast cinema market was not merely white but also a coloured one, the empire films were now caught in the basic contradictions and limitations of exploiting two hetero-geneous and opposed markets for a single product. The colonial market with its vast audiences who played a crucial role in rela-tion to the cinema, empire as well as indigenous, has not merited any critical attention so far. All work on the empire films to date has operated without significant reference to these aspects and the film text with its prioritised status has remained abstracted from the colonial context of its consumption. This work establishes the live, volatile relationship between Indian audiences (with varied identities, as active consumers and receivers of the cinematic enterprise) and empire films – through an exploration of the ways in which cinematic and other discourses were being negotiated for meaning.

Situating audiences in colonial India

The historical and national location of the audiences – white/western and coloured/colonised – is significant in understanding the construction of widely differing meanings for these films. Both social science[13] and cultural studies[14] have amply demon-strated the ability of readers and spectators to bring their different histories and subjectivities to construct varied realisations of cultural texts. In fact, it has been proved that the visual media (both television and cinema) need not necessarily be consumed hegemonically; they can be consumed oppositionally as well.

In analysing how the empire films evoked Indian colonial reactions I have found the encoding/decoding model developed by Stuart Hall useful.[15] Out of the three political responses to a media message suggested by this model – dominant, negotiated or oppositional – it is the last stance which explains Indian audiences' drastic reaction to the empire films in the 1930s. An oppositional response to a cultural product is one in which the recipient of the text (film) understands that the system that produced it is one with which she or he is fundamentally at odds.[16] The oppositional stance of Indian audiences allowed them to receive messages other than those the film-makers intended. This alternative reading, dependent upon the viewer's privileging of certain images, scenes and messages, becomes crucial in explaining how the empire films ended up mobilising Indian audiences to interrogate the political and cultural identities ascribed to them.

The Indian spectators therefore inhabited a realm of ramifying differences and contradictions. The popularity in India of empire cinema, especially the adventure genre, suggests a variety of spectatorial responses stretching from acceptance to resistance. In a direct parallel to this differentiated consumption of the empire films and their dominant imperialist ideological thrust, recent research indicates how US western genre films have been constructed by Australian aboriginal children, Native Americans and American blacks in a way that enabled them to find in the genre some articulation of their own subordination to white imperialism, and presumably to identify with instances of resistance to it. Such a reading position affected the sense these readers ascribed to the inevitability of the final narrative defeat of the Native Americans or non-whites. It was their ability to impose a non-white meaning on and find non-white pleasures in a genre of white imperialism that made it popular with them.[17]

For a variety of Indian spectators the dynamics of their situation as the recipients/consumers of the empire cinema as well as the objects of its portrayal, provided a fertile context that gave these films special meaning. The interconnection made for what

Manthia Diawara has called 'resisting spectatorship'.[18] Writing about African-American spectators in relation to the representation of blacks in Hollywood films, Diawara suggests that black spectators circumvent identification and resist the persuasive elements of Hollywood narrative and spectacle because of the components of 'difference' among the cinematic tropes of race, gender and sexuality which give rise to different readings of the same material.

In India, this work argues, the audience similarly occupied an active spectatorial position and emerged as 'meaning producers' who derived their own socially pertinent meanings from the films. In fact, the empire films emerged as serving the contradictory interests of both the producers-cum-western audience, on the one hand, and the Indian audience, on the other, by stimulating their feelings for and identification with the 'nation'. In a very crucial way the ideological thrust of imperialism demanded by the former was reversed by the latter to produce oppositional meaning. As perception itself is embedded in history, the same cinematic images and voices provoked different resonances for western and Indian audiences. The projected image clashed directly with the changing perceptions, aspirations and self-image of Indians resulting in the latter's severe criticism and rejection of western paradigms of knowledge of themselves, their race, character, history, tradition and society. They challenged the British appropriation of India's cultural space and demanded a change by exercising pressure on distributors and exhibitors, ultimately affecting subsequent productions.

The varied Indian audiences, as this work investigates, drew upon their own highly developed cultural codes and practices. Despite the colonial government's restrictions on these, in the form of censorship of print and entertainment media[19] and strict limitations on the expression of nationalist and anti-British sentiments, political messages were conveyed through covert strategies. The incipient Indian cinema, both of the silent era (1913–31) and the talkies (from 1931 onwards), was similarly articulating the growing national aspirations in a variety of ways. At a time when other national cinemas succumbed to the domination of the Hollywood film, the Indian cinema, through formal and cinematic features, constituted something like a 'nation space' against the dominant norms of Hollywood.[20] Dhundiraj

Govind Phalke (Dadasaheb Phalke), considered the pioneer of Indian cinema, conceived of film-making as a nationalist enterprise in line with the call of *swadeshi* (indigenous enterprise).[21] His initiation of the mythological genre in popular cinema was quickly followed by the emergence of several new genres. These included the costume film or the 'historical', the spectacular stunt-action dominated films, the 'devotional' film about the relationship between deity and devotee, and finally the 'social' film with its accent on social problems. By the late 1930s, Indian films had emerged as big business. Significant finance began to be invested in films and a well-consolidated, lucrative film studio system emerged, producing and marketing films on a regular basis.

This brings the Indian audience centre stage as active recipients of cinema, both the empire as well as their own; a process which has not so far received due attention from film and social historians.[22] Recent works have argued for the need to investigate the historical reception of films, in order to arrive at a fuller understanding of this phenomenon and its impact.[23] The present work engages with the historical spectatorship of empire films in the late 1930s. This analysis, however, cannot be based on empirical evidence comparable to the rich ethnographic material used by Jackie Stacey, who draws upon letters and questionnaires from over 300 zealous cinema-goers, for constructing the British female spectators of Hollywood films in the 1940s and 1950s.[24] Such source material is difficult to locate for colonial India. There is also no statistical data about cinema attendance during this period, as available for Britain, where cinema-going was recognised as a major form of leisure activity and came to be fully documented.[25]

Methodologically, I have taken recourse to archival material, where possible, making use of police commissioners' reports, Legislative Assembly and House of Commons debates and official confidential records, including observations of private and public individuals, both imperial and colonial, on the one hand, and the secret assessments and manipulations, both official and non-official, extending from British administrators in India to the highest policy-makers at the level of secretary of state for India and the viceroy, on the other. I have also used accounts of a large number of national inquiries, congresses and commissions, held on empire cinema; the major resolutions of the Motion Picture Association and the reactions of certain leading Indians to the cinematographic debates going on in this period; articles, news items, film reviews, critics' reactions, national daily newspapers of both Britain and colonial India, trade magazines and journals, popular articulations through letters to film journals, film propaganda and posters. This vast and varied material has been culled to analyse and understand the empire films and to reconstruct the multilayered responses of historically situated Indian spectators, whose class and community composition had a crucial bearing on those responses.

As a necessary prelude to the three chapters that follow, I seek to identify here the nature and level of participation of the Indian audiences with the empire cinema. The reconstruction of audience involvement, as well as the manifestation of their response, will be analysed through their regional, class and community identities in relation to the film *The Drum*, which evoked the most sustained and inflammable reaction.

The Indian audience for cinema was a rapidly growing one. The changing exhibition patterns and marketing strategies of the film exhibitors had resulted in extending cinema beyond its initial establishment as a European form of entertainment, to catering to different segments of Indian society from the first decades of this century onwards.[26] In 1931, the introduction of sound to Indian films revolutionised the audiences' reactions to the western as well as Indian films. Indeed, sound would have a detrimental impact on the popularity of western films among Indian audiences; although no figures are available of the respective popularity of western and Indian films among this audience, a possible indicator is the fact that western films were shown in fewer theatres, located in upper-class areas. For example, out of forty theatres in Bombay, only two were screening western films on a regular basis. This meant that despite the growing Indian audience for cinema, there was a much smaller audience for western films, which was primarily elite and urban.

This limited viewership did not apply, however, to western adventure films where language was hardly a deterrent, since these films depended more on spectacular action than on dialogue. This special emphasis enabled an almost unlimited viewership for this genre.[27] Films like *The Adventures of Robin*

Hood, Tarzan, Tarzan and his Mate, King Kong, Ape Man, among others of this kind, were thus enormously successful. These were films which were thematically defined by Hollywood film-makers as 'world audience films'. The Indian Cinematograph Committee noted in 1927–28 that:

> There is no prejudice against western films, which are much enjoyed and appreciated. There are certain types of western films which appeal to all classes and communities. The spectacular super-films [*sic*] and the films featuring Douglas Fairbanks, Harold Lloyd and Charlie Chaplin, have a universal appeal. A film in which any of these world-famous figures of the screen appears can be sure of an enthusiastic reception in any cinema in India. The most popular film ever shown in India was the *Thief of Baghdad*, with Douglas Fairbanks in an Oriental setting.
>
> The taste of the westernised Indian or the Indian who has some knowledge of English and acquaintance with western ideas is akin to that of the Europeans and generally the same film whether social dramas, comedies or whatever they may be, which are popular in the west are appreciated by this section of the community. The bulk of the population however, which is insufficiently acquainted with the English language and with western ideas, enjoys films with plenty of action, especially comic and adventure films, but finds no attraction in the social dramas. This is natural enough; being unable to read the captions, which are almost always in English, they derive their entertainment from watching the 'stunts', comic or adventurous. If there is plenty of action they can follow the sequences of events, and they are very quick at grasping the significance of the scenes and picking up the story. The heavy applause which is heard from the cheap seats when the hero administers summary justice to the villain or rescues the heroine in the nick of time shows a proper appreciation of the events and is seldom at fault.[28]

Films featuring Indian characters, like *The Jungle Book*, were immensely popular, and others, such as *The Lives of a Bengal Lancer, The Drum* and *Gunga Din*, which gave prominence to Indian actors (like Sabu for instance),[29] were expected to arouse a large degree of interest in the Indian market. These films were all high-adventure films with Indian locales and characters and were calculated to create spontaneous audience association with the characters and situations portrayed. They *did* attract a vast Indian audience. Performing as well at the box office as the films produced in India, they also aroused a great deal of resentment in the Indian film industry.[30]

More than half of the total feature films screened in India in 1935 were foreign films. According to an estimate of the Indian film industry the annual remittances of foreign distributors to the UK and USA were Rs 55 lakh.[31] The detailed figures available for some of the films indicate the money collections of foreign distributors from India, after deducting the exhibitors' share: Rs 2 lakh for the film *Trader Horn* in its five years of screening; Rs 2 lakh for *King Kong* in its four years of screening; Rs 1 lakh for *Robin Hood* within a year; Rs 2 lakh for *Snow White and the Seven Dwarfs* within a year; Rs 1 lakh for *Victoria* within a year and a half. Significantly these were not even the most popular films.[32]

Such films were also taken to small suburban theatres, even to those that usually exclusively showed Indian films. As the demand for films was greater than their supply and the exhibitors could not always obtain Indian films, which commanded a relatively higher price, they had to settle for foreign films. This resulted in overlapping audiences of different classes for the two categories of films, western and Indian.[33] This was recognised by *The Hindu*, which, in 1941, aptly observed: 'talkies audience knows no language barriers'.[34]

The Indian audience for cinema, especially in the 1930s, was extending over more and more classes of people.[35] By 1939, there were 1265 permanent cinemas in India and 500 touring ones.[36] Apart from these there were numerous 'seasonal' cinema houses, mostly in hill stations, which were open only for a part of the year, privately owned regimental cinemas and numerous halls, which were occasionally used for film screenings. It is difficult to estimate how many of these have been excluded from the official figures of cinema houses. The travelling cinemas went into the interior of the rural areas as film exhibitors moved from village to village for one night stands.[37] As the supply of Indian films was not equal to the demand and those available charged exorbitant rates, the travelling cinemas tended to exhibit old, second-hand western films which could be purchased very cheaply. So much so that the effects of the European and US films in the villages of India was of great concern to the British colonial authorities who not infrequently refused to issue licences to the travelling cinema, unless they undertook to show only 'Indian religious dramas'.[38] The fact that the mythological and the devotional genre lent itself easily to nationalist reading was lost on British officials. Despite restrictions the alleged 'nuisance' of the western films continued to spread fast. Even broken down touring talkies with an impoverished screen in a tent made up of 'two dirty bed sheets sewn together' were giving open air shows in places like Panipat, which attracted the nearby rural youth due to their extremely low rates of admission.[39]

The oral and written evidence from different provinces also emphasises that the 'poor classes' occupied the lower cheap seats.[40] These included not only urban workers but also 'rustic villagers' of different hues, when and where they had access. Such imported films were periodically shown to the native labourers in the Assam plantations. One plantation owner testified to the great demand for western films among his labourers in his tea garden.[41] For the urban lower classes it was observed: 'For want of amusement elsewhere, the labourers frequent cinema expending a portion of their income. A labourer may not have cooked rice to eat after his return from the cinema, but his love for films has been found to be always on the increase.'[42]

Another large and important segment of the cinema audience for western high-adventure, spectacular-action films was provided by serving Indian armymen. John Masters, who was with the British Indian army from 1934 until the transfer of power, and joined the Gurkha regiment as a subaltern posted in the NWFP, spoke of a cinema theatre within a mile of the British regiments patronised by the soldiers.[43] Indeed, the cantonment areas provided popular location bases for the cinema houses. For the armed forces, with few avenues of entertainment, cinema had proved a boon and had come to be well-patronised, especially as the soldiers were offered discount rates. This was vouched for by M. D. Puri, the proprietor of the Gaiety theatre in Lahore, who had pioneered cinema exhibition in Punjab and the NWFP and had cinemas in cantonment areas.[44]

The viewership of cinema among army personnel grew and the cinema emerged as the major form of entertainment for troops during World War II. This also meant that the large number of rural Punjabi men who contributed so substantially to the war recruitment, also formed part of the audience for the cinema throughout.[45] Khan Bahadur Nawab Muzzafar Khan, director of the information bureau in Punjab, also observed that he had noticed the villagers of Lahore suburbs visiting the cinema.[46] Similarly, the oral evidence of H. W. Hogg, secretary of the boy scouts association in Punjab, dated 25 November 1927, also told of how the 'rustic villagers' who came to Lahore to 'have a good time', generally spent their evening hours in the 'cheap cinema theatres'.[47]

Lahore under the British had emerged as the centre of educational, cultural, social and political activity, and as the country's best cantonment. Tucked away in the interior of the north-west, it was indeed the gateway to that region. During winter, a large number of Pathans, Kashmiris and others flocked to the city to escape the rigours of weather in their own homes.[48] Relatives from villages trooped in and stayed for days at a stretch. Since the city had a large number of cinema houses, they provided the major form of entertainment. Indeed, Punjab was considered 'the biggest market for films'.[49] Consequently, the audience for western films, especially for the high-adventure genre, was clearly not limited to the educated middle class but drew its viewership from different segments of Indian society.

British perceptions: conflicting viewpoints

Historically, this multilayered audience emerges as racially stratified. The colonial officialdom was markedly ambivalent in its perception of and attitude towards the Indian audience. The reception of film meaning comprised an important part of British self-perception and the ideology of racism and imperialism. Cognition and comprehension of this media was therefore assumed to be the prerogative of the enlightened British audience alone. By and large, the Indian audience was thought of as an undifferentiated whole, and popularly projected by British officials as 'child like', 'deficient of character', 'occupying a position of ignorance' and 'moral corruptability' similar to the Indian characters in the empire cinema.[50] Paternalistic notions inherent in imperial discourse reinforced this dominant perception of the 'Indian cinema audience' as projected in 1923:

The racial difference between the European and the Asiatic is fundamental and irreconcilable. The Asiatic matures easily and the development of his mentality does not keep pace with his physical growth. This is particularly true of the illiterate native, who forms nine-tenths of the population. At maturity he is still a child, and child like he remains. He never appears 'grown up'. The native of India is astonishingly credulous, and the plays (native dramas) and stories (folk-tales) he delights in would bore to death an English child of tender years by their simplicity.[51]

This perception was adopted as a general policy by the British Board of Film Censors (BBFC) in the years 1927–28, which eschewed 'undue sensitiveness to communal, racial, political and even colour considerations'.[52] The policy in its essence maintained:

We can hardly believe that a historical film which may picture incidents, say, of the French Revolution, will incite any ordinary member of an audience to attempt to overthrow the government by law established in India. Neither the commercial producer nor the exhibitor has the least desire to upset the existing order of society. Objectionable scenes may be excised, but we deprecate the idea that a film should be banned merely on the general ground that the subject matter may by over-subtle analogy be interpreted as having a possible reference to current questions. Similarly, we consider that the censor and the administrative officers should not encourage or be too sympathetic to individuals who in their private or representative capacities object to film plots or incidents. Breaches of peace must of course be guarded against, but over much tenderness to frivolous objections is more likely to encourage dissension.[53]

Clearly, the British tended to stress the childishness of the Indian mind and its inability to pierce through the outer layer of the plot. British officials were not suggesting that the cinema or its images and signs did not contain any 'damaging meanings'. What they were suggesting was that Indians would fail to perceive any subversive meaning because they lacked the mental capacity to view an image, receive its message and relate it to their concrete reality. Interestingly, this has also been the conventional viewpoint of Indian film historians and critics who

have described the 'lower-class audience' or the 'plebeian spectators' as immature, infantile, the unlettered mass, lacking the
critical ability to distinguish between image and reality. It has
been held that this mass audience would not be aware of the
veracity of the image.[54]

Despite the official perception, however, a greater sensitivity to
Indian reactions was also surfacing in many quarters due to political reasons. The government of India while deprecating 'over
sensitiveness in the political sphere', was aware of the political
fall-out of these films.[55] From time to time they were 'very
severely perturbed' about the widespread criticism that such films
were evoking in India and the inability of the authorities in
Britain to recognise it.[56]

In fact, throughout the period under consideration, there was
a difference of perception among British officials about the reception of such films in the colonial market. The available evidence
shows the conflicting currents of opinion circulating among
British officials in India and in Britain, regarding what may or
may not have been suitable for exhibition in India. Censorship in
India had been established under the Cinematograph act of 1918.
Under this, censor boards were set up in the four seaport towns
of Bombay, Calcutta, Madras and Rangoon. Lahore came to have
a censor board in 1927 because of its increased importance as a
centre for the production of Indian films and as a market. These
boards were empowered to grant certification valid for the whole
of India, but any provincial government could decertify a film
that it deemed unsuitable for public exhibition in its province.
Although the composition differed, each board of censors was
headed by the commissioner of police, invariably British, who
was assisted by other members. Half the total members of a board
were there in their ex-officio capacity and the other half were
nominated from among the different communities of a province.
The Bombay board, the most important of the five boards, had
one prominent representative from each community – a Hindu, a
Muslim and a Parsi – nominated as its functionaries. The final
decision regarding censorship was however always taken by the
chairman. In general, the boards were required to keep moral,
racial, religious and political considerations in view for censorship purposes, lest the British position in India be compromised.[57]
These boards had been severely criticised by British officials in

India and in Britain for being 'largely nominal', as well as 'weak and inexperienced'. [58]

The BBFC, as the 'mother of censors', kept in very close touch with the representatives of the empire censors through weekly and monthly correspondence, frequent meetings and 'favourable interchange of opinions', whenever they visited London. Regarding this close relationship and identity of views, Lord Tyrrell, president of the BBFC, remarked in June 1937: 'It is remarkable how closely our opinions coincide'.[59] This may have been true of the censor boards in India but so far as British officials in India were concerned, the evidence suggests the contrary and shows a wide discrepancy between the understanding of the British officials located in India and the BBFC.

The views of government of India officials were rooted in the changing political realities on the ground, although they also appeared to share the paranoia of the white viewing public stationed in India who considered the Indian audience a potentially violent one. The opinion of British civilians in India was considered important enough to be brought to the attention of the secretary of state for India. The first letter, written by 'a lady residing in India' to the editor of the London *Times*, was referred to him by H. Rowen Walker, general secretary of the British National Film League on 4 September 1923. It stated:

> I have myself seen a film in which a perfectly impossible man – supposed to be an Englishman – offends an Indian [Native American] by making love to his squaw, and the Indian finally gets him and ties him to a post, where he starves to death. This was greeted by applause by the Indians [natives of India] present. I saw another film where a drunken guest at a wedding knocks down a Negro – the Negro afterwards murders him. Again great applause from the natives. These are the cheapest, commonest films and are all we get to see in India ... The Indians go more and more to the cinema and must be thinking the British a nation to despise. [60]

The second letter was from the Manchester Diocesan Association for Preventive and Rescue Work. It was referred to the government of India by the secretary of state for India on 9 December 1924. The letter written 'after consultation with certain of the missionary societies and lay men and women returned from countries in which there is a coloured population', stated:

The film *The White Man's Grave*, was shown on the Gold Coast to a mixed audience. In the film the white man knocks out a native. As a result a riot broke out amongst the natives in the audience and there was great difficulty in preventing serious disturbances.

In Assam a screening of a film is often the annual treat given by tea-planters to their native labourers. Often the planter and his household are the only white people on the plantation of thousands of acres. The films are imported from America and from European firms. We have proof that the attitude of the natives to the white population in these plantations is rapidly degenerating after these annual displays of films purporting to show civilised English life ... It is not only a political or colour question, but one of moral welfare. It is useless to expect the coloured people to respect the white races when they see these false representations of so-called 'civilised life'.[61]

Others among them similarly tended to make an entirely simplistic correlation between western films and the behaviour of Indian audiences. For example, the kidnapping of Mollie Ellis by Afridis in 1915 was put down to the influence of western films.[62] Such connections expunged the passivity of the Indian audience and endowed them with agency, which could well prove politically dangerous.

Discerning officials in the India Office understood the potentially dangerous association of these films with contemporary events, and also recognised that censoring for the native population demanded 'different standards' than those adopted for western home audiences.[63] Yet, these officials were operating within a complex political situation, and considered it circumspect to leave the fate of these films in the hands of censor authorities in different provinces of India.[64] Part of the reason for taking this line was the fact that, allowing for the varied pulls of different interests involved in film-making, it was prudent to soft-pedal the issue because of wider political and commercial considerations. It was suggested that since certain films, like *The Charge of the Light Brigade*, had not evoked any protests among Indian audiences in the USA, Canada or England, bureaucrats consequently did not expect 'any trouble' from their Indian counterparts in Asia. Such an assessment was not entirely accurate, as I will illustrate presently, yet it was a convenient stand to assume. More importantly, however, the banning of films produced caustic comments in the foreign and Indian press.[65] The London-based officials were uneasy about the 'unfavourable publicity' that such a move could attract as 'the press etc. would get on to cases where something objectionable to Indian sentiments had been shown in a film and produce a lot of talk about it which would be equally objectionable.'[66]

Consequently, the dominant attitude of British officials in London generally remained at odds with official opinion in India. The repeated advice of the officials of the government of India – that 'Indian psychology' needed to be kept in mind while viewing these films – was essentially ignored.[67] When pressurised by the latter to keep 'Indian susceptibilities' in view, British officials retaliated by suggesting that 'a sympathetic article' about empire films might be published as an adequate answer to the 'anti-Indian charge'.[68] This was presumably to highlight those aspects in the film that were 'favourable' to Indians.

Despite these differences British officials (both in London and India) were united in their analysis of Indian society and in their belief that the British were civilising agents acting for the benefit of the colonised. There was no doubt regarding the basic thrust of the empire films, which portrayed the colonial rule as moral, positive and civilising. Any fundamental criticism of the films would have meant a critique of the very nature of colonialism itself. The discordant and cautionary voices of officials were in favour of stricter censorship, but remained within the ambit of imperial politics rather than in opposition to it.

Clearly, some British officials based in India did not necessarily read the message of the empire films within the cultural codes of their producers, as many of the London-based officials opted to do. Their decoding of the films related to the colonial situation and the possible readings (positions) of the Indian audience. Such a decoding suggests the potentiality of different reading positions, due to a variety of reasons, among the white 'master' audience. Because of their own location in India, a segment of the British official class was aware that messages encoded in one way could also be read in a different way. The question of film consumption/reception by Indian audiences had obviously emerged, to use a popular media studies' phrase, as a 'site of cultural struggle', with members of a single social class of British officials drawing their codes of understanding from differing politico-cultural contexts.

The dissident voices were ignored, however, until the reaction of the lower-class Indian audience to the film *The Drum* forced the hands of the British authorities. The reception of this film by lower-class Indian spectators showed a heightened cognitive and political disposition, indicating a more political understanding of colonial cultural representation and its ideological thrust than British officials had been willing to concede to date.

Heretofore, British officials had continued to disagree among themselves about the empire films and their impact upon an Indian audience. This incongruity of approach may be illustrated in the case of the film, *The Lives of a Bengal Lancer*. In Britain the film was passed with the following comment: 'The story is quite harmless. It has no political significance and no discredit is brought on the service.'[69] Yet, the film evoked strong protests in Lahore.[70] The Muslim community in Britain similarly protested vociferously.[71] There were questions in the Central Legislative Assembly in India and subsequently in the House of Commons.[72] Those parts of the film which evoked strong protests showed the hero, Captain Macgregor, cutting a piece of pork and throwing pig's blood on an Afridi captive to make him talk by threatening: '*Sarkar tumhe phansi dega aur tumhara badan soowar ki khal me rakha jayega, bolo badmash bolo*'. In the film it was translated as: 'talk you rascal, or you'll be hanged and your dead body will be sewn in a pig's skin.' The pig motif was repeatedly used in the film by British officers to insult the Muslim rebels in front of the Indian armymen. The abuse, 'swine', was used by them for Indian armymen and rebels alike.

Scenes such as these merited censorship in the eyes of the government of India officials who feared a 'political fall-out'. This anxiety was not merely due to the fear of hurting the 'religious sensibilities of the Muslims' in general, or those in the army in particular, but also on account of the class and racial connotations which emerged from such scenes. The under-secretary of state for foreign affairs considered these anxieties to be baseless. His opinion sums up the general viewpoint of the authorities located in Britain, who failed to understand the reactions of colonial and Indian audiences. While hailing *The Lives of a Bengal Lancer*, as the 'Jubilee year's greatest film', he maintained:

There is indeed nothing in it which an impartial observer would take to be at all derogatory to the people of India. On the contrary, the film depicts scenes in which troops of the Indian army fight with great gallantry against equally brave Afghan opponents and in which the Indian's loyalty and devotion to his officers, be they British or Indian, are portrayed with full justice. Neither is there anything in the film which might offend the religious susceptibilities of Indians. A possible criticism which might be levelled at the film is that it showed British officers engaging in what might be termed third degree methods of intimidation in order to break down the resistance of their Afghan captors into giving information. The threat was however not put into execution and the subsequent treatment of the captives was generous.[73]

Subsequently, even very pointed questions posed to the secretary of state for India in the House of Commons elicited a similar reply. On 29 April 1935 Lt.-Col. Arnold Wilson wondered if *The Lives of a Bengal Lancer*, with its mistreatment of captives by British officers, 'was in the interest of good-will between India and other countries', to which the secretary of state replied, 'It is not likely to affect the good-will between India and Great Britain.'[74]

Yet, British army officials were extremely anxious about the effects of portraying the British Indian army in the manner of these films. Well aware of the nationalist propaganda among armymen, they strongly disapproved of their own misrepresentation on the screen. Similarly, old-India hands may well have been offended by the cinematic inaccuracies of these films, signifying a sharp division of opinion among the imperialists themselves.

Such differing perceptions are seen in the controversy about the advisability of showing the film, *The Charge of the Light Brigade* to Indian audiences. The government of India took a strong stand against several scenes in this film and, in fact, to the very theme itself, which revolved around an incident from the Mutiny.[75] On military grounds alone this film had been judged as 'undesirable' by the military secretary,[76] yet R.T. Peel, secretary to the public and judicial department noted: 'I really think the Government of India are a little sensitive on the question of films.'[77]

It is undeniable that, by the late 1930s, there was greater

consensus among British officials about the inadvisability of projecting imperialist images to Indian audiences. Realising that the reading of the films could provoke a sharp negative reaction from the Indian audiences, they advised caution and change. This was confirmed by the India Office, which, in 1937, appeared to be in doubt about positive reactions from an Indian audience to British imperial symbols of royalty. W. Thompson, information officer at the India Office, wrote to Peel on 15 June 1937 maintaining that 'Inclusion of the Indian coronation contingent during the parade at Buckingham Palace for the presentation of medals, and its use in the trailer for propaganda purposes is of doubtful suitability throughout India.'[78] The Political ADC's note to Thompson, dated 23 July 1937, endorsed this stand: 'for the trailer to use the King's photograph in coronation robes with the crown on his head would not be really more effective as propaganda with the audience we are *now* considering' (emphasis in original). This correspondence was followed by a letter from the information officer to Peel, dated 2 March 1938: 'It is open to considerable doubt whether Indian cinemas especially in the Congress Provinces would be prepared to show such a trailer even if it were supplied free of charge.'

Exhibitors of films in India, suffering under the dual burden of entertainment tax and paying exorbitant rental charges for cinema houses, were naturally anxious to exhibit films which would give them profits.[79] Marketability of a film was therefore a prime concern. Especially in relation to western films, the exhibitor was in a position to choose which films to screen. Owing to the time gap which elapsed between the release of a film abroad and its arrival, he could know in advance the potential marketability of any film that he ordered or that he was due to receive, as many exhibitors had access to trade journals and other trade literature. Press comments, articles and reviews, both abroad and in India, which generated controversy had the advantage of attracting the cinema-going crowd – unless the reactions got out of hand leading to the banning of the film as in the cases of *The Drum* and *Gunga Din*. Generally speaking, 'ruthless censorship' of a film even though it might be 'a travesty of Indian life and customs', was disliked by the exhibitors, as they had to pay a heavy price for the film and knew the 'very strong attraction' the film or those scenes would have for the public.[80] Only the British owners of the Grand Opera House in Calcutta were known to 'ruthlessly censor' a film despite the risk of financial losses because of its alleged 'harmful and misleading' effects.[81]

The reaction of the audience to a film or any other screen projection was therefore of paramount interest; if they were rejecting certain images or messages, the exhibitors would be wary of exhibiting them. In actual fact, Indian audiences were known to avoid being in the cinema hall during the playing of the British national anthem at the end of foreign films.[82] The sudden rush to leave the theatre by the Indian audience suggests that they considered this to be 'blatant propaganda of the British way of life, which the natives were expected to follow', as even British officials acknowledged.[83]

Clearly, in certain quarters British officials were showing a greater sensitivity to Indian reactions for political reasons. For instance, the *Evening Standard* received a sharp rebuke for their caption – 'A native receives his award from Lady Linlithgow' – which they published on 2 June 1939 beneath a photograph of a prize-giving ceremony at the Simla horse show. The bureau of public information wrote a confidential letter dated 16 June 1939 commenting, 'To call an Indian "a native" in 1939, suggests that in matters imperial, Fleet Street is still living in the nineteenth century. The word "native" arouses the strongest resentment out here.'[84] The letter went on to suggest that 'hints' in this respect were to be 'dropped to all concerned'. Significantly, the word 'native' was commonly used in the empire films.

Awareness of Indian feelings led to voices being raised in England, advising a change in the way of looking at the exported films. Voicing such a concern was Edward Thompson, professor of Indian history at Oxford University, who in his letter to Ralph Glyn, dated 6 December 1937, summed up the situation as follows:

Indian self-respect is touched to the extreme as was shown by the nation-wide furore over *Mother India*. There is need to conciliate India's self-respect and to take steps now when peace still obtains. The films we have had, do not do this. *Elephant Boy* shows Indians in a menial capacity and as picturesque and pleasantly interesting which Indians resent as much as Scots resent being shown as 'pawky' and the Irish as being shown as chiefly remarkable for 'bulls'. The practice of a nation which delights foreigners usually infuriates the nation itself. As for the *Bengal Lancer*, the less said about it the better ... the Indian self-respect with the outside world is not won by films which broadcast the 'sahib and native' relationship or show the world that Moslem assassins are hanged in Peshawar bound up in pig-skin.[85]

The growing sensitivity to the colonised point of view can also be witnessed in an edition of *Cinema* published on 23 August 1939: 'One can imagine the feeling of an English audience if the Chinese were represented as heroes, while roles of murderers, smugglers or dope peddlers were reserved for the English.'[86] It went on to recommend that heroic roles or those of the villains should not be reserved only for one race.

Quite clearly, the British were slowly moving towards granting greater recognition to the colonised point of view *vis-à-vis* production of such films. In 1936, the foreign office in London had been asked by the public and judicial department to tell their British representatives abroad to keep a look out for films 'offensive to Indian sentiments'.[87] But nothing really was done until the British hand was forced in the wake of the agitation over *The Drum* in 1938. Prior to this, the officially catalogued report, comprising the 'objections' of India, was hardly acted upon.

This work demonstrates how the concern with the portrayal of India on screen was directly related to difficulties the British were experiencing in the late 1930s. This period coincided with the aggravated tension of an extremely uncertain internal position, and, combined with a rapidly accelerating antagonistic international situation directly preceding World War II, resulted in increased sensitivity. The situation for the British in India was so precarious that the India Office preferred not to risk having films made which might, when distributed throughout the world (not merely in India), 'stir up more trouble and cause further uprising or protest'.[88]

Yet, when the government of India put its foot down about screening films like *India Speaks*, J. Brook-Wilkinson, secretary of the BBFC, was horrified that the colonial government was 'yielding to pressure', and was taking action against the producers of 'so important a concern as RKO of New York'.[89] On the

other hand, a section of London-based British officials were apprehensive that such films actually served Indian interests. In their perception, the Indians desired these films to be shown in their country to arouse anti-British feelings. A letter from the India Office to M. Seton of the government of India, had noted as early as September 1923: 'I presume that the boards in India are mostly composed of Indians, who may not necessarily regard it as part of their duty to exclude films that bring the white man into contempt.'[90]

A more forthright reiteration of this came in the confidential letter of R. T. Peel to General Wilson, dated 4 February 1937. Written in justification of stopping the production of the film, *The Relief of Lucknow*, Peel maintained: 'Assuming that the film could be shown, Indian opinion would not object to its exhibition in England or any other foreign country. Indeed, it is quite possible that Congress leaders would welcome its exhibition in India as being likely to arouse a revolutionary mentality and a desire to experiment with another "war of independence."'[91] It was clear that the British were apprehensive of Indian audiences making 'popular cultural capital' out of empire cinema.[92]

The pre-emptive banning of *The Relief of Lucknow* was to formalise this changing perspective of British officials regarding empire films. This film was used as an occasion to lay down new policy guidelines which were noticeable in the film, *The Rains Came*, released in India in 1940.

Renegotiating ideological norms: the case of *The Relief of Lucknow*

The change in the nature of the propaganda thrust was not exclusive to Britain's Indian colony. It was a part of the wider official change made by Britain in the late 1930s, as the colonial image during the interwar period was particularly vulnerable.[93] The change in the official policy in India, following the revaluation of the imperial propaganda in cinema, was effected through the controversial film, *The Relief of Lucknow*. Its theme, the 1857 uprising, popularly referred to by the British as the Mutiny, had ample potential for cinematic exploitation. The Mutiny had become a potent symbol of conflict between British and Indian points of view and perceptions of history. For the former, the brutal acts of 'mutineers' inspired nothing but retaliatory moves, and, for the latter, it was a nationalist uprising against the British rule. British sensitivity about this period was well known, especially as the causes of the Mutiny were actually constitutive of British imperialism itself. Moreover, the 1857 revolt had become the most inflammatory memory in the nationalist agenda.

Although references to the Mutiny had not been censored or objected to, where it provided the theme or the central event around which the entire film revolved, the British felt apprehensive about likely reactions. A case in point was the film, *The Charge of the Light Brigade*, in which the crucial Mutiny incident had to be heavily camouflaged following the British censors' objections.[94] Based on Tennyson's poem of the same name, the subject of which was the Crimean War (1853–56), the entire film is located in India except for the climax in Crimea, where 600 Lancers are sent to their death. The film begins with Surat Khan, ruler of Suristan, a Frontier state, allying himself with the Russians and thus becoming a danger to the security of British India. In league with Russia, Surat Khan, on the eve of Crimean War, leads the border tribes against a British outpost, killing men, women and children. The twenty-seven Bengal Lancers avenge this massacre. This film presented the Mutiny and its colonial repression as a response to Indian subversion. It used the retaliatory Kanpur massacre of the British garrison, women and children in July 1857 for delivering a lesson: 'that no Indian can take liberties with a British regiment's women and children'. Despite being underplayed it was still considered by British officials in India a 'painful reminder of Indian history which had better be left unrecalled at the present time at least'.[95] Consequently, when another film on the Mutiny revealingly entitled *The Relief of Lucknow* was put into pre-production, it attracted the severest condemnation. Such a film by T. A. Addison and Company had already been made in 1912, but in the 1930s the British wanted no repetition of it.

In 1912, *The Siege of Lucknow* had been blatantly advertised as 'The Indian Mutiny 1857 – an actual page from the actual history of the past', and as 'historically correct – closely adhering to recorded facts'.[96] The reviews of those days had also emphasised that the film was a 'faithful reconstruction of the events'.[97]

It was claimed that the film was not fictitious but showed 'just what occurred on the night of 12 May 1857, at Lucknow'.[98]

However, there was a vast change in the Indian situation between 1912 and the late 1930s when similar claims, if made, could well prove inflammatory. Clearly, cinematic interpretations are not static but form part of a constantly changing dialectical process in which meanings are reproduced and transformed. Consequently, when the proposal for reviewing *The Relief of Lucknow* came up in 1936, BBFC stopped its production.[99] Commenting upon it, the secretary of state for India noted, 'One should be in favour of everything possible being done to stop it ... It would be a great pity to revive memories of the Mutiny and particularly inopportune just now with the Abyssinian war in progress. If the film starts with Lucknow they would be likely enough to go to other things which would be much worse.'[100]

In 1938, the proposal was again revised. By this time *The Drum* had provoked a large-scale popular agitation in Bombay followed by a ban imposed in provincial assemblies by popular ministries, along with a stringent censorship policy regarding all foreign films that featured India in any form. The British considered it politically prudent to pay attention to the vociferous objections of 'nationalist India', which at the time was considered 'peculiarly sensitive' to stories designed to emphasise the valour of British troops in a clash between them and the Indians of Mutiny days.[101]

The danger that Indian film-makers might represent the anti-colonialist movement as a response to the coloniser's violence, exploitation and repression – to express a political point of view – was heightened in the current political climate. Banning of such themes therefore forestalled the possibility of a denunciatory counter-narrative from the perspective of the colonised. This point is elaborated in a confidential letter from Lothian, additional secretary to the government of India, to Zetland, the secretary of state for India, dated 5 December 1938:

> May I say how extraordinarily dangerous, I think any such films would be in India today. In the first place young nationalist India is extraordinarily sensitive about the whole Mutiny episode. To them it was the first wave of the national movement for independence and was largely due to resentment at the suppression of the

independent state of Oudh. The Rani of Jhansi is already a popular figure on the stage. It is almost impossible for the British company, advised by British soldiers to do a film which will not cause resentment in India. To us the Mutiny was a glorious episode in our history in India in which British soldiers and civilians showed extraordinary heroism in resisting a singularly brutal collection of rebels. To the Indians – it was a heroic if unsuccessful attempt to strike for freedom.

But the effect of the film itself would be the last of the evils. It would most certainly provoke a crop of films from Indian companies setting forth the Indian version of the Mutiny and it would be extraordinarily difficult for the Government of India to censor or suppress them if it had allowed a British film of the Mutiny to appear. Further Hollywood has long been itching to use the Mutiny as a theme, as the North West Frontier Province becomes exhausted and if we are to allow a British film to appear, there will be no means of stopping Hollywood from pouring out versions of its own which would probably infuriate both Britain and India but nonetheless set fire to the stubble. India, as you know better than I do, is in a difficult state at the moment and even the Congress ministries are finding great difficulty with extremist youth. I cannot think of anything more likely to make difficulties during the next year or two when you are trying to get the constitution into operation than the kind of controversy which would almost certainly be engendered by any kind of film about the Mutiny, however carefully prepared. *It is not the film, it is the theme which is dangerous.* Use your influence to prevent any such film being manufactured.[102] (emphasis in original)

To this letter was attached a note from A. Dibdin of the public and judicial department, which revealed that in the Central Legislative Assembly of India, the commander-in-chief had come under heavy attack for unveiling a Mutiny memorial in a village near the capital, Delhi; particular objection was taken by Indians to the use of the word 'Mutineers' on the memorial.[103]

The proposal for *The Relief of Lucknow* also provoked vehement reactions in the Indian media. Picking up on these protests, the *Edinburgh Evening News* of 9 December 1938 observed, 'The majority of Indians regard the Mutiny as the first war of independence lost through treachery.' It went on to quote the *Pioneer*

of Lucknow: 'The Indians like the Irish have long memories and
have lived on them too long. Rightly or wrongly they would
resent a film on the Mutiny and for that reason consider it would
be bad policy and what is worse, bad manners to make it.'

Confirming the dangers of allowing such a film, Edward
Thompson wrote in his letter to the editor of the *Daily Telegraph*
on 19 December 1938:

> I am certain that it would be impossible to make any film on any
> episode of the Indian Mutiny which would not send a wave of fury
> throughout India, stirring Hindus and Moslems equally, to which
> the anger caused by Miss Mayo's 'Mother India' would be nothing.
> Indians have their own traditions and opinions of the Mutiny,
> which are not ours. There are interests in Hollywood, already
> living off the North West Frontier as a film region, which would
> like nothing better than to move on to the Mutiny. Our people
> know nothing of the Mutiny as it is seen from the Indian side or of
> what it still means. The film would have caused suffering to 400
> million of our fellow citizens who sent its soldiers to fight the great
> war.

Similar sentiments, echoed in other papers, advised caution in
touching upon the 'mutual savageries' of British as well as
Indians, the memories of which were considered to be alive
among 'very old people still living in India' as well as among 'the
generation which followed'.[104]

The controversy surrounding *The Relief of Lucknow* having
spilled over in to the public domain, also found a great deal of
passionate support in England. A large number of British
members of parliament, the press and publicity agents vehemently
protested against 'political censorship'.[105] Those lobbying for the
film criticised its ban on the grounds of the large amount of
money having already been spent on the film and ensuing problems of unemployment caused by throwing people out of work.
Despite mounting pressure, private and public, production of the
film was banned in early 1939.

More importantly this occasion was used to lay down a policy
regarding films which depicted India. This change virtually
brought almost all empire feature film productions relating to
India to a halt, as we shall see presently. The official statement of
Tyrell regarding *The Relief of Lucknow* stated, 'The British Board

of Film Censors has been advised by all the authorities responsible for the Government of India, both civil and military, that in their considered opinion such a film would revive memories of the days of conflict in India, which has been the earnest endeavour of both countries to obliterate, with a view to promoting harmonious co-operation between the two people.'[106]

In the parliamentary debates which took place regarding the banning of *The Relief of Lucknow*, S. Hoare, quoting the secretary of state reiterated that 'to produce a film depicting scenes of the Indian Mutiny would be undesirable at this time, when we are just embarking upon a new chapter in the constitutional development of India and when we want to get rid of differences which there have been between us in the past. I think everyone wants to see the new constitution in India a success.'[107] These were publicly touted reasons and were greatly publicised in India as well. Yet these do not adequately explain the considerations behind this shift in policy regarding the empire films, which I shall deal with later. However, an immediate issue dealing with the British Indian army may be recounted here briefly. During the year 1938, an expert committee under Lord Chatfield had been appointed to look into its deficiencies. Published in early September 1938, this committee report was sent to India in October 1938 and was accepted by the cabinet in June 1939. It came at a time when the provincial autonomy scheme was under trial in the wake of the 1935 act. The Chatfield Report feared that the Congress party might control the future federation of India and thus gain 'virtual control whether by direct or indirect means over defence policy'.[108] They were anxious to insist that the British government alone, through the governor general and the secretary of state for India, should remain responsible for the defence of India regardless of the constitutional reforms in progress. Thus the recommendations of the Chatfield Report ran almost completely contrary to the constitutional principles introduced in an India ostensibly on its road to self-government and were bound to alienate public opinion.

The British were justifiably nervous about this contradiction which made their commitment to constitutional reform and self-government suspect. Given their own vulnerability at this time, they could not afford to allow public attention to be directed at the British Indian army, which the empire film package tended to do. This was explicitly stated in a minute paper of the public and judicial department dated 9 December 1938:

> Apart from the regrettable effect a Mutiny film would have upon nationalist feelings in India, we might emphasise its probable reaction upon the Indian army. However glorious the episodes may be to the British army and to some Indian units, the reverse of the picture must be the implication of disloyalty and treachery in the Indian army of that period ... The point I would like to make is that I believe the British public, including many of those connected with the film industry are more likely to sympathise with the desire not to offend the susceptibilities of the loyal Indian army than to feel any great solicitude for the reaction upon political India, the vocal elements of which, outside the Punjab, have not exhibited a marked degree of loyalty recently.[109]

With the army's position as a highly contentious issue the British government came down with a heavy hand on the making of *The Relief of Lucknow*. This action, however, did not deter the producers from making an appeal directly to the parliamentary private secretary, Lord Beauchamp. The correspondence which followed, illuminates the finer nuances of British policy towards empire cinema, its propaganda and impact in the given socio-political situation of the late 1930s.

On 20 April 1939, John Weiner on behalf of the US Columbia studio made a second representation to Beauchamp seeking permission to make a film, *The Siege of Lucknow*, as an earlier representation had been turned down. The letter sought to reassure the British that the '*reasons* of the Mutiny will not be gone into' (emphasis in original), and 'the actual rebellion of the sepoys would be glossed over if shown at all'.[110] In an obvious attempt to assuage British apprehensions, the letter promised:

> The enemy would be shown in this picture as nothing more or less than a type of Indian bandit. Nana Sahib might be their leader, the causes could with ease be shown as the personal ambitions of this man coupled with the old business of the greased cartridges and others of a similar nature. The real question of the Indian company and their policy would be left out. The film would also show that a great number of sepoys at the siege of Lucknow *remained loyal* as well as the *majority* of the natives who lived in these parts ...

After all, the film *Gunga Din* was a great success here and in England. I am sure that one of the most important reasons for this was that 'the enemy' were bandits nothing more nothing less. This proposed film as far as 'the enemy' is concerned could be handled in a similar manner. (emphasis in original)

Beauchamp sought the advice of Zetland on this letter and later communicated parts of Zetland's advice, without naming him, to the US producer. By now the film, *Gunga Din*, released in April 1939, had also been banned by the provincial governments in India. The time had come to officially and publicly accept the stand taken by the Indian provincial governments. Zetland's letter to Beauchamp, dated 18 May 1939, put down for official and public consumption the British attitude not only towards *The Relief of Lucknow* but also other films about India in general and is therefore cited in full:

Mr. Weiner entirely misunderstands our reasons for objecting to certain films. He is at pains to explain that the proposed film would not show up British policy in India in a bad light, but it is not for that reason that any recent film about India has caused us trouble but because they portray Indians in a manner offensive to Indian sentiments. It is unfortunately a frequent characteristic of films about India produced in England or America that Indians are shown as being a subject race and as likely as not engaged in rebellion against the British which is invariably frustrated by the heroism of the latter to the discomfiture of the Indians. Mr. Weiner's suggestion, therefore, that the Mutineers should be shown as bandits actuated merely by personal ambition does not meet the main point, since it is exactly this method of presentation which offends Indians, many of whom look upon the Mutiny as the 'first Indian war of Independence', and upon the Mutineers as comparable to the followers of George Washington, only differing from them in that they were unsuccessful. It is, in fact, precisely because the Indians are posed as 'bandits' and so on that such films are so distasteful to Indian sentiments and if the Indian characters could be made more agreeable, which does not mean to say that they need be shown as excessively loyal to the British, films about India would be much more satisfactory from our point of view. Mr. Weiner mentions the film *Gunga Din*. This may have been a success in England, but it was banned in India and the Government of India was asked in the Indian Legislature whether they could take steps through the British Embassy in Washington to prevent its production and release.

Besides these general objections to so many films about India, special objections are attached to any about the Indian Mutiny. Not only does a film about the Mutiny raise unfortunate associations, no matter in what way the episodes are presented, but (it also could not fail to show part of the Indian army in the regrettable role of Mutineers) the substitution of bandits for Mutineers could not of course disguise the historical basis of the film, the production of which consequently revives memories of events which are painful and humiliating to the Indian Army with its great tradition of loyalty, as well as to the Indian public. We have on two occasions in the past been instrumental in preventing a film about the Mutiny being made in this country. In the second case production was already fairly far advanced when we came to hear of the film. But despite the inevitable inconvenience caused to the producers and the fact that some public and Parliamentary interest was shown in the case, the project had to be abandoned as a result of the Board of Film Censors informing the company that they would not be able to pass the film. It may be assumed therefore, that the Board would not for a moment think of passing a film on this subject produced on India. Since we may expect a spate of Hollywood films about India, and though I am afraid they will inevitably be of the *Gunga Din* type, I am anxious that Hollywood should at any rate be aware of our attitude.[111]

Thus wider political ramifications had brought about a near unanimity of opinion between home and colonial officialdom regarding the portrayal and effect of empire films in India.

This correspondence 'to influence the trade to the right direction sought' was sent out by Dibdin of the public and judicial department to F. H. Puckle, secretary to the government of India's home department, with strict instructions that the correspondence be kept 'highly confidential'. At the insistence of the government of India, the producers not merely of Hollywood but also the 'enlightened producers of UK' were warned that the provincial governments under Indian control were most likely to refuse certification not only to all such films but also to any company responsible for producing work 'offensive to Indian public opinion'.[112] The consequent risk of losing 'a considerable market' was also underlined.

This was followed by the circulation of detailed instructions giving specific directions regarding films, which went far beyond the four major considerations laid down in 1928 regarding assessment of imperial projects.[113] These instructions laid down certain criteria for judging whether empire films about India might be considered 'offensive' to Indians. Films that might not be sanctioned included:

1 Those which are based on episodes in British Indian history or stories in the Kipling tradition.
2 Those which show quarrelling or fighting between Europeans and Indians or between Hindus and Muslims.
3 Those in which Indian religion or social customs are brought into ridicule or contempt, for example, films tending to over-emphasise the backwardness of certain classes of people or giving undue importance to social abuses or primitive customs, which are not fairly representative of India as a whole.
4 Those in which an Indian is portrayed as the villain and a European as the hero.
5 Those which generally depict Indians as an inferior race, with a 'slave mentality', cringing and dominated by a superior white race.[114]

These instructions were sent to producers of films in the USA and Britain with a final warning: 'that a film will not be exhibited in India, is not in Indian opinion the end of the matter. What Indian sentiment particularly objects to is the lowering of Indians in the eyes of the world and the exhibition in other countries of films which would not be tolerated in India arouses for that reason no less resentment'.[115]

Film India in a shrewd comment on this changed attitude and policy of the colonial masters, observed that it was 'more as a need for imperial unity in these dangerous times than a real change of heart'.[116] *Hindu* went on to question why 'Indian feelings' could be accommodated in respect to a film on the Mutiny and not in respect to other films?[117]

This repeated private and public emphasis on 'Indian feelings' regarding films portraying India in a derogatory light served a dual purpose. On the one hand, it supported the Indian objections by portraying them sympathetically as just and fair, and, on the other hand, it supplied the British with an opportunity to set their colonial record straight (which was being roundly assailed at this time) by implying that the colony itself rejected the allegation of its backwardness under colonial domination. These new guidelines coincided with the banning of *The Drum* and *Gunga Din*.

Oriental-cum-imperialist discourse: the Hollywood stakes

The volatile controversy regarding the empire films forced the British to note with growing alarm 'America's preoccupation' with an image of India focusing on the 'exotic', 'oriental' or 'awkward' side of India. This image based itself on 'imperial glory'. The fact that the themes or backgrounds of a large proportion of Hollywood's films were made on war, conquest and political trouble, recent or historical, only served to emphasise this image.[118]

The portrayal of Eurocentric-imperialist ideology and colonialist representations on the Hollywood screen has been comprehensively investigated by writers like Robert Stam, Louise Spence and Ella Shohat in their recent works. According to them these representations and ideologies did not begin with the cinema but are rooted in a vast colonial intertext and a widely disseminated set of discursive practices which lay in philosophy, literature and history.[119] Portraying the orient or the Other on the screen tapped into the 'cultural baggage' that was deeply embedded in the discourse of the empire and which the white audience – British or American – carried with them. In fact, the birth of cinema coincided with the height of European imperialism between the late nineteenth century and World War I. Consequently, most western films about the colonies adopted the 'explorer's perspective' in which the European civilising mission is projected as 'interweaving opposing yet linked narratives of western penetration into inviting virginal landscape and resisting libidinal nature'.[120] The popularity of adventure genre films in the west, with their emphasis on masculinity, aggression and penetration in relation to the colonial world, lay in the fact that the films lent themselves perfectly to the 'gendered western gaze' described by Shohat.[121]

Historically, the USA had been a colony that had fought a

determined and successful war against imperialist Britain. It had also served as a colonising hegemonic power in relation to Native American and African peoples. This historical contradiction within the USA created an ambivalence that came to be reflected in the films. The USA came to identify with Britain in relation to its colony in India on racial grounds, but showed itself uncertain in relation to the political situation. Politically, the anti-British and anti-imperialist forces in the USA sympathised with the Indian national movement. This critique became embedded in the Hollywood films, which offered a space for alternative perceptions even while they echoed dominant imperialist messages.

Racially, however, Hollywood cinema subscribed fully to the cultural outlook that located heroes and villains in racial stereotypes. The affinity is further emphasised by the resonance between the military, racist and imperial ethics of these films and similar trends in US society. Jeffrey Richards explains this historically in terms of a deeply pervasive and strident racist society in the USA of the 1930s in which all coloured people occupied an inferior position.[122] This aspect, which, according to him, is 'the key to the link between the British empire and often unspoken and unarticulated ethos of American imperialism', found its way on to the screen not merely in empire films but in other genres as well.

The western genre, for example, came close to the imperial adventure films in conveying a similar ideological premise in its imperial-style adventure on the American frontier. It gave a specialised national form to a more widespread historical process – the general thrust of European expansion into Asia, Africa and the Americas.[123] A popular theme of the late 1930s, as seen in the classical period of the western genre, was the slow march of white settlers across the continent escorted by regiments of US cavalry to disperse the native population. The Hollywood western made the Native American appear as intruders in their own land and thus provided a paradigmatic perspective through which to view the whole of the non-white world. The domestication of their wild land is encoded in notions of civilisation, progress and manifest destiny in a striking similarity with the empire films. US identification with colonialism and imperialism was quite clear, despite certain reservations and its stand as an anti-colonial power in relation to Europe at this time.

Moreover, the imperial ideology, as Shohat and Stam suggest, was really transnational. White audiences were encouraged to identify not only with single European nations but also with the racial solidarity implied by the imperial project as a whole. Thus a British audience could identify with the heroes of French Foreign Legion films, a Euro-American audience with the heroes of the British Raj and so on. In Shohat and Stam's words:

> For the European spectator, the cinematic experience mobilised a rewarding sense of national and imperial belonging, on the backs, as it were, of otherized peoples ... The cinema's ability to 'fly' spectators around the globe gave them a subject position as film's audio-visual masters. The 'spatially mobilised visuality' of the I/eye of empire spiralled outward around the globe, creating a visceral, kinetic sense of power while turning the colonies into spectacle for the metropole's voyeuristic gaze.[124]

Each imperial country therefore emerged with its own imperial genre set in different colonies. Hollywood was thus making films not only on British imperialism but also on the French. In fact it made more films about the French Foreign Legion than the French themselves.[125] In films relating to British imperialism, Hollywood scored by using a combination of US and British actors with the former playing a central heroic role, which ensured the sympathetic identification by a Euro-American public. Yet, it is undeniable that in these carefully designed commercial productions, the US public's admiration for the British empire ideals of loyalty, courage and hard work, as pointed out by Margaret Farrand Thorp in 1939, also played its part.[126]

In projecting British imperialism, the two most popular locations for Hollywood's empire films were Africa and India. India emerged in Hollywood films in 1902 in Thomas Edison's *Hindu Fakir*, the first motion picture with an Indian theme of which there is any record.[127] It concentrated on 'mystic India' and projected an oriental land and people, full of mysterious, frightening, strange things, repulsively fascinating to a western audience due to their 'uncivilised' and 'barbaric' nature. Such films merely reproduced the orientalist discourse so attractive to the white races, a vision which the USA shared with the rest of the western white world. This film, regarded as the ancestor of a whole series of motion pictures, provided the backdrop to the cinematic adventures of the British Indian army.

Hollywood films about British troops stationed in India presented tales of racially superior white men finding adventure in a foreign land where primitive people, wild animals, poisonous snakes and a treacherous country called upon them to be brave and fearless soldiers. What emerged, therefore, was the cinematic projection of orientalist-cum-imperialist discourse by Hollywood. The first film on this theme, Twentieth-Century Fox's *The Black Watch*, was made in 1929. It was based on a story by Talbot Mundy and directed by John Ford. This enshrined the basic plot which was followed in subsequent productions.[128]

Such films had melodramatic plots revolving around primitive tribesmen (usually pictured as living just beyond the Indian North-West Frontier), who rose up against the British in India with the idea of overcoming and destroying the British army and taking over the whole country. This plot against India was defeated by the British Indian army led by gallant British officers. In defeating the wild tribesmen, the British were invariably presented as serving the cause of justice, law and order, and acting for the good of India by saving the country from being overrun by savage tribes. The 'good' elements of the Indian population were shown to work with them, the 'bad' elements against them. This theme recurred with remarkable consistency for over a quarter of a century, the dramatic element being reinforced by the contrast of white and black as convenient symbols of good and evil.

However, in this commercial peddling of British imperialism, Hollywood was aware of the pressures exercised by the British government as well as the British viewing public. During the 1930s, there was a conflict of commercial interests between Britain and the USA in the struggle for world trade. In film-making especially, the Americans had left the British way behind. In 1926, for example, eighty per cent of the films shown in India were from the USA and only ten per cent were British. The British film industry had been steadily declining and was severely handicapped due to shortage of material and staff.[129] The Americans' forging ahead of the British was a source of much heart-burning in British film and official circles. In view of this resentment and the possibility of the British government introducing fresh policies or further tightening the existing protectionist policy with its quota rules, it was important for US producers to make films that were acceptable to the British in terms of projecting politically and ideologically correct messages and images. It also made them very careful about not offending 'British susceptibilities'.[130]

Along with the British government, the susceptibilities of the British public had also to be kept in mind because success at the box office could be obtained only by producing films arousing popular interest. The British public, with forty per cent of the population regularly attending the cinema, accounted for a weekly sale of twenty million tickets, providing Hollywood with its largest overseas market.[131] A still larger market awaited Hollywood in Britain's world-wide empire. The importance of the British empire was testified to by film director Frank Capra, who recalled in his autobiography that only two of his major films failed to make money and this was because they were banned in the British empire.[132] The desire to capture this lucrative film market made US film-makers situate their films in various territories of the empire, for it was a well-known fact that if a film was located in a specific colony it had a far greater chance of being a commercial success there.

The British, on the other hand, encouraged the making of such films for their own reasons, particularly as the British official attempts in non-feature film propaganda about India had not been very effective. This failure was not merely due to lack of resources and a reluctance to use state intervention in private enterprise, as argued by Philip Woods,[133] but also to the commercial non-viability of such an enterprise. Propaganda films focusing on developmental aspects such as irrigation, agricultural improvements, education and industrial progress in India had no audience. Whereas feature films easily attracted enthusiastic distributors and exhibitors, not to mention a popular viewership.

Moreover, there was considerable pressure both inside and outside the government for the production of feature films promoting the imperial agenda.[134] Although the British government remained reluctant to become directly involved in feature film production until World War II, private producers were certainly encouraged to adopt the British empire as a fruitful field for cinematography. From about 1932 onwards the BBFC moved from post-censorship to pre-censorship. It encouraged producers first to submit to the board for general advice on draft scripts. This was followed by the submission of suitably amended scripts, which received detailed comments and amendments prior to the commencement of actual production.[135] This exercise obviated the need for drastic censorship if not outright bans later on. Such close association between the state and the cinema also had its effect on production and its thrust. As scripts were officially vetted and both Hollywood and its counterpart in Britain made these films with the active co-operation of the colonial authorities and the British Indian army, the images-cum-ideological content of the films had the stamp of approval of the authorities. A spate of films thus came to be produced in which the focus on the British Indian army projected a combination of militarist, patriotic, imperialist and masculinist values.

With time, the films made by Hollywood became increasingly important to Britain, especially in view of the rising Indian objections; objections which could be disregarded in the case of Hollywood films but not British ones. It was pointed out that due to the pressure brought about by the Indian government on the India Office and, consequently, on the BBFC, more films about India could not be produced in England.[136] Hollywood films were considered comparatively safe from this pressure.

Zetland, acknowledging England's need for the production of such films, explained to the chairman of the BBFC why and how Hollywood (and not the British) could continue the production of such films, arguing that 'we in this country could not be held responsible for what was done in the States and could not be attacked by Indians on account of it.'[137] Moreover, if the film for some reason had to be banned or withdrawn, it was felt that it would be politically 'easier to exclude an American film from India, than an English one'.[138] The Americans on their side continued to glorify 'British feats of arms', show 'soldiers in a eulogistic manner' and 'endorse the imperial ideology'.[139] However, this orientalist-cum-imperialist ideological thrust in the empire films produced its own contradictions for, ultimately, the empire films were not successful in endorsing either imperialism or colonial policy. They backfired.

A shift of policy: shelving of films

The imperatives for change in orientalist-cum-imperialist representations came from the changing historical requirements of colonial rule. This change was not exclusive to Britain's Indian colony and was part of a wider official policy adopted in the late 1930s. The changed policy regarding India was fully evident in the British guided and controlled film, *The Rains Came*, which departed from the hitherto adopted adventure genre and its stock characters. This film proved to be the sole exception. The pressures of a changed policy combined with material and political interests to force Hollywood into either abandoning or shelving thirty-seven such films relating to India, which were announced in the 1939–40 schedules.

Consequently, a remake of *The King of the Khyber Rifles*, previously filmed in 1929 as *The Khyber Rifles*, was shelved,[140] and proposed film adaptations of two of Kipling's imperialist works, *Kim* and *Soldiers Three*, were also banned and made only after India's independence. *The Bengal Border* and *Storm over India* similarly had to be put into cold storage, and a reissue of *Gunga Din* was banned. Even Alexander Korda was reported to have dropped, in September 1939, the idea of acquiring film rights to a historical novel about India.

Hollywood's feature films of the adventure genre dealing with India as their theme re-emerged only after independence. In view of the drastically changed socio-political context of the triumph of colonial nationalisms and decolonisation, and their ideological requirements, there was continuity as well as change in cinematic representations and ideological formations (of both western and Indian cinema) in the post-colonial period.

Throughout World War II, a plea for a change of policy and image in relation to the colonies was stressed. The need for such a change for the British public was emphasised. For example, Alexander Shaw, a British film producer, who spent a year in India during the war wrote:

> But please remember, India belongs to you and me and the next Englishman. It is no good you sitting back and being funny about *Pukka* Sahibs and the cabinet's attitude to India. Indians don't laugh about you any more, they take you very seriously. If you who are reading this article were to go to India you would be held personally responsible for every unpleasant thing that has happened in the country since Clive; it was you who put down the so called Mutiny, who killed the Rani of Jhansi, as she led her

troops in to battle, it was you who imprisoned Nehru because he objected to his country being brought in to the war without being asked.[141]

In view of these observations Alexander Shaw made certain recommendations to the British government reiterating what had already been officially accepted and implemented.[142] He emphasised that 'care should be taken that these films (catalogued as peoples of India, primitive tribes, cults, villages, religions), are brought up to date and that subjects are not presented from a "dead past point of view."'[143]

Endorsing these recommendations and summing up the new perspective, a sub-committee on films officially announced on 27 March 1942 a shift of emphasis 'from the British Indian army to portraying Indian armed forces to indicate India's war efforts'.[144] The shift in cinematic emphasis towards 'recent developments in India in industrial, educational, military fields etc.', which was to have 'immediate value in connection with war' and also 'would be of permanent interest', had already started.[145]

British policy was compelled to change in response to new social and political pressures, both colonial and international. This dramatic shift in theme and ideology highlighted the tussle between the contrary perceptions of colonisers and colonised. The empire cinema had emerged in the 1930s as an arena for debate and discussion on matters of imperialist concern and thus as a new site for the formation of public opinion. In this, the media, both Indian and western, played a significant role. A subversion of symbols and meanings effected an expose which successfully transformed the pro-British propaganda of the empire films and made them counter-productive.

Colonial India and the making of empire cinema investigates this important cultural shift in British policy regarding British and colonial images and ideology. It unravels neglected aspects of the unofficial and official attempts to manipulate and control a vastly influential and popular communication mass medium like the cinema. In doing so it also locates the cinema in relation to other significant media such as print and broadcasting. The scale of interest the cinema generated in the colonising and colonised country indicates its historical importance. This work foregrounds certain hidden facts and nuances of the interaction between colonial society and the cinema at a very crucial stage of its historical development.

Notes

1 By 'discourse' is meant an 'organised and regulated as well as regulating and constituting' domain of language use, a 'truth-producing system in which propositions, concepts and representations generally assign value and meaning to the objects of the various disciplines that treat them'. The concept of 'discourse' would suggest 'linkages between power, knowledge, institutions, intellectuals, control of populations and the ... State as these intersect in the functioning of systems of thought'. See Paul A. Bove, 'Discourse', in Frank Lentricchia and Thomas McLaughlin (eds), *Critical Terms for Literary Study* (Chicago, Chicago University Press, 1990), pp. 50–65.

2 For the classic account of the Other under the impact of colonialism and the role of the creation of knowledge in this colonial enterprise, see Edward Said, *Orientalism* (New York, Routledge & Kegan Paul, 1978). For an essay that relates Said's general insights to British scholarship on India, see Ronald Inden, 'Orientalist construction of India', *Modern Asian Studies*, 20 (1986), pp. 401–46. See also Inden's *Imagining India* (Massachusetts, Basil Blackwell, 1990).

3 See, for example, John M. Mackenzie (ed.), *Imperialism and Popular Culture* (Manchester, Manchester University Press, 1986).

4 John M. Mackenzie gives a comprehensive compilation of the most important research work in this connection. See *Imperialism and Popular Culture*, and *Propaganda and Empire: The Manipulation of British Public Opinion, 1880–1960* (Manchester, Manchester University Press, 1984).

5 S. Theodore Baskaran, *The Message Bearers: The Nationalist Politics and the Entertainment Media in South India, 1880–1945* (Madras, Cre-A: 268 Roypettah High Road, 1981); M. S. S. Pandian, *The Image Trap: M. G. Ramachandran in Films and Politics* (New Delhi, Sage Publications, 1992); Pandian, '*Parasakthi*: life and times of a DMK film', *Economic and Political Weekly*, 26: 11–12 (Mar. 1991), pp. 759–70; Sumita S. Chakravarty, *National Identity in Indian Popular Cinema, 1947–1987* (Delhi, Oxford University Press, 1996); and M. Madhava Prasad, *Ideology of the Hindi Film: A Historical Construction* (Delhi, Oxford University Press, 1998). The other scholars currently engaged in the study of Indian films offering fresh insights in this field are Geeta Kapur, 'Mythic material in Indian cinema', *The Journal of Arts and Ideas*,

3 (Jul.–Dec. 1987), pp. 79–109; Ravi S. Vasudevan, whose articles have been very useful in understanding Indian cinema of early 1940s and 1950s; Ashish Rajadhyaksha, 'The Phalke era: conflict of traditional form and modern technology', *Journal of Arts and Ideas*, 14–15 (Jul.–Dec. 1987), pp. 44–77; and Rosie Thomas, 'Sanctity and scandal: the mythologization of *Mother India*', *Quarterly Review of Film and Video*, 2:3 (1989), pp. 11–30.

6 'Subjectivities' is used here in a strictly limited sense: the meanings ascribed to being an individual with a given identity by a cinematic text.

7 Thomas R. Metcalf, *Ideologies of the Raj* (Cambridge, Cambridge University Press, 1995), p. x.

8 Tytti Soila, 'Valborgsmassoafton: melodrama and gender politics in Swedish cinema', in Richard Dyer and Ginette Vincendeau (eds), *Popular European Cinema* (London & New York, Routledge, 1992), pp. 232–44.

9 The ideologies of empire are varied and complex with different motivations and justifications all at odds with one another or working simultaneously. They are rejected by the subordinate all over the world. For most of the nineteenth and twentieth centuries the British ruled over a colossal empire. This extended over a large part of Africa, the whole of the Indian subcontinent and Australasia, territories in south-east Asia and the Pacific and even, for a time, much of the Middle East. The empire's diverse character, with particularities of different types of people, culture and civilisation and rapidly changing equations with imperial power in the wake of the rise of nationalist forces ensured that imperialism meant different things to different people at different times, making definition of the empire ideology difficult and contradictory.

10 Ella Shohat and Robert Stam, *Unthinking Eurocentricism: Multiculturalism and the Media* (London & New York, Routledge, 1994), p. 110.

11 Richard Dyer, 'White', *Screen*, 29:4 (Autumn 1988), pp. 44–64.

12 Janet Staiger, 'The handmaiden of villainy: methods and problems in studying historical reception of films', *Wide Angle*, 8:1 (1986), pp. 19–28.

13 It is now widely accepted that audiences recreate their own meaning from reading or seeing text or images. Ginsburg shows how 'a man of the people' uses his own experience to read or draw out the meaning of a text entirely in a differently context to the one intended. Chartier similarly maintains the possibility of a narrative, written or oral, permitting a plurality of meaning. He explains this in terms of the logic of cultural consumption in which recipients or people as

cultural consumers are not passive but construct their own reading and interpretations. See Carlo Ginsburg, *The Cheese and the Worm* (London, Routledge & Kegan Paul, 1980); Roger Chartier, 'Intellectual history or sociocultural history: the French trajectories', in his collection of essays, *Cultural History: Between Practice and Representations* (Cambridge, Polity Press, 1988), pp. 19–52.

14 For different theories and a comprehensive debate on audience studies see, Ellen Seiter, Hans Borchers, Gabriele Kreutzner and Eva-Maria Warth (eds), *Remote Control: Television, Audience and Cultural Power* (London & New York, Routledge, 1989); and Paul Marris and Sue Thornham (eds), *Media Studies: A Reader* (Edinburgh, Edinburgh University Press, 1996).

15 This model was developed by the University of Birmingham Centre for Contemporary Cultural Studies under the direction of Stuart Hall. See David Morley, 'Changing paradigms in audience studies', in Seiter *et al.*, *Remote Control*, pp. 16–43.

16 Lawrence Grossberg, 'Strategies of Marxist cultural interpretation', *Critical Studies in Mass Communication*, 1:4 (1984), pp. 392–421.

17 The example cited by John Fiske is drawn from Robert Hodge and David Tripp, *Children and Television* (Cambridge, Polity Press, 1986). John Fiske explains that the popularity of Westerns is due to the aboriginals' ability to be the producers of their own culture and makers of their own meaning and pleasures. See Fiske, 'Movements of television: neither the text nor the audience', in Seiter *et al.*, *Remote Control*, pp. 56–78.

18 Manthia Diawara, 'Black spectatorship: problems of identification and resistance', *Screen*, 29:4 (Autumn 1988), pp. 66–76.

19 The colonial government legislation which imposed restrictions and censorship on the print and entertainment media with severe consequences for any activity deemed seditious, incorporated the *Registration Act* (1867), the *Dramatic Performance Control Act* (1878), the *Vernacular Press Act* (1878), and the *Press Act* (1910).

20 See Ravi S. Vasudevan's pioneering work on the cinema of 1940s and 1950s, which is also relevant for this period. Among his other articles, see especially 'Shifting codes, dissolving identities: the Hindi social film of the 1950s as popular culture', Nehru Memorial Museum and Library, New Delhi, Research-in-Progress Papers, second series, no. 74; and 'Addressing the spectator of a "third world" national cinema: the Bombay "social" film of the 1940s and 1950s', *Screen*, 35:4 (Winter 1995), pp. 305–24.

21 Rajadhyaksha, 'The Phalke era', pp. 44–77

22 The recent work of Stephen P. Hughes, dealing with the growth of film audiences in the city of Madras during the first decade of this

century is an exception to this. See his 'The pre-Phalke era in south India: reflections on the formation of film audiences in Madras', *South Indian Studies*, 2 (Jul.–Dec. 1996), pp. 161–204. The few other works on audience studies that exist deal with the contemporary period and with highly specialised cinema audiences. For example, the work of Pfleiderer and Lutze is based upon participation observation of a rural audience at a special screening: see Beatrix Pfleiderer and Lothar Lutze, *The Hindi Film: Agent and Reagent of Cultural Change* (New Delhi, Manohar Publications, 1985). Sara Dickey's work, *Cinema and Urban Poor in South India* (Cambridge, Cambridge University Press, 1993), deals with fan clubs among the poorer sections of society in South India and is essentially a sociological study. Pandian's article '*Parasakthi*' deals with agitational politics around this film in 1952. However, the identification and actual participation of the audience/agitators remain elusive, subsumed under the politics which they represented. The major emphasis of the work remains on the ideological trends represented in the film in the given logic of electoral politics of Tamil Nadu.

23 Robert C. Allen, 'From exhibition to reception: reflections on the audience in film history', *Screen*, 31:4 (Winter 1990), pp. 347–56; and Barbara Klinger, 'Film history terminable and interminable: recovering the past in reception studies', *Screen*, 38:2 (Summer 1997), pp. 107–28.

24 Jackie Stacey, *Star Gazing: Hollywood Cinema and Female Spectatorship* (London & New York, Routledge, 1994).

25 A unique project was started in Britain in 1930 called 'mass observation' to assess different aspects of everyday life of British citizens. The cinema proved to be an important aspect of everyday life in Britain at that time and the *Mass Observation Archives* in Sussex has more files on cinema than on any other single topic. This vast collection has several reports on audiences' behaviour, preference, family life, cinema impact and so forth.

26 Hughes, 'The pre-Phalke era in south India', pp. 161–204.

27 *Hindu* (10 Dec. 1937), p. 5.

28 *Indian Cinematograph Committee Report*, 1927–28 (Madras, Government of India, Central Publication Branch, 1928), pp. 21–2.

29 The advertisement for *The Drum* in India, for example, mentioned Sabu as the 'star' of the film; other actors were dismissed as 'many others'. See *Bombay Chronicle* (10 Sep. 1938), p. 14.

30 There was a great deal of resentment in the Indian film industry because they felt that US and British films were being 'dumped' in the Indian market, when they had already earned their cost at home.

31 *Film India* (May 1939), p. 39.

32 Culled from *Bombay Chronicle* (26 Feb. 1939), p. 8; *Hindu* (7 Sep. 1934), p. 5; *Hindu* (11 Aug. 1933), p. 12; and *Film India* (May 1939), p. 39.

33 Panna Shah, *The Indian Film* (Bombay, Motion Picture Society of India, 1950), p. 45.

34 *Hindu* (14 Nov. 1941), p. 3.

35 *Film India* (Jan. 1939), p. 29, and *Film India* (May 1939), p. 39.

36 Shah, *The Indian Film*, p. 68.

37 Indian Cinematograph Committee, *Evidence, 1927–28*, vol. II (Calcutta, Government of India, Central Publication Branch, 1928), p. 212.

38 Maharashtra State Archives, Mumbai, Home Poll, F. no. 75 (1928), p. 3.

39 *Film India* (Jan. 1939), p. 29.

40 ICC Evidence, vol. I, p. 50.

41 ICC Report, p. 23.

42 ICC Evidence, vol. IV, p. 235.

43 John Masters, *Bugles and a Tiger* (New York, Viking Press, 1956), p. 115. Interestingly, one of the empire films located in the Frontier was being screened at the time of Masters' visit to the cinema in the cantonment area of the NWFP where he was posted.

44 ICC Evidence, vol. IV, pp. 78–9. Also see oral evidence of Badri Prasad Mathur, professor of English, Radha Swami Educational Institution, Agra (13 Feb. 1928), pp. 894–95.

45 ICC Evidence, vol. II. See oral evidence of Lala Lajpat Rai, member of the Central Legislative Council (28 Nov. 1927), p. 205.

46 ICC Evidence, vol. I, pp. 14–15.

47 *Ibid.*, vol. II, p. 72.

48 For a fascinating recapitulation of the past see V. S. Mahajan 'Down memory lane', *Tribune* (6 Dec. 1992), p. 5.

49 *Film India* (Jan. 1939), p. 29

50 From 1927–28 onwards, there is a vast literature on the Indian audience in the form of letters, observations by different strata of British society in India and articles, all of which underline the 'unsuitability' and 'gullibility' of Indian audiences. See India Office Records, London, L/P&J/6/1747, pp. 452–622. Part of this vehement condemnation of the Indian audience was geared towards a demand for more stringent censorship to discourage the exhibition of US films in India. For the British opinion of the Indian audience see also Aruna Vasudev, *Liberty and Licence in the Indian Cinema* (Delhi, Vikas Publishing House, 1978), pp. 20–2.

51 IOR, L/P&J/6/1747, 1922–1930. See 'Films in the east', *The Times* (23 Aug. 1923), p. 582.

52 IOR, L/P&J/6/1995, 1930–1938, p. 621.
53 *Ibid.* The film in question was *The Triumph of the Scarlet Pimpernel.* This film was certified after excision of scenes dealing with violence and 'ruthlessness of mob rule'.
54 For the conventional viewpoints addressing the nature of spectators of the commercial films in India and its critique see Vasudevan, Addressing the spectator', pp. 305–24, and 'Shifting codes, dissolving identities'.
55 IOR, L/P&J/7/831, 1935, Punjab government to the home secretary, 10 Jan. 1944.
56 IOR, L/P&J/8/127, Coll. no. 105-A, pt. VII, Feb. 1936–Jul. 1938, government of India to the home secretary, public and judicial department letter no. 5/2/3/36-Poll., 10 Mar. 1936.
57 Vasudev, *Liberty and Licence*, pp. 17–18.
58 ICC Report, pp. 2–9.
59 British Film Institute, London. See paper read by Tyrrell at the summer conference of the cinematograph exhibitors association of Great Britain and Ireland on 23 Jun. 1937.
60 IOR, L/P&J/6/1747, 1922–1930.
61 *Ibid.*
62 *Ibid.* See Constance Bromley, 'Censorship and propaganda: influence of foreign films', *The Times Cinema Supplement* (21 Feb. 1922).
63 IOR, L/P&J/6/1747, 1922–1930.
64 *Ibid.*, R. T. Peel to the under-secretary of state for India, 7–12 Mar. 1937.
65 MSA, Home-Poll, F. no. 274, 1933–1934, p. 31.
66 IOR, L/P&J/8/126, Coll. no. 105-A, pt. I, Oct. 1935–Aug. 1940. See handwritten remark on letter no. P. 1850/128/150, foreign office to P&J department, dated 12 Jun. 1936.
67 *Ibid.* See handwritten comment on a note to the secretary of state, dated 19 Aug. 1939.
68 *Ibid.* See minute paper of the P&J department, dated 16 Aug. 1939.
69 IOR, L/P&J/7/831, 1935. See P&J department to G. E. Shepherd, 22 May 1935.
70 *Ibid.*, R.T. Peel to J. Brooke-Wilkinson, secretary of the BBFC, 6 Jun. 1935. See also telegram from government of India to secretary of state for India, dated 1 Jun. 1935.
71 *Ibid.*, Aftab-ud-Din, Imam, the Shah Jahan mosque, Surrey, England, 7 May 1935.
72 *Ibid.* See extracts from the Central Legislative Assembly debates of Sep. 1935 and the House of Commons debates of 29 Apr. 1935.

73 *Ibid.* John Simon, under-secretary of state for foreign affairs to under-secretary of state for India , 25 Apr. 1935.
74 IOR, L/P&J/8/127, Coll. no. 105-A, pt. VIII, Apr. 1937. See note dated 9 Mar. 1937.
75 *Ibid.* See government of India home department to R. T. Peel, secretary of the P&J department, confidential DO no. 1, 2/3/63-poll, 18 Feb. 1937.
76 *Ibid.* See confidential paper of the military secretary, dated 17 Feb. 1936.
77 *Ibid.* See note dated 9 Mar. 1937.
78 IOR, L/P&J/8/129, Coll. no. 105-B, Feb. 1936–Jul. 1939.
79 ICC Report, p. 24.
80 IOR, L/P&J/6/1747, 1922–1930. See Bromley, 'Censorship and propaganda', *The Times Cinema Supplement* (21 Feb. 1922).
81 IOR, L/P&J/6/1747, 1922–1930.
82 Personal interview conducted in May 1992 with N. V. K. Murthy, former director of the Film and Television Institute of India at Pune. Murthy remembers several such occasions in the film theatres. A counter demand was being made at this time that the Indian nationalist song '*Vande Mataram*' should be played at the end of Indian talkies. See *Hindu* (10 Dec. 1937), p. 5.
83 Murthy interview. See also IOR, L/P&J/8/129, Coll. no. 105-B, Feb. 1936–Jul. 1939.
84 IOR, L/P&J/8/131, Coll. no. 105-D. See letter no. F.49/8/39, bureau of information, home department, Simla, to A. M. Joyce, India Office, London, 16 Jun. 1939.
85 IOR, L/P&J/8/130, Coll. no. 105-B, Oct. 1937–Jul. 1938.
86 IOR, L/P&J/8/126, Coll. no. 105-A, pt. I, Oct. 1935–May 1940.
87 *Ibid.*, J. W. Chidell to R. W. A. Leeper, foreign office, London, 16 Aug. 1939.
88 *Ibid.*
89 *Ibid.* See minute paper of P&J department, dated 16 Mar. 1936.
90 IOR, L/P&J/6/1747, 1922–1930. See letter dated 11 Sep. 1923.
91 IOR, L/P&J/8/128, Coll. no. 105-A, pt. XIII, Apr. 1936–1939.
92 John Fiske has adopted the term 'cultural capital', borrowed from Pierre Bourdieu's work, and added to it the notion of cultural power in the hands of cultural categories other than the dominant bourgeoisie. In the colonial context, these other 'cultural categories' may be defined as the colonised. See his 'Moments of television', pp. 56–78.
93 For details see Rosaleen Smyth, 'Britain's African colonies and British propaganda during the Second World War', *Journal of Imperial and Commonwealth History*, 14:1 (Oct. 1985), pp. 65–82.

94 IOR, L/P&J/8/127, Coll. no. 105-A, pt. VII, Feb. 1936–Jul. 1938.
95 *Ibid.*
96 See *Bioscope* (15 Aug. 1912), p. 461, *Bioscope* (29 Aug. 1912), pp. 664–65, and *Kinetogram* (2 Sep. 1912), p. 8.
97 *Bioscope* (29 Aug. 1912), pp. 664–65.
98 *Kinetogram* (2 Sep. 1912), p. 8.
99 Other proposals on making Mutiny films were also rejected at the scenario-vetting stage in 1936. One such scenario was that of *The Prime of Empire* proposed by Paramount Film Service Ltd.
100 IOR, L/P&J/8/127, Coll. no. 105-A, pt. VII, 1939. See letter from P&J department to the secretary of state for India, 7 Apr. 1936, and a handwritten note of the secretary of state, dated 6 Apr. 1936, which stated: 'It may start with Lucknow, Cawnpore will follow. We ought to do all we can to stop it'.
101 *Ibid.* Private letter from Zetland to Linlithgow, dated 6 Dec. 1938.
102 IOR, L/P&J/8/128, Coll. no. 105-A, pt. XIII, Apr. 1936–1939, 1939, Lothian to Zetland, 5 Dec. 1938.
103 *Ibid.* See note by A. Dibdin dated 5 Dec. 1938.
104 *Ibid.* See *West Africa* (10 Dec. 1938).
105 *Ibid.* For details of objections from different segments of British society and the critical comments of the press see P&J department papers dated Dec. 1938; *Daily Herald* (2 Dec. 1938); *Daily Telegraph* and *Morning Post* (3, 6 & 19 Dec. 1938); *New Chronicle* (6 Dec. 1938); *Daily Despatch* (7 Dec. 1938); *Daily Film Reuter* (7 Dec. 1938); *Edinburgh Evening News* (9 Dec. 1938); and *Bystander* (14 Dec. 1938).
106 Cited in *The Cine-Technician*, 4:19 (1939), p. 144.
107 IOR, L/P&J/8/126, Coll. no. 105-A, pt. I, Oct. 1935–May 1940. See also *House of Commons Debates*, 342:22 (7 Dec. 1938).
108 For details of the Chatfield Report see Milan Hauner, *India in Axis Strategy: Germany, Japan and Indian Nationalists in the Second World War* (London, German Historical Institute, 1981), pp. 126–28.
109 IOR, L/P&J/8/128, Coll. no. 105-A, pt. XIII, Apr. 1936–1939.
110 IOR, L/P&J/8/126, Coll. no. 105-A, pt. I, Oct. 1935–May 1940. See letter of John Weiner dated 20 Apr. 1939.
111 *Ibid.* Zetland to Beauchamp, 18 May 1939. The words in the parenthesis existed in the first draft but were subsequently dropped in the final draft perhaps because they were too revealing of the official intent.
112 *Ibid.*, government of India, home department, to P&J department India Office, London, no. 20/40/39-Poll, 2 Jun. 1939.
113 The 1928 guidelines maintained that films should not adversely

reflect on the British army or the white race as that might imperil the British prestige, which was vital to the maintenance of British rule; films should not offend foreign contenders; film-makers should consider the political expediency of the film and whether it was likely to inflame the indigenous population; and, finally, films should not deal with miscegenation. In subjects dealing with India, it was further laid down that films should not portray British officers in an odious light, neither should they suggest disloyalty of native states or in any way undermine British prestige in the empire. Scenes of 'white men in a state of degradation amidst native surroundings', or 'equivocal situations between white girls and men of other races', or British possessions represented as 'lawless sinks of iniquity', or 'conflict between armed forces of a state and the populace', were especially mentioned in the instructions as projections which were to be avoided. See BBFC, annual report, 1928, p. 5.

114 IOR, L/P&J/8/126, Coll. no. 105-A, pt. I, Oct. 1935–May 1940. See foreign office circular memorandum dated 31 Jul. 1936. Significantly, these instructions had been prepared in Jul. 1936 itself on the basis of government of India recommendations but had neither been implemented nor heeded seriously.

115 *Ibid.* J. W. P. Chidwell, P&J department, to R. W. A. Leeper, foreign office, London, 10 May 1939.

116 *Film India* (Aug. 1939), p. 5.

117 *Hindu* (8 Sep. 1939), p. 3.

118 IOR, L/I/1/691, 1940–1942, information department, F. no. 462/14E, 1942. See note of Burton Leach, empire division, to Hodson, 5 Sep. 1940.

119 Robert Stam and Louise Spence, 'Colonialism, racism and representation: an introduction', in Bill Nicholas (ed.), *Movies and Methods*, vol. II (Berkeley & Los Angeles, University of California Press, 1985), pp. 632–49; Shohat and Stam, *Unthinking Eurocentricism,* pp. 45–83; Ella Shohat, 'Gender and culture of empire: towards a feminist ethnography of the cinema', in Hamid Naficy and Teshome H. Gabriel (eds), *Otherness and the Media: The Ethnography of the Imagined and the Imaged* (Langhorn, Harwood Academic Publishers, 1993), pp. 45–84.

120 Shohat, 'Gender and culture of empire', p. 46.

121 *Ibid.*

122 For details see Jeffrey Richards, 'Boys own empire: feature films and imperialism in the 1930s', in Mackenzie (ed.) *Imperialism and Popular Culture*, pp. 140–64.

123 Shohat and Stam, *Unthinking Eurocentricism*, pp. 114–21

124 *Ibid.*, pp. 103–4.

125 *Ibid.*, p. 151.

126 See reprint of her article in *Daily Telegraph* (8 Apr. 1987), p. 10.

127 For details of early films centring around India, see Dorothy B. Jones, 'The portrayal of China and India on the American screen, 1896–1955' (Massachusetts, Center for International Studies dissertation, Massachusetts Institute of Technology, 1955), pp. 52–5.

128 This film concerned a 'holy war' planned by tribesmen living in the Afghanistan frontier under the leadership of a woman called Yasmini, who was regarded by them as a goddess. Her plan was to overcome the British while Britain was preoccupied on the continent during World War I, and with her tribesmen to sweep over and conquer all India. The hero aided by 'loyal Indian subjects' uncovers the plot and prevents the uprising.

129 Clive Coultass, 'British feature films and the Second World War', *Journal of Contemporary History*, 19:1 (Jan. 1984), pp. 7–22. See also the introduction to Nicholas Pronay and D. W. Spring (eds), *Propaganda, Politics and Films, 1918–45* (London, Macmillan, 1982).

130 IOR, L/P&J/8/127, Coll. no. 105-A, pt. IV, Aug. 1935–Apr. 1936. See memorandum from the British consulate, Los Angeles, California, 22 Nov. 1935.

131 Peter Stead, 'The people and the picture: the British working class and film in the 1930s', in Pronay and Spring (eds), *Propaganda, Politics and Films*, p. 77.

132 These were *The Miracle Woman* (1931), which was considered to offend religious susceptibilities of certain viewers, and *The Bitter Tea of General Yen* (1933), which dealt with miscegenation. Films that dealt with the British empire therefore must have seemed a safe box-office gamble. Frank Capra cited in Jeffrey Richards, 'Imperial images: the British empire and monarchy on films', *Cultures*, 2:1 (1974), pp. 79–114.

133 Philip Woods, 'Film propaganda in India, 1914–1923', *Historical Journal of Films, Radio and Television*, 15:4 (1995), pp. 543–53.

134 In 1930, the Imperial Conference had accepted the need for offering positive propaganda, especially through feature films, for the projection of the British empire. See Richards, *Dream Palace*, pp. 134–52. Also see Jeffery Richards and Anthony Aldgate, *Best of British Cinema and Society, 1930–1970* (London, Basil Blackwell, 1983), pp. 22–3.

135 See Nicholas Pronay and Jeremy Croft, 'British film censorship and propaganda policy during the Second World War', in James Curran and Vincent Porter (eds), *British Cinema History* (London, Weidenfeld & Nicholson, 1983), pp. 144–64.

136 IOR, L/P&J/8/128, Coll. no. 105-A. pt. XIII, Apr. 1936–1939. See J. D. Coleridge to the secretary of state for India, 15 Apr. 1936.

137 *Ibid*. See minute paper of A. Dibdin dated 5 Dec. 1938.

138 *Ibid*., J. D. Coleridge to the secretary of state for India, 15 Apr. 1936.

139 *Picture Goer* (6 Feb. 1936).

140 *Film India* (Jul. 1939), p. 32, and *Hindu* (8 Sep. 1939), p. 3.

141 IOR, L/I/1/691, 1940–1942, F. no. 462/14E, 1942. See Alexander Shaw, 'India', *The Cine-Technician* (Feb.–Mar. 1942), pp. 19–21.

142 At the outbreak of World War II, the ministry of information was formally established to pursue this line of propaganda regarding the colonies in the print, broadcasting and visual media.

143 IOR, L/I/1/691, 1940–1942, F. no. 462/14E. See recommendations dated 27 Sep. 1942.

144 *Ibid*. See report of the film sub-committee, consisting of H. R. Gough and A. Walgough, dated 27 Mar. 1942.

145 *Ibid*., Burton Leach, empire division, to Hodson, information department, 5 Sep. 1940.

2

The Drum (1938):
the myth of the Muslim menace

On 1 September 1938, *The Drum*, one of the most successful British empire films, both in terms of box office receipts and of prestige, was released in the city of Bombay.[1] Based on a story by A. E. W. Mason, *The Drum* was produced by Alexander Korda, directed by his brother Zoltan Korda, and featured Sabu, Raymond Massey, Desmond Tester, Roger Livesey and Valerie Robson. Within a week there was a wide-scale agitation against the film which brought the uptown commercial and business areas of Bombay city to a virtual halt and created a severe law and order situation. It took the police more than a week to bring it under control, something made possible only by the withdrawal of the film from exhibition. This chapter investigates the nature and ramifications of this little known but significant agitation.[2] I use the film, *The Drum*, to explore the burgeoning contradictions between imperialism and the emerging nationalist agenda which generated this conflict.

The Drum is a landmark in selectively recreating ideology and imagery in the history, culture, religion and politics of the colonies. It relaunched the myth of Muslim menace in India, constructed a Muslim communal identity, and depicted Muslims as fundamentalist, backward and anti-national. The primary contradiction in India in 1938 was not shown as being between nationalism and imperialism but within nationalism itself. The film strengthened the ideological field that had been long-nurtured by the British in India and which sought to exclude the Muslims from the image of composite India in a policy of divide and rule. It was an attempt to strengthen the communal as well as 'loyalist' forces in the North-West Frontier Province (NWFP), with the aim of checkmating the Hindu–Muslim unity of the Red Shirts and the Congress in this region, which defied the understanding of colonial rulers and was assuming a threatening form.

The Indian socio-political situation in the 1930s provided a receptive ground to the escalating counter-propaganda drive of the fascists as well as the British, US and Indian critics, contradicting these cinematic constructs, making them counter-productive. The interaction of these cinematic constructions, which built up a justification of the British North-West Frontier policy, with counter-publicity, criticism and the pressure of counter-cultural production from the colonial and international forces, brought to the surface the inherent contradiction of such a portrayal in the form of widespread agitation. The initiative for this agitation came from Muslims drawn from the urban underclass and lumpen proletariat of Bombay city, who were supported in their demands by wider sections of society cutting across community and class. In analysing this agitation, I shall show a more direct correlation between a lower-class plebeian audience in a colonial setting and the sharp political and social understanding of popular cultural representations and its ideological thrust, hitherto denied to this class both by the British as well as latter-day Indian opinion.

The political response countered effectively the communalised myth of the Muslim and his 'menace' to India. In the days of communal propaganda and consciousness, the agitation became an assertion of national identity even as it consolidated a 'Muslim constituency' to defend a 'Muslim identity'. It showed the ability of 'a large crowd'[3] to successfully apply a national-political critique of the British colonial power. Ideas critical of Britain were applied in new fields to give expression to anti-colonialism and anti-imperialism and new symbols were coming into use as focal points of unity and protest which cut across community and class identities.

The success of the agitation lay not only in the withdrawal of the film or in making way for the withdrawal of all such films, but in compelling both the colonial government as well as the Congress to rethink their stand on cultural representation and articulation of new cultural traditions which impinged on politics. It went far beyond an anti-imperialist agitation that politically challenged the British appropriation of India's cultural space and production of knowledge about India, while exposing the political motivations of the colonial government. The agitation challenged not only the white man's selective construction of the Muslims but also that of the Congress, then at the helm of affairs under the provincial autonomy. It underlined a heightened consciousness among different urban groups in the process of self-assertion forming a force for change, which was directed as much at the imperial masters as at its own leadership.

The film essentially shows the establishment of British influence in an imaginary independent state of Tokot situated in the tribal belt of the NWFP of India. Underlying this is the abiding fear of Russian infiltration of the Khyber pass and its ambition to replace Britain as the ruler of India. Voicing this danger, the hero, Captain Carruthers, says to the governor of the NWFP, 'from China to Afghanistan there is a movement to get all the little kingdoms into one great confederacy against us'. He reveals that for this purpose mountain battalions were trained and machine guns supplied by the Russians. To counter-check this, Carruthers leads a mission to Tokot, in a move reminiscent of the subsidiary alliance system of Wellesley, to sign a treaty of friendship with the old ruler. The ruler of Tokot, eager to secure the succession of his minor son, Prince Azim, played by Sabu, signs this 'treaty of peace'. Making clear the conditions of this treaty, Carruthers points out to the old Khan, 'My Government will establish an agency at Tokot with a British Resident and it will protect your country against its enemies. On the other hand, as understood, you will suppress the passage of arms through your State.'

In return the old ruler Khan and the heir apparent are given a very generous subsidy for life. The former, grateful for this gesture of good will declares, 'England has offered her friendship. If England is our friend we shall have peace.' The state subjects are shown as jubilant and happy having been rendered 'safe' from all danger to their 'peace'. The ruler, however, is murdered by his brother, Gul Khan, who usurps the throne. Carruthers returns to Tokot as the British resident. He is accompanied by his wife, Marjorie. Gul Khan plots with the Russians to plan the massacre of the residency staff. To this end, he invites Carruthers and his men for the feast of *muharram*. At the crucial moment, however, Azim, the rightful heir to the throne and a friend of the British, beats out a flourish on the drum to warn them. Azim had learned to play the drum from a Scottish boy employed as a drummer in the British Indian army. The class of the former enabled the racial divide to be transcended. Their friendship plays a crucial role in the film. It establishes the British as 'natural friends and allies' of the Pathans (illustration 3). Mason, the author of the story and the film script, confirmed this by disclosing that their friendship was the reason why this film was ever made.[4] Finally, the British troops with the aid of this young loyal Pathan prince, defeat native treachery. Gul Khan is killed and young Azim placed on the throne (illustration 4).

Creating myths: the North-West Frontier

The Drum deals with the policy adopted by the British in the NWFP of India and offers a justification for it. This justification is not given any recognition by the leading film historian, Jeffrey Richards, who argues that Korda's film offered no concrete political, economic or constitutional justification for the empire's existence. Jeffrey sets films of this genre firmly in the nineteenth century, which looked back to the pioneering days of exploitation, construction and profit, construed and legitimised as adventure, along with an older, nobler and altogether more potent concept: 'the white man's burden', involving hard work, self-sacrifice, duty and death. My own argument analyses the film in its contemporary socio-political situation, and in relation to its reception in India, the reaction it evoked and the criticism and condemnation it attracted. It suggests that the film made in the troublesome interwar period, was an answer to certain problems that Britain was facing in national, international and colonial spheres and seeks to understand its varied ramifications not only in relation to the colonists but also to the nationalists.

The importance of this film for the colonial government at this historical juncture is underlined in the choice of Mason to script the film and the close links which Korda enjoyed with the British government. A. E. W. Mason (1868–1948), was one of the more successful novelists and short story writers of his generation. He had come to India in the early years of the twentieth century. Later on among British members of parliament he came to be fully accepted as an 'authority on India'. Advertised in the media as an 'India specialist', the extensive interviews and write-ups on him emphasised his India connection and 'special first hand knowledge of India'. He was obviously familiar with the troubles the British were facing in the Frontier region. Similarly, Korda's close links with the British government and its individual functionaries were significant. Not only did these links secure him the co-operation of the British Indian army and colonial authorities,[5] but also determined the nature of his film's propaganda thrust. As a cinematic exercise, this film propagated certain viewpoints far more forcefully and clearly than any other film in the empire cinema package and elicited the strongest reaction from Indian audiences.

Indeed, *The Drum*, alone among the other empire films of this genre, was openly claimed to have been set in the contemporary India of 1938. Immediately after the credits a globe is shown spinning slowly; the splashes of red indicating the British dominated colonies are accompanied by the very popular floating tune of 'Rule Britannia'. This is followed by the repeated use of a map of India, specifically indicating the NWFP in British India and the territories beyond. Images of maps and globes, as Shohat and Stam argue, helped 'suture the white western spectator into the omniscient cosmic perspective of the European master-subject'; they emphasised physical possession, domination and western technological power over vast and varied geographical areas.[6] Thus the unfolding reality is impressed upon the viewer from the start. What follows is the merging of this reality with fiction. Open thanks are also expressed to 'His Highness, the Mehtar of Chitral' for his 'valuable assistance during the making of this picture'. Film publicity would also highlight the vast amount of establishing footage that was allowed to be shot in Chitral, greatly contributing to providing authenticity to the film, and much advance publicity of *The Drum* also focused on the location shooting of the film in the NWFP, brought about with the co-operation of the India Office.[7] When the press books emphasised 'a Pathan tribe in revolt', they also underlined the location of this revolt in the 'Khyber – bloody frontier of empire – the historic gateway to India'.

Some discerning voices among the British in India were able to comprehend what they termed as 'the delicate position' of all such films depicting life on the North-West Frontier as projecting 'a mixture of reality and imagination', which was 'treading on dangerous ground'.[8] Significantly, films considered topical in relation to the contemporary situation in India or creating an impression of authenticity by the use of maps or reference to historical happenings were not generally allowed to be screened in India. For example, the Hollywood film, *Storm Over Bengal* (1938) was greatly frowned upon by British officials, and was prevented by the India Office and the public and judicial department from being sent to India.[9] Strong objection was taken to the use of a map of India, which, according to the officials, 'threatened the fictional atmosphere of the whole affair set in the north west frontier province'. Yet, in Korda's film, *The Drum*, these objections were never raised or were overruled. The connection with contemporary India was stressed rather than denied. Korda's close links with British government and censor authorities certainly explain the differential treatment meted out to his film. The following account will indicate that this link also determined the ideas, attitude and message that were sought to be conveyed through this film as a representation of a particular historical period.

The resultant portrayal showed India in imminent danger of a Muslim take-over and the British as the only hope of maintaining peace. Danger to this peace had certain dimensions. In delineating the source and nature of this danger, the film made a comment on the Indian socio-political situation by cinematically recreating the imperial myth of a divided India. This conflictive premise, which Britain alone could override, was imaged both in *The Drum* as well as in *Gunga Din*. For portraying this aspect, *The Drum* picked up the official propaganda that 'but for the British army in the north west frontier province, the Hindus and Sikhs of the province would be annihilated either by the Muslims of the settled districts who constitute the majority community in the province or by their trans-border brethren from whom they are separated not even by a day's journey on foot.'[10]

This argument had undoubtedly found favour with the communalised sections of Hindus and Sikhs in this region. It is undeniable that over the years communalisation of the NWFP had occurred and communal bodies like the Hindu Sabha and Sanatan Dharam Sabha were active in places like Dera Ismail Khan. The violent impact of communalism on life, property and law and order supplied the British with justification for securing support for their aggressive operations in the NWFP to maintain peace.

Cinematically, this justification was sought by constructing a set of communal identities. In the film the arch villain, Gul Khan, dreams of creating an 'anti-British confederacy' of small independent tribal Pathan states as a prelude to conquering the whole of India. Here the personal ambitions of Gul Khan are metonymically those of the Muslims. In a crucial scene in the film, he articulates his plans:

> See my dreams spring to life. I see a wave of men, lean, hard, hungry, freemen from the hills, whooping down on the soft comfortable slaves of the plains. Their throats ripe for the knife. A story as old as time. I see a river, the river Jhelum – the Jhelum where the old Mughal empire thrived. I see the mosques and domes rise again – the palaces of Shah Jahan.

The Muslims, then, are constructed in a communal mould as the enemies of India, aiming to reconstruct their old Mughal empire, which stretched across the map of India. Gul Khan's words evoke images of the Muslim conquest of India from the North-West Frontier through the centuries. The notion of Muslims as invaders, outsiders, aliens and non-Indians fed actively on their image as anti-national, not against the British (as the white western audience would understand) but in relation to India and Indians. The locus of struggle remained the Indian mainland, and the film suggested that if the British were the outsiders – the invaders – then so too were the Muslims.

In the Frontier, the Pathans lived in harmony with the non-Muslims (Hindus and Sikhs), who were, in fact, considered 'insiders' by them.[11] The non-Muslims, for their part, considered themselves as much Pathans as the Muslims.[12] In this region the construction of national identity was through the regional component. Nationalism was defined by an aggressive posture to outsiders, who were British and not Hindus. Consequently, the Pathans could hardly be dubbed as communal because their religious fervour was against the imperial power – the encroaching outsider.

The British, while pursuing what they termed a 'scientific frontier', had brought several tribal areas, which had never known conquest, into the fold of the British empire. The tribal uprisings were a reaction to the encroachment over their land and colonial intrusion expressed through the presence of foreign troops and administrators. These uprisings certainly unfurled the banner of Islam, and the word *jehad* (holy war) appeared as a unifying creed to the warring tribes, which rallied around religious leaders to prepare to throw back the foreigners.[13] The film tried to deflect this by positing the Hindu as the outsider to the Pathan, to be conquered and subjugated. This is portrayed in the film as the 'high dream' of the Pathans or Muslims in India. Significantly this coincided with the Hindu communalist projection of the 'Muslim dream' in India.

The film implicitly visualised India as a primarily Hindu India and made an ostensible bid at arousing latent fears of the Hindus against Muslim domination. This was an ideological stand which reinforced that strand of socio-political ideology that insisted on dividing India into Hindu and Muslim categories.[14] The film acted as a double-edged sword that cut both ways to the benefit of the colonial power. For the Hindus, it projected an image which kept the Muslims outside a composite India and, for the Muslims, it sought to confirm the image of a Hindu dominated India.

Moreover, in the eyes of the Indian audience, it was not only the rebel Muslim who stood exposed as anti-national for harbouring such dreams, but also the loyal Muslim for extending support to the British leading to their domination in this region. This support was also an explicit support of the British policies adopted in the NWFP. As such, it was also an anti-national move and, as the rest of India was implied to be Hindu, it could be perceived as an anti-Hindu move. In a manner of speaking, therefore, the film recreated the Muslim as a communal stereotype that was both anti-national and anti-Hindu.

This implicit colouring of the Muslims with a communal and anti-national bias did not go unnoticed. The educated middle-class audience in India, which was showing itself more and more alive to what it had termed the 'insidious propaganda' of the film, related the cinematic images to the contemporary situation, and made a frontal attack on its anti-India thrust and content. The September 1938 edition of *Film India* warned the nation against 'the shameful fling at the Frontier Pathans, who poor souls do not even know how they have been defamed and exposed to ridicule'. It went on to appeal to Dr Khan Sahib, the 'enlightened' Congress

premier of the NWFP 'to take notice of the dirty propaganda that
is being carried on against his men', urging him to seek the imposition of a ban on *The Drum*, in order to prevent 'further malice
and defamation of a brave and chivalrous race of men.' The film
was declared to show 'a complete mistrust of the frontier
people'.[15] This charge of mistrust has to be understood in relation
to India and Indians and not to its British rulers. S. H. Jhabvala,
a labour leader and the Railway Union representative in the
Bombay Legislative Assembly, openly declared in the House, 'the
people of north west frontier province are depicted as being
treacherous'.[16] Once again, 'treacherous' is used in relation to
India and not its colonial masters

The condemnation of the film for attempting to malign the
Pathans was accompanied by an attack on it for offering a justification of the British Frontier policy. Making a direct connection
between the NWFP and the film portrayal, an article in *Film India*
of September 1938 argued: '*The Drum* is an argument for the
British policy in north-west frontier province. It is anti-Indian in
spirit and there is enough suggestive material in the picture, if
viewed from the correct nationalist angle, which would justify a
ban by the censors'.

A lengthy letter of protest from Aziz Mohammed Lallji, who
later spearheaded the agitation against this film, was published in
the *Bombay Chronicle* on 8 September 1938:

> It is well known that Indians totally disapprove of the British
> policy in regard to the independent tribes of the north west fron-
> tier. Hence it is the bounded duty of Indians and particularly
> Muslims of India firmly to protest against any propaganda consti-
> tuted to justify such imperialist policy. Especially when the
> propaganda takes the powerful and effective form of a screen-
> picture, the necessity of making a severe and immediate protest
> cannot be exaggerated.
>
> The British film *The Drum* being at present simultaneously
> shown at the Excelsior and the New Empire clearly and openly
> propagates in favour of imperialist Britain and against the inde-
> pendent tribes. That this is done under the pretext of depicting
> Frontier life enhances its bitterness, as the producers of the film
> industry in depicting the life of the Frontier people have openly
> justified the imperialist policy of Britain enforced there. The

picture aims at showing that what ever is done there is done for the benefit of the Frontier people. The picture shows the Frontier people to be treacherous, wily and ferocious.

It is quite clear that such a picture would only rouse the feeling of contempt towards Frontier people in the hearts of those who see it. *The Drum* through its propaganda wounds the feelings of Indians and particularly of Muslims.

This was followed by a protest in the *Bombay Chronicle,* a popular Bombay-based daily newspaper reflecting nationalist opinion, which had been in the forefront of condemning the film on similar grounds. Taking a strong editorial line in its issue of 14 October 1938, it maintained, 'The film [*The Drum*] is objectionable, because it is a very insidious attempt at pro-British propaganda, the danger of which will be realised by those who know something of the present Frontier policy of the British Government, of the criticism it has evoked in India and outside and above all, the character of the tribesmen themselves.'

While defending the Frontier policy, the film seeks to deflect the political danger to the British empire in India on to the colonised themselves through a combination of ideological thrusts. The political discourse in the film is made to mesh with the religious discourse, one feeding into the other in a fatal combination. It challenges the ideological tenets of a modern age as projected by the colonial government. Although it is the *mullah* (the religious head), who is shown to be contemptuous of those who were humble and welcoming to the British, and who dreams of leading a *jehad*, finally, it is Gul Khan, the chief villain, well-equipped with modern weapons, who initiates all the action. Gul Khan reprimands the *mullah* by saying that 'holy war doesn't make men invulnerable to bullets'. According to him 'victories are won by an army, marching to one man's order, fighting to one man's plan'. Yet, this modernised warfare, a motivated gift from the enemies of the British empire, is not only discounted because it is to be used against 'legitimate authority', but more importantly, because its real target is the modern state apparatus. Introduced by the British, the act of 1935 was proudly flaunted in the international arena as a modern, democratic exercise in responsible government in India. Consequently the danger of a fundamental Islamist attack within India, backed by an up-to-date army, was infinitely greater. In effect, it meant that a power-hungry despot sought to replace the modern constitutional and democratic advance introduced by the British by an anti-modern, anti-western, retrograde, fundamentalist regime, which would prey on its own people.

The visual imagery gives primacy to a fundamentalist religious discourse, which is then placed at the heart of this political intrigue to condemn both. For example, there are prolonged scenes of Muslims offering prayers, intercut with two significant scenes depicting Muslim barbarity. The first insert shows Muslims at machine-gun practice firing at targets made up of puppets resembling British soldiers in sitting postures. The second insert shows a severed head of a Muslim informant, in the service of the British Indian army, flung amidst a gathering of officials at the British Residency. Further, the sacred festival of *moharram* is used in the film as an occasion for the planned massacre of British troops, as an additional commentary on the inherently barbaric nature of Islam and a concrete instance of *jehad*.

This brutal depiction makes a mockery of the famed code of honour said to be rigidly observed by Pathans. This code, according to British officials, imposed upon a Pathan three obligations: to shelter and protect even an enemy who comes as a supplicant; to seek revenge by means of retaliation; and to offer open-handed hospitality to all who may demand it.[17] In addition, Pathan values included equality, mutual respect, righteousness, pride, bravery, defence of the honour of women, worship of God and devoted love for a friend. Colonial intervention severely disrupted this code. Indeed, a code which set up an ideal type and ideal standards of behaviour could hardly be observed when confronted with the severely deviant behaviour of a foreign enemy bent upon subjugating the Pathans. For example, no British record speaks of the striking hospitality of the ordinary Pathan villager to any passing stranger or foreigner. The threat of the enemy froze their hospitality. *The Drum*, projecting the imperialist knowledge of the colonial world, showed an open breach of this code. Gul Khan observes the code only until the feast of *moharram* is over, when he seeks to destroy the British guests – a blatant betrayal of a host's code of honour – creating a greater sense of treachery, villainy and betrayal in the minds of the viewers and justifying the brutal retaliation by the British.

Such scenes had their basis in an incident that took place in the north Waziristan Agency in 1897.[18] A British political officer, Gee, entered the village without prior warning. His purpose was to select a site for a small fort the British wanted to erect in the neighbourhood. The Waziris were suspicious. They thought he intended to confiscate their lands in lieu of a fine, which they had not paid. They were surprised and frightened by Gee's sudden arrival with an unusually large escort. The tribesmen laid out a feast for the British party, then, when their guard was down, attacked them, killing several officers. The incident triggered the Frontier uprising of 1897, the most serious the British faced in the region.

Commenting on this incident, James W. Spain observed that the Pathans could not be convicted of a breach of their traditional obligation of hospitality.[19] In fact, Spain argued that it was Gee who should have been censured for not observing any ethics. By arriving suddenly with an unusually large escort, he failed to understand the ground rules of tribal territory; namely, that there is an emotional principle underlying hospitality, and that there are certain behavioural requirements on the part of the outsider for the obligation to be upheld by the Pathan. Spain suggested that had Gee requested protection or even informed the Waziris of his impending arrival, the uprising of 1897 need never have happened. The fact that the code operated upon both the host Pathan and the British guests was either not understood or ignored by the imperialists, with the result that the film, *The Drum*, reproduced the familiar imperialist discourse popularised by the ethnographer-cum-administrators, who categorised Pathans as 'bloodthirsty', 'cruel' and 'vindictive', given to 'stabbing from behind' and 'striking stealthily to win'.[20] Considered to be the innate characteristics of Pathans, these were highlighted in the film.

This 'inherent violence' of Islam is displayed in the film when Gul Khan discloses his plans for the captured British resident: 'I will put you in a wooden cage I have and it will be carried through all the mountain states, so that the people may know how the British are to be feared!' Gul Khan also inflicts a wholly barbaric punishment on Mohammed Khan, a tribal chief and a faithful friend and ally of the British, for having passed on his secret plans to them, by throwing him in to a dungeon and cutting off his tongue. This barbaric and violent presentation of Muslims is contrasted with the pacifist and civilised image of the British. Indeed, when the notorious villain, Gul Khan, is killed, it is not the British but a vengeful fellow Muslim, Mohammed Khan, who performs the deed. To these stereotypical qualities are added yet others. In a scene between Carruthers and young prince Azim, the essential characteristics of the Pathans are sought to be corrected in a patronising way. Carruthers, asserting his authority over Azim, backed up with the threat of a spanking, insists that he must tell the truth at all times.

CARRUTHERS: Will you promise to tell me the truth.
AZIM: Always? That will be very hard.
CARRUTHERS: Yes, I expect it will. But, promise to try, will you?
AZIM: To tell the truth? All right, I promise.
CARRUTHERS: That's fine.
AZIM: But nobody in Tokot ever does.
CARRUTHERS: Oh well, you'll teach them. Come on.

Having been taught the British virtues of truth, Azim is considered fit to provide the assimilationist role model to others in his community. These scenes, however, were deleted at the insistence of the censors in Britain when the film was sent to India.

In several other ways, the film sought to underline the backwardness of the Muslims as contrasted with the progressiveness of the British. Gul Khan, for instance, refuses to accept a British doctor for his sick friend by maintaining, 'Dr Murphy is an unbeliever. When we are ill or in pain we write a few prayers on a piece of parchment and burn it in the fire. Sometimes, it does not succeed, unfortunately we die.' Moreover, the film adopted a condescending British attitude towards aspects of Indian culture – the habit of belching after eating, for example, as a form of compliment to the hosts – while allowing no room for equally horrified Indian reactions to European table manners and standards of personal hygiene.[21]

Masculinity and femininity: positing gender relations

This backwardness, uncivilised behaviour and tribal nature of the Muslims were more prominently underlined by positing masculinity and gender relations at the centre of the ideological evaluation of oriental and western civilisation and culture. The film foregrounds the social position both of oriental (Muslim) and western (British) women, by means of image and dialogue, to indicate the progressiveness of the latter and the backwardness of the former. This dichotomy then serves as a commentary upon the oriental male, his degenerate masculinity and tribal social structure harshly contrasted with the honourable, upright and respectful masculinity of the white male, with his modernised progressive western society and its civilisational bounties. Curiously, these highly negative stereotypical images of Muslims continue to be propagated in the western media even to this day.[22]

The Drum is overwhelmingly a male film. Among the natives, except for a brief dance sequence of a *nautch* girl, and an even briefer appearance of a Hindu *ayah* (maid) of the white memsahib, no female character is portrayed. This invisibility of women is not accidental but may be looked at as an intentional erasure, which makes its own statement. It highlights a variety of white, western contentions about the Other – both male and female. The assumptions work on different planes. In relation to colonial masculinity, this all-male projection suggests an important aspect associated with the Pathans – that of homosexuality. In a society with marked sexual segregation in most contexts, conditions for the practice of homosexuality are laid out.[23] Whereas, in western Anglo-American society, heterosexual relations are seen as the norm and homosexual relations have been stigmatised. Indeed, under the influence of Judaeo-Christian teaching and fear of dissent, the west has long abhorred overt sex between males. Consequently, there has been a sustained attack on homosexuality in the west, particularly in England. In fact, Britain had 'an ultra-squeamishness and hyper-prudery' towards sex, which it all too successfully imposed on the rest of the world.[24] Non-conformity to the norms of heterosexuality threatens the dominant ideology's view of sexuality as innate and natural. This naturalness was underlined in *The Drum* in the celebration of the central heterosexual monogamous couple, the Carruthers

This imposition ignores the fact that other societies have allowed homosexuality to occur without strong negative sanctions. A long tradition of homosexuality is present in many Muslim countries. Although homosexuality is forbidden in the Koran, the popular literature of this region and beyond contains both stories about homosexuality and fine love poetry about and addressed to homosexuals.[25] Significantly, homosexuality in these regions did not compromise masculinity or generate anything like a fixed self-conscious homosexual identity such as emerged, for example, in eighteenth-century Europe.[26] The pre-colonial concept of masculinity under the Mughals accommodated even eunuchs as soldiers and warriors, many of whom rose to the position of generals in the Mughal army and commanded fortresses.[27]

Under the colonial government, the concept of masculinity was much more narrowly and physically defined. Yet, at the same time, in the British Indian army, hailed as symbolising masculinity at its best, homosexuality was rampant.[28] John Masters, who belonged to the Gurkha Regiment, described the army as a 'one-sexed society'.[29] The subaltern in the army could not marry, among the officers only a very small percentage could marry, and among them still fewer could keep their wives in the barracks. In such a situation, sexual behaviour gravitated towards the use of prostitutes and the practice of homosexuality. The colonies, with greater space, privacy and relaxed inhibitions, provided ample opportunities for both. This was especially true of the Frontier situation with its traditionally open attitude towards homosexuality. Karachi, for example, even boasted of boy-brothels used by the British troops. All attempts to close them down by the British, as early as 1845, were successfully resisted by the Amirs.[30]

Deeply uncomfortable with and unwilling to accept or acknowledge rampant homosexuality among its military personnel, the British put the onus of corrupting the British army on the colonised. This attitude assumed a seduction by the Other which feminised the colonised and masculinised the colonisers. The male gaze of the servicemen, because of the power equation between the dominant and subordinate, feminised their object of desire, while retaining the masculine status for themselves. Therefore, whatever the claims of Frontier men to masculinity, they were, by suggestion, condemned in the film, represented as low-ranking, impotent and lacking in 'masculine' qualities. Consequently, the Frontier male, although shown as martial – imagined in terms of supposedly resolute virility, so as to strengthen the colonial argument for the brutal suppression – was also construed as a degenerate. He was portrayed as a debauch prone to torture and rape, on the one hand, and to homosexuality, on the other. This complex imagery effectively played down his warlike qualities as well as the homosocial form of male bonding against colonialism.[31]

This portrayal was further reinforced by the natives' attitude towards their women. The film uses the Indian woman's image to cast reflection upon Indian men and society and indicate the level of civilisation it has achieved.[32] The publicity drive of *The Drum* highlighted the oriental woman in three prominent ways as '*purdah* system, veiled women, and *nautch* dancers'. Hidden in harems and heavily veiled in public, they were understood to be treated as mere objects of male desire and sexuality. Regarding *purdah* the film succeeded in conveying both the sexual attraction as well as repulsion of the white races for observers of *purdah* as a custom. In a scene preceding the feast of *moharram*, considered 'the most amusing passage of the film', the sergeant giving instructions to the British soldiers says, 'In this part of the country the ladies 'ave their lovely features veiled, and you're to leave them veiled.' The film envisages the western spectatorial position as that of a lone male who had the enticing oriental female at his disposal and mercy to unveil and penetrate. Experientially, the unveiling of the women of this region indulged in by the British soldiers – a particularly disgraceful kind of behaviour, which challenged and breached the Frontier code of honour – was in part responsible for the violence of the retaliatory moves by Frontier men.[33]

The sergeant follows his previous instructions by adding: 'We shall be the guests of a Mohammadan prince, and any nosy parking round the harem doors will be met with severe and painful punishment.' For the western audience, the reference to a harem suggested a voyeuristic entrance into an inaccessible private space where their fantasies of sexual domination could be played out. The harem has been described in eurocentric discourse as a male dominated space, signifying oriental despotism. Recent historical accounts have emphasised the harem largely as an upper-class phenomenon and a site of contradiction, which, despite female subordination, existed as a privileged site of female interaction.[34] For some Indian audiences, moreover, these veiled references to the army's behaviour towards oriental women may well have recalled 'the undisciplined lust' with which British soldiers had fallen upon the women of Kabul in 1841.[35] British soldiers, coming from the lower classes, were considered by the elite British to lack continence. According to Ballhatchet, the need to supply these men with an outlet for their 'virile energies' was given official recognition, leading to the provision of facilities for sexual relations with native women.[36] Such an attitude perhaps enabled the officer class in the army to overlook the unruly and immoral behaviour of their men when, in a war situation, they sexually preyed upon the vanquished, both female and male. The inclusion of such scenes in the film were intended to appeal to the British lower classes, who constituted the major cinema-going public of the 1930s and 1940s.

In *The Drum*, the stereotype of the veiled woman, depicting an extreme form of sexual segregation and containment of females, is counterpoised by the extremely libertine behaviour of the oriental male. He is shown to patronise *nautch* girls, popularly associated with prostitution. In a tense scene, serving as a prelude to the planned massacre, where the British guests are being entertained by a *nautch* girl, the conversation between Gul Khan and Carruthers is revealing:

GUL KHAN: When I was in London and Paris, the ballroom dancing always impressed me as something unspeakably vulgar and barbaric.

CARRUTHERS: Probably, because your Highness feels that women should never dance with men.

GUL KHAN: Only for men.

CARRUTHERS: You think that if they dance together the man loses a great deal of his dignity.

GUL KHAN: And the woman something of her chastity.

The sexist and racist clichés used in the film show the colonisers' hostility to cultural differences rather than their understanding. The portrayal of gender and sexuality in the film revealed more about the colonisers' assumptions – at variance with western social expectations – than about those of the colonised.[37] Gul Khan's remarks are used to reinforce the colonial reading rather than contradict or contest it.

This scene can be contrasted with an earlier scene of a ballroom dance. Shown as the glamorous social highlight of the evening, the latter demands the full participation of both sexes. The freedom and pleasure afforded to western women, participating in social entertainment, is counterpoised by the *nautch* girl dancing for the pleasure of men alone. A *nautch* dance was an expression of hospitality traditionally offered to guests by the ruling class,[38] but was looked upon by colonists as a deplorable entertainment, obscene and suggestive of the grossest immorality. Yet, at the same time, depicting this oriental stereotype for the benefit of a white audience, the cinematic portrayal successfully played upon both the sexual attraction of the dance and the white audience's condemnation of it. In the film, this dance is dismissed contemptuously as an entertainment and described as 'stomach waggling' by the British sergeant, who instructs the British soldiers to nevertheless show an appropriate 'look of rapture' on their faces. *The Drum* also embodies a racist attitude, as it implies that no white woman would appease a man through such a demeaning exhibition of herself.

The representation of white femininity in the film articulates a powerful, if subtle, racist message confirming not only cultural differences but also the cultural superiority of the white. The image of the liberated western woman who ostensibly enjoys equality with men, together with the freedom to dress, behave and work as she likes, is thrown into sharp relief by that of the Muslim woman in *purdah*, who is deprived of any social, economic or political rights to selfhood. In western eyes *purdah* underlined the confinement of women, their oppression and unequal gender relations. *Purdah* and the concept of *purdah*[39] denied the fact that the Pathan women were active participants in the Frontier national movement; women volunteers formed a significant part of the *Khudai Khidmadgars* of Abdul Gaffar Khan.[40] The qualities of fearlessness, courage, initiative and truth applied in this region to all Pathans, men as well as women.[41] Moreover, under the aggressive thrust of British colonialism in this region, *purdah* provided an opportunity of preserving one's identity and a certain status in the face of external pressures.[42] Clearly women's invisibility and isolation from the public world outside in the colonial situation had certain justification, which was lost on the western world.

More importantly, the custom of *purdah* was not as wide-spread as some the west would believe. The village and nomadic women in this region seldom observed *purdah* or wore the *chadri* (veil) as it would have interfered with their many daily activities. In the cities, however, among the landowning classes and the aristocracy, it was known to be observed; even here this custom did not go uncontested, as educated city women and the reformists raised their voices against it.[43] In the tribal areas there was no *Purdah* at all.[44]

Similar use was made of the harems and the practice of polygamy in the publicity drive of this film and others of its kind, with the aim of inferiorising a society by highlighting its repressive social practices. *The Drum* carried the theological overtones of the inferiority of the polygamous Islamic world to the Christian world as encapsulated by the monogamous couple. Yet in a region with an adverse female sex-ratio this practice was not exactly widespread.[45] Although polygamy was permissible, in practice the competition for brides and rising bride prices made monogamy the rule. Yet, the film posits, the polygamous custom as the norm in India and is to be contrasted with the western norm of monogamous marriage and egalitarian relations, mutual trust and partnership.

The dual projection of *purdah* and polygamy, in combination with the brief appearance of the female dancer and the voiced concerns of the native male about female chastity, created an image of oriental woman with an unbounded sexuality that needed to be contained and hidden. The film reduced the Muslim woman to a sexualised inferiorised Other and set her up in binary opposition to the 'chaste pure white woman'.[46] The chaste white woman in the film is considered sexually safe even alone among several men of her own race. In one crucial scene, for example, a toast is made to the captain's wife 'and all the other women of the empire for bringing feminine grace to the hard task of defending civilisation'. Her safety is questioned only in relation to the native male. In this sense, the kidnapping of Mollie Ellis by Afridis in 1915 provided a form of 'racial memory' of the sexual threat that Indian men posed to white women.[47]

The British had always been conscious of the white woman's image as a direct reflection upon themselves. Although European women clearly held an ambiguous position in the colonies – both conforming to and subverting the imperial agenda and colonial order[48] – the film presents an idealised picture of colonial women in the role of chaste wife, whose only agenda is to further her husband's mission and work. The colonial army, therefore, accommodated the wife as a symbol of heterosexual, monogamous patriarchy. It celebrated her role, which, instead of impinging on male prestige, furthered it.

The white heroine is shown as a person in her own right. Described in the publicity handouts as a 'brave woman' who followed 'the brave men'. She knows the hazards of life in a colony like India, but willingly backs the male enterprise wholeheartedly and 'follows him into the forbidden Himalayas sharing the perils of a seething borderland'. The posters of the film showed the heroine with the caption: 'One woman who dared. A thrilling drama of a woman whose courage carried her beyond the Frontier into strange adventure.' This image of bravery and steadfastness was upheld both for white men, who were made to feel proud of her, and as an example for other white women in Britain. Marjorie Carruthers justifying her desire to accompany her husband to the NWFP, despite 'known dangers' says, 'How shall I face other women if I run away from it?' Colonial wives were indeed looked upon as bearers of a special civilising mission to both the colonised and their own men. They were not merely representatives of home culture, but also that culture's moral standard. The colonial wife helped to maintain civilised standards of behaviour in general by socialising the native into British ways of thinking and living. In a crucial scene in *The Drum*, Marjorie feeds the young prince at her table.

The only occasion she transgresses her brief is when she physically touches the naked shoulder of a native, bandages his wound and saves his life (illustration 1). This calculated gesture in the film seeks to dissolve the social segregation shown in the army, which suggests racial exclusiveness and superiority. The occasion is provided by the boy prince masquerading in the garb of a menial, as a low caste commoner who takes shelter in her house in order to escape the assassins. The imagery evoked is that of the compassion of a white *memsahib* for one of the servant class. In reality, the contact of white *memsahib* with natives was primarily confined to native male servants who provided many white women with the chief if not the only model of gender and race relations in the colony.[49] These male servants were likely to have been treated with a mixture of familiarity and crudeness rather than distance and firmness as was usual in domestic service. The dark skin of these semi-naked, lower-status Indian household servants had the unusual effect of dress in European eyes.[50] In this one gesture she reaches across the racial boundaries, described in the posters as 'a dramatic' and 'a tense' moment in the film (illustration 1). Yet, in view of the rumoured cases of assault or attempted assault on white women by natives, usually by the class of coolies, *khansamas* (cooks) and other menial servants,[51] this reach across races could very well be read otherwise among its white audience. This transgression seemed to have evoked some criticism in England.[52]

Yet the film actually negated this transgression: the native was not only a mere boy but a prince. As a saviour of the native prince, Marjorie emerges as a mother figure. Moreover, the native is shown to acknowledge this act of bravery. Prince Azim, for instance, calls her brave for this act. Marjorie's gesture also shifts the focus from the imposed military protection of the British male to parental protection bestowed by a benevolent mother. The image of the white woman as both chaste wife and good mother is threatened by Gul Khan, the villainous Other. A clue to his libidinous nature is introduced when, while admiring the white heroine he pontificates, 'The western world, Madame, refuses to learn our scant virtues, the chief of which is the grateful admiration of beauty.' Shown to be covetous, his lustful nature is essentialised when he declares, 'Madame, I kiss your feet, I am your slave.' Although made to speak in a voice, clearly not his own, it heightens the deliberate depiction of the perverse and wanton sexuality of the oriental male. The posters of the film publicised in bold letters: 'Fighting for their Women and their Empire'.

This threatening sexuality of the Muslim Pathan was suggested not only in relation to the white female but its menace was transferred even to Hindus. The historical realities of a number of Hindu women eloping with Muslim men in 1936 – cases which were treated as kidnapping cases[53] – and the abduction of Hindus (men, women and children) by Pathan tribals especially in the years 1937–38, lent this menace a communal colour.[54] The Hindu inhabitants were successful traders, property owners and moneylenders enjoying a lucrative business connected with the army. As the major beneficiaries of British military operations, they were targeted in the periodic raids from the independent territory of Waziristan, undertaken to 'deliver a counter-blast to the military operations of the British and its punitive measures'.[55] Consequently, kidnapping with its ransom demands was regarded as a trade in this region, and Hindus were made to pay for the British military operations in the tribal territories.[56] However, although the Hindus suffered more than the Muslims as far as kidnapping was concerned, the majority of those killed and wounded were Muslims. The cumulative effect was a deterioration in communal relations, reinforced greatly by British propaganda.

In such a situation the implicit suggestion of the sexual menace of the Muslim male reinforced the communal assumptions, which assigned him aggressive sexuality, essentialising it as inherent to Islam. Consequently, the invisibility of native women as a 'subject' category turned them into what Paola Bacchetta calls an 'unfixed' category to be sexually appropriated, a common tactic in most war-like situations.[57] The filmic depiction, therefore, reflected the growing insecurity of the minority population of Hindus who occupied nine per cent of the total population of this region. The threatening sexuality of the Pathan added to the uncivilised and backward depiction of the Muslim, and emphasised the need to control it.

This aspect added yet another dimension to the threat of Muslims and the nature of this threat. It sought to reinforce the fears that the communal Hindus were propagating. Conversely, the British emerge as benevolent and humane, their aggressive policy, bent upon creating imperial hegemony over independent tribal territories, fully justified.

Anti-British propaganda: British apprehensions

The justification of Britain's Frontier policies offered in this film was not new but it was certainly sharper and more consciously done.[58] However, it assumed an importance and urgency in view of the extremely troublesome phase of confrontation that the British were facing in this region. Their policies had created a conflagration in the entire region and had come under scathing attacks by the Indian National Congress. In pre-World War II days, it had also provided much needed fodder for anti-British propaganda forces elsewhere in Europe.

In 1937–38 Germany and Italy stepped up their anti-British propaganda in the print media and films, creating panic in Britain.[59] This propaganda concentrated in part on inciting the Muslims of India to revolt. The British were accused of 'carrying on a ruthless policy of terrorism' in the NWFP of India. Furnishing details, Lt.-Comm. Fletcher disclosed in the House of Commons that this propaganda of 'brutal British repression' involving 'searching harems and outraging women' was spreading 'destruction and devastation' in India.[60] The highly 'libellous and abusive radio talks' were holding the British to 'the scorn and hatred of the Muslims'. The running theme asserted that 'the empire of the British was decadent' and 'will soon break up'. This propaganda, according to British information, was reported to be having 'the desired effect' in the 'Muslim world'.[61]

The Frontier was identified by the Germans as a particularly vulnerable target:

> The mountain people of Waziristan have felt the severity of British punitive measures when it [Waziristan] tried to gain its independence. The British colonial authorities did not answer with legislature but sent back tanks and aeroplanes into the rebel territory and killed thousands of women and children with bombs and shells. World history has not forgotten the cruelties of the British in India where they tied helpless prisoners to the canon's mouth and then fired.[62]

What was so effective about German propaganda was the fact that it had some basis in reality, as evidenced by a confidential report from Waziristan dated 17 September 1939.[63] This described in detail the 'instigating activities' of the Faqir of Ipi, one of the most popular religious and tribal leaders in north Waziristan, against the British. To curb this uprising the British used their military forces in strength, leading to heavy casualties among the tribesmen as well as their own troops. Instances of aerial bombing were given. The report also disclosed how similar confrontations were taking place in other parts of the NWFP, especially the tribal belt. The British penalised the Frontier people by imposing heavy fines on them. Significantly, this confidential report was attached to a report on German propaganda, to underline the disturbing similarity between the two.

The Nazi propaganda listed the bombing of civilian populations and the imposition of collective fines on the NWFP among the widespread crimes committed by the British in India. The House of Commons was flooded with questions regarding the growing anti-British propaganda, especially in relation to India. The Germans were also very effective in influencing the Afghans by screening special propaganda films. Examples of these showed atrocities perpetrated by the British on the Arabs, such as the blowing up of their houses.[64] These propaganda films were not merely shown in Kabul to the restricted audience of European and high government officials but to the people at large, and they were supplemented by radio broadcasts and printed leaflets.

Secret reports confirmed the sharply escalating anti-British propaganda by Fascist forces in India. A telegram from the government of India external affairs office, to the secretary of state for India, dated 28 November 1939, mentioned a committee of five members of the Gestapo conducting Nazi propaganda in India:

[The] main task of this body is production of anti-British pamphlets and other literature which is printed in Urdu and Bengali amongst other languages. It is further reported that the opposition party [in the Punjab Legislative Assembly] of the All India Congress in Lahore has ordered 150,000 copies of the pamphlet entitled 'The Tory Party and its History' from this source. So far as India and the Indian borders are concerned it is important to prevent by every possible means the dissemination of this type of propaganda.

The use of Urdu and Bengali languages for anti-British propaganda purposes in India highlights the two crucial states of India in which Muslims formed the majority populations. These had special importance for the colonial government because they were the only two non-Congress states. These were also providing unstinted support for British Indian army recruitment. Both premiers, Sikander Hayat Khan of Punjab and Fazlul-Huq of Bengal, had declared 'their loyal devotion to the crown'.[65] The precious loyalty of the Muslims, so assiduously cultivated in these pockets of India, stood threatened by the escalating counter-propaganda of the Fascists in 1938–39.

This propaganda was greatly reinforced by the reaction to and criticisms evoked by the empire films both in the USA and Britain. In fact, in the reigning political climate of the late 1930s even the pro-British propaganda became counter-productive and an embarrassment to the British. Hollywood's pushing of the British line, forwarding and endorsing their imperial ideology, did not go unnoticed in the British newspapers and it was widely commented upon.[66] These comments were reproduced verbatim in the Indian press with the explicit purpose of showing how the empire cinema was propagating British imperialism, applauding its attempts at empire building and its tradition of Britain's supremacy in India. Such media comments and discussions of the film were considered 'highly objectionable' by the India Office officials who became more and more uncomfortable with the propaganda and publicity of what were openly accepted as British propaganda films, advocating British imperialism.[67] It instructed its New York consul staff not to use or encourage the phrase British propaganda films, or its associated description, considering all such projection as 'most libellous'.[68]

The empire films were not without staunch critics in Britain and the USA. In the latter, the growing sentiments of anti-imperialism subjected these films to a lot of criticism. It was with growing alarm that the British noted 'America's preoccupation with the disturbed state of the rest of the world.'[69] In the USA the growing anti-imperialism, as seen in both the print and broadcasting media, found the touting of British imperialism embarrassing, especially as it also showed disinclination to become involved in war to defend British imperialism. Consequently, there had been critical write-ups and reviews in the press.[70] In keeping with the USA's larger stand on the question of democracy and foreign rule, US critics, even urged a boycott of these films. *The Film Survey*, a monthly organ of Film Audience for Democracy, an organisation of progressive film-goers in the USA, claimed: 'On occasion we have been criticised for our comments on most of the films about India. We have usually maintained that these movies were not only an untrue picture of those people, but furthermore, an open glorification of the worst aspects of British imperialism.'[71]

The Indian media similarly condemned the propagation of empire films as British propaganda. In *Film India*'s opinion, 'the imperialist propaganda was the crudest and the most vulgar sort' in which Indians were depicted as nothing better than 'sadistic barbarians'. Considered 'revolting and nauseating', these propaganda films were said to make 'the stomachs of every Indian and every fair minded foreigner turn with disgust'.[72] The *Bombay Chronicle* commenting in the same vein maintained: 'Our national respect is deliberately sought to be injured every time a film depicting Indian life is produced abroad.'[73] The *Hindu* took it as 'vilification of India through screen, which lowers us in the estimation of the world and these films shown in India inflame us.'[74]

In their critical attacks, the Indian media highlighted how the screen portrayal of the Muslims in western films was ridiculing Muslim religious practices. For example, a film like *Real Glory* was severely criticised for scenes in which the hides of pigs were flaunted in front of members of an Arab tribe before the Muslims were made to bury their faces in them. Such depictions, it was observed, 'will naturally cause resentment in the Muslim world, particularly among seventy million Muslims in India'.[75] Similar objections to the film, *Belladonna*, were publicised, with the film's 'lowering of Egyptian marriage customs' exposed in detail.[76] Objections were also raised against *The Lives of a Bengal Lancer* in sections of the Indian press.[77] The reaction of the Muslims to films that offended their religious susceptibilities was of concern to British officials in India, who had issued standing instructions to be careful about them.[78]

The British were very sensitive to the possible reaction of the Muslims, especially as they contributed significant resources, in terms of manpower, to the British Indian army. By World War I they were contributing sixty-five per cent of the troops.[79] Their contribution to the Indian manned ships registered in the United Kingdom was also substantial.[80] The British stakes in the loyalty of their armed forces were very high. They could not afford to take any chances, especially as men in the armed forces comprised an important sector of the Indian film audience for western films.

Moreover, the British experience of their Muslim recruits in the army during World War I had not been entirely happy. It had created a sense of insecurity and uncertainty about their attitudes. 'The seditious behaviour' of some of the Muslim soldiers during World War I was put down to the effect of propaganda and rumours implying that it was sinful to help the Christian British fight the Muslim Turks.[81] The need was to contain and counter-act this kind of propaganda by positing a favourable image of Muslims as loyal and natural allies of British.

The British identified the Pathans as being particularly vulner-able among the Muslims, and feared their alienation. The Pathans had been recruited not only for the British Indian army but also for the armed militia and local auxiliaries known as Frontier Scouts. Acting under the political officers they enforced commu-nity justice, punished offences and levied fines. They were also the first line of defence. As such, British fears centred on Pathan prox-imity and susceptibility to enemy propaganda.[82]

The alienation of the Pathans, whether in the army or the Frontier Scout force could have proved disastrous for the British in India, as the NWFP had emerged as one of the 'really hostile provinces of India' by the 1930s. This was a period of greatly heightened nationalist propaganda in this region. Indeed, during this period it was flooded by pamphlets, literature, poetry and drama that exhorted all Pathans – men, women and children – to sacrifice their lives in the cause of nation and country.[83] The Frontier inhabitants came out of their seclusion, carefully main-tained for so long by the British, and were prominent in joining the mainstream of the Indian national movement. The 'blood-thirsty' tribes of the Frontier had successfully belied their past and come together.

In the NWFP local pride and regionalism were transformed into nationalism. The Pathans had developed a concept of the nation beyond that of the tribe or tribal. The bonds of solidarity with other Muslims of British India were emphasised and some of the contradictory elements were contained in the mythical unity of the idea of nation. The Khudai Khidmadgars (the servants of God) or the Red Shirts, organised by Abdul Ghaffar Khan in 1929, led the way, with full independence as their goal. It was a very well-organised movement, with a network of committees in every village among the Afghan *Jirga* (tribal assembly), that conducted a highly successful subversive campaign on both sides of the border. Deeply influenced by the non-violent *satyagraha* and the creed of Hindu–Muslim unity of Mahatma Gandhi, they joined the Congress within a year in its civil disobedience move-ment. So close was the identification and ideological formation of

Abdul Gaffar Khan with Gandhi that he came to be popularly hailed as the 'Frontier Gandhi'. The British were publicly proclaimed 'the common enemies of the Congress and the Pathans'.[84] At a time when communal passions ran high elsewhere in India, this expression of national solidarity proved unnerving for the British who consequently reacted by inflicting further repressive measures from 1930–37 in an attempt to break the movement.[85] Yet the nationalist forces grew steadily in strength.

The successful Congress-Khudai Khidmadgar movement was strengthened by prolonged troubles in the non-administered tribal territory situated between the NWFP of India and the Afghanistan border (Durand line). During the interwar period, the British Indian army was engaged in extensive operations in the NWFP, quelling tribal insurrections and maintaining order. The Pathan hill tribes in their barren and inaccessible region, wedged in between British India and Afghanistan, were cut off by the army presence from their traditional source of livelihood, raiding the fertile valleys running down from the Indus. The barren hills were too poor to maintain their inhabitants and there was hardly any alternative source of income.

Waziristan was the most notorious area of tribal unrest. The years 1936–38 were particularly troublesome for the British, requiring as many troops in this region as in the rest of the Indian subcontinent.[86] The British followed a forward aggressive policy involving indiscriminate bombing of villages to curb the seditious activities of religious leaders who amassed wide support as champions of Islam, using it to defy the British. Extremely popular, these leaders succeeded in knitting different Pathan tribes together, playing the British and Afghans against each other, and keeping the Frontier in a constant state of turbulence and unrest.

In fact, these two movements, one in the independent tribal belt and the other in the controlled territories in the NWFP, became firmly linked up with the national movement in their anti-imperialist, anti-British drive. This common anti-British front was stressed by the Faqir of Ipi who wrote to Jawaharlal Nehru in September 1937, addressing him as 'the leader of the liberty loving people and the distinguished head of the Indian state'.[87] Nehru, for his part, hailed the Faqir of Ipi in all his meetings in the NWFP as a 'freedom fighter' who, like the Congress, was protecting and defending his country from the continuing incursions of the British.

The Congress had emerged as the severest critic of the British Frontier policy which they termed 'swinging backwards and forwards'. A very widely circulated 1938 report of the Congress, critiqued this policy very succinctly:

> Every inch of ground, which the government seizes for strategic purposes is treated by tribesmen in Waziristan and elsewhere as an act of unprovoked aggression and its natural consequences follow in rapid succession. Sniping, blockades and punitive expeditions are all connected to the same chain of cause and effect. Appeal to tribal pride in the name of religion, honour or freedom are but the usual levers which those who resent hostile in-roads into the independent territory, avail themselves of to mobilise their otherwise disorganised forces. The central motive of the tribal organisations in almost all cases is always their passionate and burning hatred of 'slavery'. In every advance from the British side even when it is clothed in friendliness, the freedom loving tribesman (who is not aware of the dis-armed dacoity of his next door cousin in the settled territories, and who has reached his own conclusions in the settled territories regarding the civilising missions of the British) sees only the greed and gory talons of the earth-hungry, and power-thirsty monster of British imperialism. He fights it with every available weapon, and he has scant regard for 'the whining and squealing' British Indian subjects, who, he is convinced, provide men and money for aggression into his land and the ruthless massacre and subjugation of his kith and kin. He desires to be left alone, and therefore, when he finds that he is not going to be left alone, he uses his powers in defence and offence, and in doing so he does not spare those who he feels are instrumental in a course of activity which is intended to enslave him.[88]

Further it was pointed out that India, already fighting for its freedom, could not be expected to be a party to the enslavement of its independent borders. This policy involved maintaining a huge army for the purpose of conquest and subjugation of their territories, consequently placing enormous financial burden on the Indian tax payers. Altogether, it meant a regular drain of India's material and manpower resources.

Repeated questions regarding the Frontier were raised in the

Central Legislative Assembly. These attacks not only cut through party lines but also curiously echoed the German propaganda. For example, the British were taken to task for their aerial bombing of civilian populations in the Frontier, as part of a campaign to enable British troops to advance and facilitate road-building activity.[89] The *modus operandi* adopted by the British to evacuate the villagers before bombing – dropping handbills from aircraft to an illiterate Frontier population – was severely condemned. Maulana Sakat Ali, a Mohammadan urban member, representing the cities of United Provinces, summed up the situation: 'I know the Muslim feeling is very bitter now. We cannot give a price for troops that might be employed to kill our own people in Waziristan. We have no quarrel in Waziristan.'[90] The peace claimed to have been brought by this military policy was declared to be the 'peace of the graveyard'.

The 1937 installation of the Congress ministry in the NWFP under the premiership of Dr Khan Sahib increased the thrust of this criticism and the consequent pressure felt by the British. Politically, it became inevitable that any fresh nationalist outburst in India would profoundly affect the Frontier province.

Protest and agitation: crystallising nationalist concerns

In such a sensitive climate, combined with the need to counter the nationalist and Fascist propaganda, the contemporary situation in the NWFP was obscured by *The Drum*. It ignored the nationalist characters and privileged an image of the loyalist that, in their opinion, had a greater chance of acceptability among the Muslims. The attempt, in the words of Mason, the film's screenwriter, was to make *The Drum* 'pro-Muslim' and 'pro-Frontier'.[91] The resultant portrayal encompassing a justification of the British Frontier policy and construction of loyalist as well as communal stereotypes among the Muslims was to evoke mammoth opposition among different sections of Indians. The peddling of British imperialism through cinema had continued over the years without arousing the kind of sharp reaction from the Indians that occurred when *The Drum* was released. This resulted in much British disquiet.

Protests against the empire cinema had been building up for a long time. This film genre with the British Indian army and military conquest at its centre was so much more than simple adventure films. The colonial context exposed them as ideologically loaded. In 1927, Muslims in Delhi protested over the screening of *Moon of Israel*, and the film had to be withdrawn.[92] Similarly, in Karachi, there was a furore over the exhibition of a film depicting a scene in the life of the prophet.[93] The local Muslims sued the theatre manager for alleged insult to their prophet and religion. The protests of Muslims against *The Lives of a Bengal Lancer* in Lahore and Britain, which evoked considerable discussion in the Indian Central Legislative Assembly and the House of Commons, has already been commented upon. Although little is known about these protests, colonial records suggest that such protests had grown over the years. This growth coincided in the 1930s with the growth of Muslim religious identity.

At the same time the images of Muslims as depicted in the indigenous films made by Hindu film-makers came under attack for their motivated and negative portrayal; sections of the regional languages press, both Urdu and Gujarati, were instrumental in arousing communal passions.[94] On the other hand, the All India Film Censorship League, a little-known body, with wide claims, had taken to protest against films that tended to 'ridicule the Hindu religion, culture and society.'[95] Yet, despite these conflicting viewpoints, there was unanimous condemnation of the screen images of Muslims in western films, which many Indians believed ridiculed Muslim religious and social practices.[96]

The crystallisation of a sustained political agitation against *The Drum* was enabled by the brief interlude of provincial autonomy introduced under the act of 1935, when popular national governments took over the reins in the provinces of British India. Thus the possibility of influencing the government through democratic participation and protest became viable. *The Drum*, when released, provoked a kind of agitation in India, which fed off older resentments and proved to be very unsettling for the colonial masters. Moreover, the nature and intensity of this protest were significantly different from the earlier protests. It came at a time when a combination of factors, both colonial and international, could prove to be very damaging for the British in India. The unity it displayed cut across several categories of community and class and was built upon the basis of a deeply shared concern at this time.

The film was both preceded and succeeded by a great deal of criticism and adverse propaganda in the media, which succeeded in mobilising popular opinion against the film. Ably supported by the Bombay film industry, the media led in arousing nationalist opinion against the empire films. For the film industry their national and business interests came together. Their demand for protection against the 'unfair competition' that Indian films faced in relation to foreign films had been a long standing one.[97] According to them, excessive duties on imported machinery and raw stock in combination with the imposition of entertainment tax and high costs of exhibition gave them a permanent handicap. They demanded cancellation of all rebates and other advantages allowed to foreign films, producers, distributors and exhibitors and asked for facilities for their industry to put them on at par with foreign competition.[98] Demand for taxing foreign films was also made.

The national media took up this demand as part of their *swadeshi* demands. The *Hindu*, for example, pointed out that in 1935, of the films screened in India, 42.2 per cent of feature films and 16 per cent of short films were actually made in India, as opposed to a foreign share of the market of 51.8 per cent of feature films and 84 per cent of short films.[99] Accordingly, the profits appropriated by foreign countries and the capital generated 'rightly belonged to them [Indian producers]'. The *Bombay Chronicle* declared the earnings of foreign film companies a 'real drain on the country's resources'.[100] In making these demands the distinct anti-India slant of foreign films strengthened the hands of the film industry. The resultant movement against this image and ideology found an enthusiastic reception and echo among wider public and nationalist interests. In the interwar period, in view of the international situation and the vulnerability of the Indo-British relationship, the film industry mounted yet greater pressure upon the colonial government. With the advent of the Congress ministries, these efforts multiplied manifold as did the tirade of criticisms and condemnation of anti-Indian films.

The exhibition of *The Drum*, therefore, saw the national and the film media leading the protest among different sections of the Bombay public. It was this media coverage with photographs and long critical articles, excerpts of which were published by the regional languages press, which was responsible for laying the groundwork for the public support generated against the film. The *Bombay Chronicle*, for example, gave lengthy and daily coverage to this theme for a whole week and in its 13 September issue the controversial film and the protest against it appeared on its front page as a news item of important national interest. Consequently, what emerged was an agitation in which the educated middle class was speaking for the Pathans and the lower-class Muslims were acting on behalf of them – a Muslim constituency was being created to defend the Muslim identity.

In this collapse of the Pathan and Muslim identities the casting of Sabu (under contract to Alexander Korda), in the role of a dark exotic oriental prince, may well have been significant. The life story of Sabu, who had scored a great hit in *The Elephant Boy* (1937), was well publicised by the foreign and Indian media. Sabu, a lower-class Muslim boy from south India was discovered by Korda in the stables of the Maharaja of Mysore at the age of nine and went on to become a popular film personality. His casting in *The Drum* proved a propaganda master-stroke in more than one way. In Technicolor, the film highlighted brilliantly the natural contrast of the British and Indian skin colour, a contrast heightened by the image of Sabu's bare torso, which was maintained throughout much of the film (illustrations 1, 3, 4). The employment of Technicolor was a factor that not only explains part of this film's huge success in Britain[101] but also a great deal of the resentment it provoked in India. It projected racism more blatantly and obviously. This dark image of Sabu as a Pathan prince in *The Drum* created a bond of identity with the lower-class agitators of Bombay, even as his obsequious loyalty repulsed them. *Film India* observed:

> The technicolour [sic] seems to have been used to show the skin colour of Sabu who plays an important part of the Prince in the story. When everyone, including some thousand extras are shown as dressed or overdressed, Sabu, the Prince of his people is shown with a half naked body. Was it a subtle use to dab Sabu's dark colour on the minds of the white people? The majority of Pathans are a fairer race than the British. How then does a Prince happen to be darker than his people?[102]

Sabu's dark skin also came in handy to illustrate an old maxim: that an Englishman could pass off as an Indian, as demonstrated by Captain Carruthers, but the reverse was not possible. Sabu could not change his skin colour, he could only change his habits. This emphasis on colour assumes importance in view of the fact that there was, in the opinion of John Masters, 'an increasing strong colour bar in the thirties'. Commenting upon it Masters maintained, 'the Englishman's initial aversion was from Indian customs and habits, especially those connected with Hinduism and he gradually transferred this feeling to the colour of the Indians' skin because, whereas the former could be explained, the latter could not and was thus indefensible.'[103] This adds a fresh dimension to the prejudice of the British in India and its portrayal in cinematic terms.

The over-blown posters of *The Drum* showed what was described as 'a tiny Sabu' riding a 'milk-white' Arab stallion at full gallop 'to save his cherished British friends and regain his throne'. This brought the white–black contrast into a sharper relief and made its own comment. The inherent racism implicit in the image was not lost on the audience. It totally decried the possibilities of genuine friendship and respect suggested by the interaction of the young Sabu and the Scottish drummer boy, in which class as well as race is forgotten. The hope of A. E. W Mason of portraying this relationship as 'a symbol of the friendship which is common between British people and the Pathans of north-west India', was rejected by Indian audience.[104] The western audience, however, accepted this, showing a two-faced reception of the film. They also accepted Sabu as a symbol of loyal India.

The bounties of the British to loyal Indians were then highlighted. The propaganda of the film played up in bold letters:

Hollywood's rags to riches
All pale before the saga of Sabu
Small east-Indian film star once roamed the
Jungle and lived on a handful of rice.

These bold captions were followed by a detailed story as to how Sabu used to 'roam about the jungle in a loin cloth and turban and lived on a handful of rice a day'. The prominence given to such acute social and civilisational differences underlined the power of the superior white races to transform the loyalists, of whom Sabu was an example, and bring them within the light of civilisation to bestow its benefits on them. The real-life 'reality' of Sabu was superimposed on the fictional reality of the screen, both merging into one another to validate and authenticate its portrayal.

For the Indian audience on the other hand the stark reality of their own humiliation, segregation and exploitation were never brought more forcefully to the fore than in the case of Sabu. Sabu's claim to fame, his acceptance by colonial masters, his depiction as the hero of *The Drum* and top billing in the publicity campaign lay in his loyalty to the British. K. A. Abbas summed up the situation from the point of view of Indian viewers: 'Sabu perhaps may be popular in America (and in Britain) but this popularity is based on the imperial axiom that Indians as a rule are unscrupulous and uncivilised except the few who have learnt the virtues from the British. The popularity of Sabu in *The Drum* is the popularity of a faithful dog or a house-hold servant, not of ordinary human beings.'[105]

This reversal of the loyalist category combined with a running subtext in the film to subvert the British ideological thrust and provide a comment on British colonial domination of India. For example, Carruthers, the newly appointed British resident, comments on the activities of the chief rebel, Gul Khan:

CARRUTHERS: This is the old story of the mad dreamer of this
    world who are half empire builders and half gangsters If they
    succeed, history books call them great.
MARJORIE: And if they don't?
CARRUTHERS: Another gangster sinks into oblivion.

If on the one hand this conversation evokes the empire building of the Muslims in India and condemns their renewed attempts as that of gangsters, it may also be subverted by an Indian audience to make a comment on the British empire building itself.

In yet another scene, Gul Khan delivers a hard-hitting condemnation and exposé of the professed and much-touted principles of the British governing human relationships and politics. To Carruthers' assertion that 'We believe in equality of rights', Gul Khan responds, 'Equality of rights! Have you ever heard of the lamb persuading the tiger to live in peace with him and respect his equality of rights? Has the musket equal rights with the machine gun?' Gul Khan is also shown to be aware of the British policy of protection and subsidy under British army, which he describes as 'the army of occupation'. It is significant to note here that the British Indian army was repeatedly and publically described as 'the army of occupation' by the Congress.[106]

The frailty of the British possession of India is also commented upon by Gul Khan who says to Mohammed Khan, a loyalist of the British, 'I tell you the empire is ready to be carved out to pieces. Don't you want to help yourself?' The British fear of a violent overthrow and their vulnerability in the face of such a challenge to their domination is indeed the rock upon which all the empire films dealing with the NWFP were made. The fear that runs through *The Drum* and other films of its ilk, is informed as much by historical events, where entire British regiments had been annihilated, as by contemporary social and political upheaval.

Fear as an emotion and a concept is crucially used in *The Drum* to define the relationship between the colonisers and colonised. Yet, curiously in the film this concept works as much for the British as against them. The film reverses the fear complex, applying it to the colonised rather than the colonisers, its basic premise being that Indians should be fearful of the British, so that the British may continue to rule them. When the villain, Gul Khan, repeatedly asserts that 'the British will be killed to show that they are no longer feared any more', when he argues that the 'tribes must know that [the] English are not to be feared, then they'll all rise', and when he claims that he will carry Carruthers in a wooden cage through all the mountain states 'so that people may know how the English are to be feared', it leaves an ambiguous impression. Particularly in the colonial context of 1938 by which time Mahatma Gandhi had made significant advancements in countering the 'fear' of the British.

Clearly, the film was being received in ways that had not been the intention of the film-makers. The fact that the reading of the film by Indian audiences proved extremely problematic is evidenced in the agitation that followed the release of *The Drum* on 1 September 1938, in two Bombay theatres, the New Empire and the Excelsior. The British commissioner of police in his letters dated 12 and 15 September 1938 to the secretary of the home department at Bombay, gave lengthy descriptions of this agitation.[107] On the 8 September, a deputation of five Muslims, headed by Aziz Mohammed Lalljee, leader of the 'Muslim

Naujawans', made a representation to the commissioner of police on the ground that, 'it [*The Drum*] was a propaganda in favour of the British policy in regard to the relations with the Frontier tribes and, as such, was contrary to the beliefs both of the Muslim League and the Congress.' Significantly, the Muslim League's major attack on the British (and the Congress) was on their attempt to divide the Muslims as a community.[108] When asked by the police commissioner whether they represented any particular body in Bombay, they replied that they were making their request on behalf of 'the Bombay public'. He told them that according to the Bombay Film Censor Board, the film did not appear to be objectionable and suggested that if they did not agree with its exhibition, they were at liberty to carry on counter propaganda, correcting any misapprehensions that might be raised in the minds of the film audience owing to possible departures from the fact.

This virtual dismissal by the police commissioner signalled the start of a determined agitation in the city of Bombay. On the same night, a public meeting attended by about seventy-five Muslims was held. Mohammed Amin Azad, Aziz Mohammed Lalljee, Mohammed Daud Ghoghari and others made speeches criticising the exhibition of the film on the ground that it was propaganda in favour of the aggressive policy adopted by the British government on the Frontier. It was decided to organise a procession the following day, which was to proceed to the New Empire theatre and picket its entrance.

On 9 September, at about 2.45 p.m., a procession carrying banners against the film, estimated to be of about two hundred Muslims, headed by Aziz Mohammed Lalljee, Mohammed Amin and others, proceeded from Mohammed Ali Road to the New Empire and Excelsior theatres. En route several more people joined the procession. They shouted slogans outside both the cinema houses and had to be dispersed by the police from the immediate vicinity of the theatres. The crowd proceeded to the Esplanade Maidan where a meeting was held and a deputation of five persons was appointed to talk to the management of the cinemas to persuade them to discontinue the screening of the film. The cinema authorities expressed their inability to accede to the request of the deputation on the ground that they were bound by their contract with the producers to show the film in Bombay.

It was then decided to take recourse to direct action by picketing the cinema entrances and volunteers were called for; picketing of the evening and night shows began later that day.

The following day, five picketers laid themselves on the ground outside the entrances of the Excelsior theatre. They were forcibly removed by the police to the Esplanade police station. Picketing continued on 11 September. Two processions attempted to approach the cinema houses before the evening show, but police with *lathis* (wooden staff) were placed at strategic points near the entrance and on the roads leading to the theatres, and they moved the crowd on. Again, at 10.00 p.m., efforts were made to take a procession past the Excelsior; this time the police had to disperse them forcibly. In all, forty-six people were arrested for causing obstruction and taken to the Esplanade police station, where they were called upon to furnish bail deposits of Rs 5 each. In a significant move, they refused to pay and had to be remanded in police custody. On the morning of 12 September they appeared before the honorary magistrate at the Esplanade police station. As they pleaded not guilty, the case was postponed at the request of the defence counsel to 19 September and the accused remained in custody.

On 12 September picketing at the Excelsior cinema was resumed at 3.00 p.m. Picketers approached the theatre in pairs, stood at the main entrance of the theatre, shouted '*Allah-o-Akbar*' and obstructed the passage of those wishing to gain admittance. Twelve picketers were arrested for causing obstruction. The cinema house was surrounded by a vast crowd of demonstrators. Police, mounted and armed, had to be employed to forcibly disperse the crowd and cordon off the theatre from them. This crowd could only be dispersed by 10.30 at night.

On the same night, a meeting of some Muslims was held in the Daud Building behind Pydhoni police station. A 'Drum Boycott Committee' was organised under the presidency of Maulana Mohammed Ahsan. Several others like Yusuf Moledina, Habibul Haq, Maulana Mustaq Ahmed, Maulana Hamid Ahmed, Usman Mohammed Merchant and Maulvi Fazullah expressed their resentment against the screening of the film in Bombay on the grounds that 'it was insulting not only to the self-respecting Pathans but to all Indians'. They also condemned the police action in arresting picketers and interfering with the civil liberties of the public; congratulated the arrested Muslim youths and assured them of their support; and lambasted the members of the Bombay Film Censor Board as 'incompetent' and 'anti-national'. The two Muslim members of the board, Sultan Chinoy and Dr T. M. Kajiji, came under severe criticism for not objecting to the screening of this film, and a call was made for a demonstration against them outside their residences. The commissioner of police, an Englishman, came under heavy attack and it was suggested that he should not be the president of the board as he had no sympathy with the 'Indian national cause'. Finally, and importantly, the speakers also criticised the attitude adopted by the Congress ministry for treating their peaceful picketing as a lawless activity and in incarcerating the picketers. The major points of criticism were then passed as resolutions in the meeting.

The picketing continued. On 13 September, twenty-one more people were arrested for causing obstruction outside the Excelsior during the evening and night shows. From 11–13 September, mobilisation of opinion had clearly taken place through word of mouth, the press, and public meetings arranged in the Maidan. Consequently, a large crowd collected on Marzban Road near the two cinema houses at 6.00 p.m. and shouted slogans. They were diverted to the Esplanade Maidan where they held a huge meeting, which was presided over by the leading labour leaders, Purshotamdas Tricumdas and R. S. Nimbkar. The prominent involvement of these two labour leaders reflects the class nature of this growing crowd.

A large number of speeches were made and the resolutions passed at the earlier meeting were confirmed. The meeting concluded at 7.15 p.m. and those who had attended it attempted to proceed in a procession southwards along Hornby Road with a view to demonstrating outside the cinema. The police did not allow them to do so. The crowd eventually marched in a procession to Mohammed Ali Road. At about 10 p.m. a large crowd shouting anti-British and anti-film slogans collected near the New Empire and attempted to proceed to the Excelsior but was prevented from doing so by the police who forcibly dispersed the crowd and cordoned off the theatres. According to the police estimates seventy picketers were arrested. The public estimate and rumours turned these into hundreds of arrests. The assembled crowd, diverted to the Esplanade Maidan, where escorted by armed mounted police, they eventually moved along Hornby Road and proceeded to Nagdevi Street before being dispersed. The police action against the demonstrators had succeeded in enlarging the geographical space of their agitation from the immediate vicinity of the cinema halls to the entire upmarket commercial and residential areas.

On 14 September about a dozen people collected in the Daud building and, after protesting against the arrest of picketers, they proceeded to a meeting, which was to be held on the Esplanade Maidan. This had to be abandoned due to heavy rain, but picketing for the evening show was resumed at the Excelsior at about 5.30 p.m. Four picketers, more vocal than the others, who were shouting anti-British and anti-film slogans at the main entrance of the cinema houses, were arrested and removed to the Esplanade police station. They were released after the last show of the film was over. Despite these arrests the picketing continued, led by Mohammed Ahsan and Abdul Rehman Mitha, but no action was taken against them as they were not shouting slogans. They withdrew after the film was over.

This proved to be the last of the film shows. *The Drum* was withdrawn and later banned. With growing support the agitation clearly had the potential of becoming a larger movement. The government was flooded with appeals and telegrams from different quarters ranging from members of the Legislative Assembly, editors of daily newspapers and film magazines and representatives of different associations demanding the release of the arrested and withdrawal of the film on national grounds.

Identifying prime actors: audience and agitators

Significantly, the agitators were described by the police as 'mostly young Mussalmans of no importance' who neither belonged to the Congress nor were supported by the Muslim League.[109] This description imparts an interesting dimension to the agitation, as clearly certain strata of society were stirred and galvanised into action, who were politically and culturally not identifiable. Yet, they formed an enlightened audience as readers and critics of screen images and ideology, they reacted consciously to a western foreign-language film, and they saw the film as propaganda and did not dismiss it as inconsequential.

The reception of this film among the lower-class spectators shows their political and social understanding of colonial cultural representation and its ideological thrust. Their ability to formulate their own meaning out of the empire package of films was buttressed by the fact that not only did they have their own highly developed socio-cultural codes to draw upon, but the indigenous cinema was also articulating contemporary nationalist discourse. In this connection, I propose to discuss here the adventure-stunt genre which ran parallel to its corresponding genre in the empire films.

The adventure genre has special importance as the mixed social audience of the 1930s and 1940s, the uprooted, lumpen and working class, were considered to be more attracted to the stunt, mythology and adventure films.[110] The stunt and the high-adventure films made in India took their immediate inspiration from Hollywood. In fact, the swash-buckling screen persona of Douglas Fairbanks, whose *Thief of Bagdad* had proved a popular success all over India in 1925, was also adapted by the Indian films. The Wadia brothers, Homi Boman and Jamshed Boman Homi Wadia, made a series of silent films inspired by Fairbanks, including *Diler Daku* (1931), a direct adaptation of *Mark of Zoro* (1920), which was followed by *Lal-e-Yaman* and *Dilruba Daku* in 1933.[111] In the Indian-made films of this genre, the plot was successfully reversed and used in an entirely different direction. J. B. H Wadia, the director and producer of the famous Wadia Movietone, which produced several big hits in this genre, maintained that a 'revolt against a tyrannical king or a minister for *Azadi* (freedom) was nothing if not against the British Raj, although indirectly.'[112]

The female counterpart of this adventurous hero was the 'warrior woman'. The depiction of the warrior woman on the screen has its ancestry in the folk songs and legends, popular literature and poetry, which celebrated the concept of *virangana* (warrior woman).[113] In popular iconography she is usually depicted riding on a horse, wearing a turban and tunic with flowing trousers and brandishing a sword high above her head. This warrior woman was a popular figure in the folk theatre (*nautanki*) of northern India, especially in the years 1910–1940. Her popularity is linked, according to Kathryn Hansen, to the restrictions imposed by colonial government on nationalist messages in the print and entertainment media.[114] Denied open reference to heroes like Lakshmibai – who had emerged as a popular symbol of resistance to colonial rule – the public turned to fictional heroines from popular culture to voice their anti-colonial sentiments. The screen adoption of the *virangana* concept resulted in a series of films beginning in the silent era itself.[115]

The more popular of the *virangana* concept movies were made by the Wadia brothers. J. B. H. Wadia introduced the 'fearless Nadia' as the warrior woman who masqueraded as a male to fight against injustice and oppression. Her films had an unmistakable nationalist message, and included *Toofan Mail* (1932), *Hunterwali* (1935), *Miss Frontier Mail* (1936), *Deccan Queen* (1936), *Hurricane Hansa* (1937), *Toofan Express* (1938), *Flying Ranee* (1939), *Punjab Mail* (1939) and *Hurricane Special* (1939), most of which were big hits.[116]

It may be noted here that the agency granted to a woman, although well within patriarchal codes, provided a counterpoint to the image of the *purdah* woman of the empire films and visibilised their active role in the national movement. The Indian audience was clearly being fed on what were termed *swadeshi* theme films. This was generally true of a large number of films produced in India. There were complaints in England about such films, which had become a 'profitable business proposition' by 'exploiting public sympathy on national grounds'.[117] It is not difficult to appreciate the application of this understanding by the lower strata to the western films that sought to negate the national message.

Although *The Drum* was exhibited at the New Empire and Excelsior film theatres, both known to exhibit only English-language films and situated in the elite upmarket area of Bombay, it still attracted a lower-class audience. Indeed, although located in the Hornby estate (now Dada Bhai Naroji Road), the cinemas were also close to the pier, the railway station, and the general post office,[118] as well as the 'dense, dark and congested' Bazaar Gate area, rounded by the Parel and Mohammed Ali Road, where the lower classes were concentrated. Also nearby was the Esplanade Maidan, which was the favourite haunt of different classes of people ranging from workers looking for jobs to petty vendors and middle-class idlers to soldiers who used it for their manoeuvers. The higher priced seats were certainly the preserve of elite urbanites and Europeans but the lower stalls at five annas per seat (consisting roughly of twenty per cent of the hall),[119] with separate entrances, drew its audience from the lower classes located minutes away from the fashionable upmarket area. The location of these two halls and the fact that they were frequented by Europeans may well have contributed towards triggering an intense reaction among the lower-class Indian audience against the negative way in which Indians were represented in the film. Frantz Fanon, for example, points to the shifting, situational nature of colonised spectatorship and the difficulty of identification experienced by them in a theatre with a predominantly white audience who would automatically identify them with the 'savages on the screen'.[120] Significantly, *The Drum* was screened to full houses from the 1–8 September before the agitation crystallised.

The lack of alternative kinds of entertainment in the urban centres resulted in the cinema emerging as a popular and comparatively cheap form of entertainment for the lower classes whose only other mode of relaxation was roaming the streets of Bombay.[121] The fact that the principal players in the disturbances were not the dominant groups but the urban underclass, imparts a greater significance. Bombay, in 1938, had a huge labour surplus, which was mainly unskilled. One of the major nodes of industrial development in the colonial period, Bombay stimulated migration from the rural periphery and other parts of India. Due to migration and a higher birth rate, Bombay city underwent a growth of thirty-three per cent from 1931 to 1941.[122] The inability of the colonial economic system to absorb this growing population made the urban occupational structure during the interwar period extremely unpredictable.

Subject to the fullest rigours of the urban market, this segment of population was willing to take up any job. Many became construction labourers, hired daily, as construction activity in the city in the late 1930s was taking place at a frenzied pace.[123] Significantly, there was a lot of construction going on in and around the core business area where the protest against the film took place. It was such a portion of the workforce – the lumpen proletariat – who formed the backbone of the protest movement. It was illiterate and tended to maintain rural links because it had no choice.

Unlike the industrial trade unions in Bombay, which during the colonial period were closely linked with the demand for political independence, under the leadership of middle-class professionals and intellectuals, the lumpen elements had remained unorganised.[124] Cosmopolitan in character they showed differences of language, region, creed and tradition. Yet, a substantial chunk of them were composed of Muslims from the Konkan region, which gave it a more cohesive look.[125]

This was the underclass, practically homeless or mushrooming in the slums, overlapping the heavily congested inner areas, which formed the floating population of urban Bombay.[126] Officially described as 'riff-raffs of the city', *'mawalis'* and 'hooligans',[127] they made their political presence felt. Considered to have been in the forefront of the ten riots, officially termed as communal riots, which took place in Bombay city from February 1929 to April 1938, they were held responsible for the breakdown in the city's law and order.[128] In order to contain this hooligan element, the Congress ministry in Bombay introduced in March 1938 a bill to amend the City of Bombay Police Act of 1902. This empowered the city police with emergency powers to deport any suspected hooligan outside Bombay for a certain period of time.

Significantly, these riots were designated and accepted as communal riots not only by British officials but by the Congress leadership as well. This depiction necessarily imparts a communalised consciousness to this social group. This contention had been challenged by S. H. Jhabvala who considered these riots 'more or less of a political and economic nature' rather than due to 'any religious fanaticism'.[129] Although the Bombay city riots and the nature of these riots have not been adequately researched, the existing evidence suggests the use of communalism to break the individual strikes leading to riots, rather than communalisation of this strata of society.[130] Yet, it is clear that different identities were crystallising and clashing at a time of economic and industrial instability, severe unemployment and low wages. Extensive mobilisation on caste, *mohalla*, region, language, religion, and class were also taking place.[131] It would be hard to say when religious identity assumed dominance, if at all, at the cost of other identities and with what effects. The initiative taken by the Bombay city's underclass Muslims in the case of *The Drum* effectively contradicts its communalised, violent and riot-prone nature, which had posed a danger to law and order, necessitating anti-hooligan legislation.

It is undeniable that for these 'nobodies', religion was crucial to their identity and protest, which was triggered off by the widely perceived insult to the Muslims and their identity in the film. The universalising messages of cinema transcended the regional diversity and cultural specificity of the Pathans into that of Islamic and Muslim. The depiction of the Pathan tribal culture had certain key religious features like the festival of *moharram*. This made it a Muslim depiction rather than tribal – a depiction which was but a western, homogenised, essentialist reproduction of the Muslim.

It may be noted here that Pathans in Bombay held an ambiguous position: frequently employed as strike breakers by the industrial management, as moneylenders they were also necessary for the workers' survival.[132] Hated both by the Hindus and Muslims alike, their houses and records were objects of attack in riot situations. Yet, in relation to colonialism, their depiction in the film became a *cause célèbre*. *The Drum* was perceived as an attempt to divide the Muslims by denying a common Pathan Muslim identity. It had asserted a Pathan tribal identity as different from that of the plains – different both from that of the Muslim and the Hindu – by emphasising 'fiercely and murderously antagonistic warring Pathan tribes' that praised the practice of barbaric head-hunting. The film posited economic as well as cultural hierarchies between not only the white western world and the coloured colonised world but also between the colonised and the tribal world.

However, the protesters were clearly agitating not merely on a matter concerning their own creed but on wider feelings. They were rejecting a cultural symbol that insisted on dividing them into categories of fundamentalist, communalist, backward and, above all, loyal to the British, hence, in their eyes, anti-national. This positing of a religious identity to constitute the highly questionable social and political level of the on-screen narrative fed into the looming communal propaganda of Maharashtra in the late 1930s. The communal charges had put Muslims under suspicion. Their loyalty to the nation was being challenged in the crucial days of the independence movement. Their protest demonstrated their readiness to rise in defence of their national claims and self-respect. It was not only an outright rejection of the value put on loyalty to the British but also a self-assertion of their nationalism. Their selfhood and nationhood were conflated in their response to imperial hegemony.

Moreover, the film was seen as a virtual testimony to British coercive domination over the Pathans and Muslims through their scheming manipulations and brutal army repression. It was also perceived as an attempt to conceal their intervention and exonerate their criminal record in the Frontier. This was a critique of British policies not only in the NWFP but in the entire subcontinent, which operated on a divide and rule basis.

Although the agitation was officially described as 'wholly Muslim' it was supported most vociferously by members of other communities as well, who used it as an occasion to put across their anti-colonial and nationalist viewpoints. Several resolutions were passed at the public meetings, presided over by middle-class intelligentsia and professionals, during the course of this agitation. These repeatedly:

a expressed resentment against the screening of the film, *The Drum*, in Bombay on the grounds that it was insulting not only to the 'self-respecting Pathans' but to 'all Indians' and demanded its withdrawal;
b condemned the police action in arresting picketers and thereby interfering with the civil liberties of the public;
c demanded the immediate release of the arrested picketers;
d congratulated the arrested Muslim youths and assured them full support;
e expressed 'no-confidence' in the Bombay Board of Film Censors consisting of persons without 'national and religious traditions'.

The film provided a platform for different sections and communities to come together. The agitators' complete identification with the national cause, which rose above party politics, was highly significant. The *Bombay Chronicle* was to put this feeling most succinctly when it maintained in its issue of 8 February 1939: 'In the matter of national prestige there should not be any communal or party aspect and there should not be any half measures. The pictures that offend our national pride should straightway be banned without the slightest consideration for the feeling of those producers who choose to offend our country without any provocation'.

Reaction and action: the Congress ministry

A ban on *The Drum* and others of its kind was demanded on national grounds. The Indian National Congress which had formed the ministry in Bombay was repeatedly petitioned to take action. Expectations from the Provincial Congress government to uphold 'national pride and prestige' were openly voiced.[133]

The Congress had not formulated any specific cultural policy in relation to the empire films. Although questions were raised repeatedly by individual members in the Indian legislature, both in the Council of States and the Central Legislative Assembly, regarding production of 'anti-Indian' films and what the government proposed to do about them, nothing concrete had been on the Congress agenda.[134] The existing evidence suggests that, apart from the documentaries, the Congress leadership was unable to realise the importance of film as an instrument of mass media.[135] Consequently, film was not used as part of its agenda of struggle, and so the Congress was unable to provide leadership to those who were agitating against *The Drum*.

Significantly, all the earlier protests against the empire films had remained primarily confined to the educated middle classes. Their forms of protests were limited to petitions, deputations and other types of supplication made through the media and channels like the Legislative Assembly. The direct action of the urban underclass changed the nature of the protest as well as its reception by the authorities whether colonial or national. The direct action showed an independent initiative even though it was fragmented in scale and distant from the core of the articulate political society. Since the Congress and the Muslim League had not taken any cognisance of the cultural onslaught of the empire films, which degraded Indian nationalism, it is significant that their critique of the British Frontier policy was picked up by the protesters and applied in a larger context.

This was apparently made possible due to the wide coverage of NWFP and its leadership in the national and local media.[135] There was a flood of news items on this region accompanied by severe criticism of the British policy during its troublesome phase extending from 1936–39. The emphasis of the regional language newspapers was on the common identity of the Muslims in India and the Frontier, as well as on their mutual bond of the anti-colonial struggle against the British.[137]

It is significant that the lumpen proletariat, which lacked the unity, solidarity and organisational skills to come together on economic grounds and fight for their survival on basic issues like employment and wages, used the cinema as a symbol of imperialism to act as a cohesive group. Their anti-imperialist thrust, however, was not divorced from or a denial of their harsh economic conditions and demands. Rather, it was a confirmation. It brought them and their cause to the forefront. In the given circumstances of industrial unease and unemployment, when a national government was at the provincial helm, it was as much an assertion for recognition of their existence, as an anti-colonial move and an attack on a popular symbol of imperialism. It is important to note here that, at this popular mass level, the film was not seen as inconsequential but was used to articulate a multiplicity of messages. This imparts greater complexity to the popular reception of cultural imperialism. The agitation showed an effective adoption of different forms of political struggle. Not integrated in the mainstream of political life and dismissed as hooliganism, this agitation underlined the potential of their social class not only to the colonial government but also to an interim national government.

The Congress intervened only when the agitation had become full-blown. Until then it was treated as a law-and-order problem. In this regard, the Congress had already passed an anti-hooligan act against this under-section of the working class in Bombay. The Congress, in fact, shared a very uneasy and uneven relationship with the working class. During its stint as a provincial ministry, the Congress, according to Claude Markovits, displayed a strong anti-labour, pro-capitalist bias.[138] In the period preceding provincial autonomy, starting with the Karachi declaration, the Congress had shown itself sympathetic to workers. It now found itself suddenly confronted with an unprecedented wave of labour unrest[139] as well as high expectations of recognition from the Congress leadership. When *The Drum* was released, the relations between the two were particularly tense. The Congress had drafted its Industrial Disputes Bill of 1938 in January of that year, and had circulated it for consultation.[140] The bill had 'deeply stirred the labour world' in Bombay. Elaborate preparations were being made by the Bombay Province Trade Union Congress to call for a one-day strike on 7 November in the event of the Industrial Disputes Bill being passed. Workers in other trades and industries like the tramways, railways, municipal workshops, port trust and docks, as well as taxi and Victoria drivers, washermen, saloon workers, hawkers and even hotel servants were being approached. There was intensive propaganda. September and October of 1938 were months of agitation against the bill, along with mammoth meetings and demonstrations, both peaceful and non-violent.

The protest movement against the film is consequently located amid a great deal of tension. Initially, the agitation, considered by the British police commissioner as 'wholly artificial' and 'sponsored by irresponsible youths', was tackled as a law-and-order problem, undoubtedly under the instructions of the Congress ministry, which acted to contain it.[141] The minister in charge of home affairs, K. M. Munshi, by far the most important member of the Congress ministry, was well-acknowledged as a conservative sharing interests with big industrial houses and business concerns and who looked upon labour and other lumpen elements with suspicion.[142] The fact that this lumpen element was drawn from among the Muslims may well have strengthened this suspicion.

More importantly, the geographical location of the two cinema houses on the Hornby and Marzban streets, an upmarket commercial area, was surrounded by residences of upper-class Indians like the Tatas.[143] The Hornby estate was the nerve centre of business, finance and insurance in the 1930s. Sir Jamsetjee Jeejeebhoy's Fort House, the upmarket shopping centre patronised by the elite, was on Hornby Street. It is not difficult to visualise that any agitation in and around this area was treated by the police as constituting a potential danger to the life and property of an elite section of the city, which had to close down its commercial and business activities during the agitation.

The Congress ministry was under pressure not only from the commercial and business class to intervene, but also from different sections of Bombay society who took up the cause of the agitators. Appeals were even addressed to the members of opposition parties in the legislature to put pressure upon the Congress in this matter.[144] As the pressure from the legislature and the press mounted, the home minister made a public statement regretting that the matter was brought to his attention only after the agitation had begun. An attempt was made to appease the agitators on 20 September, after twelve days of agitation, and only after ascertaining that they did not belong to the Muslim League. On the home minister's personal orders, the agitators were asked to sign a pledge as a condition of withdrawing the cases against them. The statement, an exercise in co-opting the agitators in to the Congress fold, read:

> Recently we have found that foreign producers have been producing films which depict Indians and Indian life in a manner which is offensive to our national self-respect. When we went to see the film 'Drum' we found that this picture was calculated to wound our self-respect by showing among other things Frontier Pathans in a bad light.
>
> In order to draw attention of the country to this class of films we decided to peacefully picket the theatre. Our object has been served by the Government of Bombay deciding to look into such films in the future before sanction is given by the Censor Board. We also find that our protest has attracted the attention of the Madras Government.
>
> Our object was to carry on only peaceful picketing and we have conducted the picketing very peacefully. In doing so if we did anything which would amount to any breach of law we want to make it clear that we had no intention of breaking the law or any order – lawfully given to us.
>
> We, however, take this opportunity of expressing our regret that we should have precipitately resorted to direct action of picketing without having exhausted all constitutional means of seeking relief by approaching the Government on this question. We are sorry that we should have done so particularly as the present Government is our own Government whose decision on the matter we should have accepted with the greatest pleasure.[145]

The arrested agitators who had expected endorsement from the Congress government rather than their penalisation at the hands of the police, rejected this offer. The legitimacy of their anti-imperialist agitation had been taken away by treating it as a law-

and-order problem. Law and order had been enforced by the coercive apparatus of the colonial state to muzzle free speech, curb the individual freedom of movement and deny the right of assembly to the people. A similar treatment by the national government identified it with some of the most repugnant aspects of colonial rule, and helped to designate it as an autocracy in their eyes. It brought to the surface the growing tension between the bourgeois leadership of the Indian national movement, which sought to come to terms with the working class, the urban labouring poor and the under-class in general, in order to enlist their participation in a mass movement against the colonial power.

The failure to integrate and hegemonise these sections of society was due not only to the dichotomy of interest between the national bourgeois leadership, dominant in the Congress and the lower orders, and the apprehensions of a self-generating movement getting out of hand, but also because of the inadequacy of the former to recognise the nature of the anti-imperialist thrust of the latter's movement. The leadership was unable to comprehend a lower-class, non-economic agitation that understood the cultural assault of the empire films as an assault on their life, honour and dignity, a movement which succeeded in transcending the narrow confines of an imposed identity to articulate a larger national identity, and acted autonomously rather than as an appendage of the reigning political parties.

The indecision of the Congress ministry meant that the situation remained tense, compelling the home minister's personal intervention. He viewed the film on 27 September and recorded his objections.[146] These objections reflect the viewpoint of an educated, middle-class Indian audience in relation to the empire films and how these were received and interpreted in colonial India. The objections were listed under two heads. First, from the point of view of the 'religious Muslims', scenes showing the Muslims at prayer and the Mullah preaching a holy war were mentioned, and, second, from the 'national point of view', the following six objections were listed:

1 Sabu's flunkeyish attitude to Captain Carruthers at their first meeting.
2 Sabu's preference for being a member of the Pathan regiment rather than a free chief.

3 Gul's statement of descending on India.
4 The conversation where Captain and Mrs Carruthers refer to their stay on the frontier.
5 Sabu's becoming an instrument of destroying his own people for the sake of personal gratitude to Captain Carruthers
6 Sabu's attempts to destroy Gul, who represents freedom, for the sake of personal gratitude to Captain Carruthers and the Governor's conversation with him.

The terms of debate on censorship no longer remained in the hands of the censor authorities. New norms were coming into existence dictated by the Indian audience. The logic and reading of the film had reached beyond its intent. The Congress ministry banned the film in Bombay. The distributors of *The Drum* were sent instructions to remove two thousand feet of the 'objectionable parts' of the film before offering the film for exhibition elsewhere.[147]

The producers, with the idea of counteracting the agitation against the film, submitted it to the Bengal Board of Film Censors, and expected it to get an easy passage because of the non-Congress complexion of the Bengal ministry.[148] The effort was in vain. The Bengal and Punjab governments followed the Bombay example by banning the film, and Madras, which had been following the controversy closely, excised more than two thousand feet of the film, leaving it incomprehensible to the viewer. In Delhi – the central location of the colonial government – the censor authorities decided to ignore the agitation and its objections, and exhibit the film. This attempt aroused such violent protests that the cinema owners were allegedly compelled to flee to Ceylon.[149] The pattern of protest against such films had been firmly set.

This controversy around the empire cinema had clearly added to the colonial masters' discomfiture since the emerging contours of a cultural policy among Indians were discernible. A unanimous resolution was passed by the Indian Motion Picture Congress in Bombay in April 1939 under the presidentship of S. Satyamurthy, who significantly was also the deputy leader of the Congress party in the Central Legislature. It chalked out a set of instructions to be followed: first, the provincial governments were to adopt an 'Indian point of view' for judging the empire films made by the British, European or American producers and were to refuse certificates of exhibition, if this was found wanting; second, the public was instructed to adopt the most obvious form of resistance, the weapon of boycott, if this was breached.[150] Satyamurthy also demanded in the assembly that the BBFC should appoint a person 'with experience and knowledge of Indian conditions, Indian feelings and Indian sentiments', in order to guarantee that films were 'properly excised', and no scenes were exhibited that could affect the 'sentiments of the people of this country'.

In the spirit of these recommendations made in the wake of the widespread agitation against *The Drum*, the Bombay government had already issued a notification dated 15 October 1938 that laid down the basis of future policy to be followed in relation to all foreign films. The notification instructed:

> Government takes this opportunity to warn the importers of foreign made films, part of which offend the Indian sentiments or national self-respect, may not receive in future the indulgence which the film *The Drum* has received. In this case the film had been passed by the Bombay Board of Film Censors, and exhibited to the public some days before the attention of Government was drawn to the objectionable features of the film. Government have now instructed the Board that thereafter it should submit to Government its report and opinion on every foreign film depicting Indian life or dealing with Indian subject matter, wholly or in part, with a synopsis before it is certified.[151]

These instructions became a landmark, for such films had to seek thereafter the government's permission before their release. The instructions also applied to travelogues and newsreels, leading to several excisions being made in such films, which had earlier been exhibited almost uncut.[152]

The crystallisation of such a policy stood to overrule the western stereotyping of Indian culture and society. It was a refusal by the Bombay government to allow the Indian people to be insulted or injured by the derogation and denial of their identity and integrity as the colonised – a refusal, that is, to allow the colonisers to colonise their cultural space. The agitation around *The Drum* had consequences for the Congress as well as the colonial government: both were compelled to re-assess the impact of empire cinema. For the British this assumed an urgency especially as *The Drum* was followed closely by *Gunga Din*. The need to break with the set formula of adventure genre films had become dire.

Notes

1 *The Drum* was a popular and artistic success. It won the City of Venice Cup at the film festival in Sep. 1938 and grossed over $170,000 in the USA alone. Rachael Low, *The History of the British Film 1929–1939: Film Making in 1930 Britain* (London, George Allen & Unwin, 1985), p. 223.

2 Very little is known about this agitation. The contemporary press in the USA and the UK mentioned the agitation as 'riots' but gave out no details. Consequently, later writers also dismiss it in one line. There has not been any investigation of its nature and extent. No academic analysis of this agitation has been undertaken so far.

3 MSA, Home-Poll. F, no. 237-I, 1938, p. 69. This was the police description of agitators.

4 A. E. W. Mason cited in the *Bombay Chronicle* (15 Feb. 1939), p. 10.

5 For the close links of Korda with the British government see Jeffrey Richards, *The Age of the Dream Palace: Cinema and Society in Britain 1930–1939* (London, Routledge & Kegan Paul, 1984), pp. 136–7. See also Jeffrey Richards, 'Boys own cinema: feature films and imperialism in the 1930s', in John M. Mackenzie (ed.), *Imperialism and Popular Culture* (Manchester, Manchester University Press, 1986), p. 150.

6 See Ella Shohat and Robert Stam, *Unthinking Eurocentricism: Multiculturalism and the Media* (London & New York, Routledge, 1994), p. 114; and Ella Shohat, 'Gender and culture of empire': towards a feminist ethnography of the cinema', in H. Naficy and T. H. Gabriel (eds), *Otherness and the Media: The Imagination of the Imagined and the Imaged* (Langhorn, Harwood Academic Publishers, 1993), pp. 45–84.

7 IOR, L/P&J/ 8/127, Coll. no. 105-A, pt. IX, Jun. 1937–Apr. 1939. See *Cinema* (12 May 1937), p. 5. For the close cooperation of the India Office also see the letters dated 29 Oct. 1937 and 4 Nov. 1937 to Brook-Wilkinson of the BBFC from the India Office.

8 *Ibid*. See India Office to Brook-Wilkinson, 29 Oct. 1937 and 4 Nov. 1937.

9 *Ibid*. See minute paper, P&J department, 13 Dec. 1938.

10 NMML, All India Congress Committee Papers (AICC Papers), F. no. P-16, 1939–40, pp. 87, 99–101.

11 Akbar S. Ahmed, *Pukhtun Economy and Society: Traditional Structure and Economic Development in a Tribal Society* (London, Routledge & Kegan Paul, 1980), p. 66.

12 Impressions of Prithvi Raj Kapoor, the noted theatre and film personality, recorded by Jai Dayal in his *Go South with Prithvi Raj and his Prithvi Theatre* (Bombay, Prithvi Theatre Publication, 1950), p. 10. Significantly, the enormously popular play of the Prithvi theatre, *Pathan*, which was staged in the early years of independence, portrayed this brotherhood between Hindu and Muslim Pathans.

13 Explaining the rise of religious leaders dubbed 'fanatical', Akbar S. Ahmed states that among the Pathans the distinction between the spiritual and the secular order – theoretically made between 'men of God' and 'men of spear' – is hardly maintained. Empirically, this division is rarely sustained and its boundaries constantly crossed and recrossed. A Pathan's 'ideal leader' combines both a spiritual and temporal authority. There is no compartmentalisation of the two. See Akbar S. Ahmed, *Millennium and Charisma Among Pathans: A Critical Essay in Social Anthropology* (London, Routledge & Kegan Paul, 1976), pp. 51–3.

14 The most lasting and fundamental of the orientalist contribution to knowledge about India was the essentialisation of the Hindu Muslim opposition. See David Ludden, 'Orientalist empiricism: transformation of colonial knowledge', and Arjun Appadurai, 'Number in the colonial imagination', both in Carol A. Breckenridge and Peter van der Veer (eds), *Orientalism and the Postcolonial Predicament* (Delhi, Oxford University Press, 1994), pp. 250–78 and pp. 314–40 respectively.

15 *Film India* (Oct. 1938), pp. 25–7.

16 The Bombay Legislative Assembly debates were given a great deal of prominence in *Film India* (Dec. 1938), pp. 53–4.

17 Denzil Ibbetson, *Punjab Castes: Races, Castes and Tribes of the Peoples of Punjab* (Delhi, Cosmos Publication, 1981 [1916]), p. 58. For details of value orientation of the Pathans in their tribal code known as *Pukhtunwali*, see Ahmed, *Millennium*, pp. 56–7; and Ahmed, *Pukhtun Economy and Society*, p. 64.

18 Cited in James W. Spain, *Peoples of the Khyber: The Pathans of Pakistan* (New York, Frederick A. Praeger, 1962), pp. 130–1.

19 *Ibid.*

20 Ibbetson, *Punjab Castes*, p. 58.

21 Kenneth Ballhatchet, *Race, Sex and Class under the Raj: Imperial Attitudes and Policies and their Critics, 1793–1905* (London, Weidenfeld & Nicolson, 1980), p. 5.

22 See Howard Brasted, 'The politics of stereotyping: western images of Islam', *Manushi*, No. 98 (Jan.–Feb. 1997), pp. 6–16.

23 This is a viewpoint which, despite certain reservations, continues to be accepted even now. See, for example, Gill Shepard who argues in her case study of Swahili Muslims of Mombassa, Kenya, that, empirically, where young men and women do not have easy sexual access to each other, homosexuality is more likely to occur. See Gill Shepard, 'Rank, gender and homosexuality: Mombassa as a key to understanding sexual practice', in Pat Caplan (ed.), *The Cultural Construction of Sexuality* (London & New York, Tavistock Publications, 1987), pp. 240–70.

24 See Ronald Hyam, 'Empire and sexual opportunity', *Journal of Imperial and Commonwealth History*, 14:2 (Jan. 1986), pp. 34–89.

25 Afghanistan, with more than half of its Pushtun population ethnically corresponding with the Pushtun population of the North-West Frontier and the tribal regions, has several proverbs, folk tales and songs which deal with homosexuality. 'A woman for mating, a boy for love' is one example. A song narrates a tale in which 'a beautiful boy with a bottom like a peach stands across the river, and I can't swim.' There is also open banter between males concerning homosexual activities. See Louis Dupree, *Afghanistan* (Princeton, New Jersey, Princeton University Press, 1973), p. 198. The open attitude of different societies to homosexuality can be seen in relation to sixteenth-century Japanese society, which regarded it as 'effeminate' to refuse sodomy. See Hyam, 'Empire and sexual opportunity', p. 43.

26 Zahirud-din Mohammed Babur, the first Mughal emperor, for example, wrote in his autobiography about his 'frothing up of desire and passion' for a 'fairy-faced' young boy called Baburi and composed several love couplets for him. See *Babur-Nama* (Memoirs of Babur), translated from the original text of Zahirud-din Mohammed Babur Padshah Ghazi by Annette Susannah Beveridge (New Delhi, Orient Books Reprint Corporation, 1970 [1922]), pp. 120–1. Rosalind O'Hanlan similarly argues that homosexuality was a familiar feature of the social landscape in pre-colonial India, especially of the Mughal army. Many noted warriors and commanders were known homosexuals. The ties between military servants and their personal slaves and eunuchs often included strong sexual elements without compromising masculinity. This acceptance, however, did not go uncontested. Emperor Akbar, who regarded homosexual love as transgressive, tried to discourage and repress it, but without success. See Rosalind O'Hanlan, 'Imperial masculinities: gender and the construction of imperial service under Akbar', unpublished paper, 1996.

27 There is documentary evidence in the eighteenth century regarding this. Rosalind O'Hanlan, 'Warriors, gentlemen and eunuchs: maleness in Mughal north India', paper presented at the Department of History, Delhi University, 5 Feb. 1997.

28 Hyam suggests that with the growing moralistic-cum-legal restraints in Britain in the wake of the purity campaign of 1880, the homosexuals found an outlet in the colonies especially through the army. According to Hyam 'the predominant forms of male prostitution were military'. See his 'Empire and sexual opportunity', pp. 34–89.

29 John Masters, *Bugles and a Tiger* (New York, Viking Press, 1956), pp. 153–4.

30 Hyam, 'Empire and sexual opportunity', p. 72.

31 Both Mosse and Anderson argue that nationalism favours affinity for male society. See George Mosse, *Nationalism and Sexuality: Middle Class Morality and Sexual Norms in Modern Europe* (Madison, University of Wisconsin Press, 1985), p. 67; and Benedict Anderson, *Imagined Communities: Reflections on the Origin and Spread of Nationalism* (London, Verso, 1983), p. 16.

32 For the use of the low position of women by the British to denigrate the Hindu civilisation, see Uma Chakravarti, 'What ever happened to the Vedic *Dasi*: orientalism, nationalism and a script for the past', in Kumkum Sangari and Sudesh Vaid (eds), *Recasting Women: Essays in Colonial History* (New Delhi, Kali for Women, 1989), pp. 27–87.

33 Abdul Gaffar Khan, in his conversation with Pyarelal, the secretary of Mahatma Gandhi, recalled the kidnapping of Mollie Ellis, an English woman, by Ajab Khan in 1915. According to him, this incident was attested to by an eyewitness who knew all the parties concerned. Ajab Khan, according to this eyewitness, was a gunrunner whose house was raided by a major of the British Indian army. During the course of this raid the officer rudely unveiled the women of the *zenana* (a separate living quarters for women). Ajab settled his score by kidnapping Ellis. See E. G. Tendulkar, *Abdul Gaffar Khan: Faith is a Battle* (Bombay, Popular Prakashan, 1967), p. 259.

34 For different historical accounts and a critique of Eurocentric representations of harem see Shohat, 'Gender and culture of empire', pp. 45–83.

35 Hyam, 'Empire and sexual opportunity', pp. 34–89.

36 Ballhatchet, *Race, Sex and Class*, pp. 164–7.

37 This position took no cognisance of the fact that Indians were shocked at the 'indecorous behaviour of western ladies baring their

shoulders and dancing on social occasions.' Such things, according to Ballhatchet, did not encourage Indians to loosen the restraints of caste or to abandon the traditional seclusion of respectable women. See Ballhatchet, *Race, Sex and Class*, p. 5.

38 This is not to deny the patriarchal assumptions underpinning the feudal ethic of the ruling class in India

39 There is already a latent bias in the selection of the *burqa* as the only sign of *purdah*, and the implication that *purdah* is therefore restricted to Muslim women. Other symbols and modes of *purdah* operating among Hindu women, for example, get obscured.

40 Tendulkar, *Abdul Gaffar Khan*, pp. 88, 100–1, 192, 223.

41 Joan L. Erdman with Zohra Segal, *Stages: The Art and Adventures of Zohra Segal* (New Delhi, Kali for Women, 1997), p. 67.

42 This interesting parallel is drawn from the observations of Kathleen Howard-Merriam, who spoke with women in the Peshawar refugee camps about *purdah* and their exclusion from public space. She argues that the 'westerners who have been quick to impose their own ethnocentric perceptions should note the value of this seemingly anachronistic custom for a people under siege whose very survival is at stake'. Cited in Valentine M. Moghadam, 'Revolution, Islam and women: sexual politics in Iran and Afghanistan', in Andrew Parker, Mary Russo, Doris Summer and Patricia Yaeger (eds), *Nationalisms and Sexualities* (New York & London, Routledge, 1992), pp. 424–46.

43 Tendulkar, *Abdul Gaffar Khan*, pp. 52–3. See extracts from an article by a Pathan woman in the monthly Pushtu journal *Pakhtun* launched in Mar. 1928.

44 *Ibid.* See observations made by Jawaharlal Nehru about this region in Feb. 1937, p. 223. See also pp. 53 and 231.

45 Moghadam, 'Revolution, Islam and women', fn. 46.

46 Contemporary white supremacist discourse in the USA assigns African-American women's 'primitive sexuality' as opposed to the 'chaste and pure white woman.' See Charles Herbert, *Sexual Racism: The Emotional Barrier to an Integrated Society* (New York, Harper Colophon Books, 1976), pp. 57–144.

47 Jenny Sharpe uses this term in relation to the Mutiny. See her *Allegories of Empire: The Figure of Woman in the Colonial Text* (Minneapolis & London, University of Minnesota Press, 1993), pp. 61–154.

48 A large number of scholars have written on this theme. See, for example, the collection of essays in Nupur Chaudhury and Margaret Strobel (eds), *Western Women and Imperialism: Complicity and Resistance* (Bloomington & Indianapolis, Indiana

University Press, 1993); Kumkum Sangari, 'Rethinking histories: definitions of literacy, literature, gender in nineteenth century Calcutta and England', in Swati Joshi (ed.), *Rethinking British: Essays in Literature, Language, History* (New Delhi, Trianka, 1991), pp. 32–123; Indrani Sen, 'Between power and *'purdah'*: The white women in British India, 1858–1900', *The Economic and Social History Review*, 34:3 (Jul.–Sep. 1997), pp. 355–76; Kumari Jayawardena, *The White Woman's Other Burdens: Western Women and South Asia during British Rule* (New York & London, Routledge, 1995); Ann Stoler 'Making empire respectable: the politics of race and sexual morality in 20th-century colonial cultures', in Jan Breman (ed.), *Imperial Monkey Business: Racial Supremacy in Social Darwininist Theory and Colonial Practice* (Amsterdam, V. U. University Press, 1990), pp. 35–70; Helen Callaway, *Gender, Culture and Empire: European Women in Colonial Nigeria* (London, Macmillan Press, 1987); and Hilary Callan and Shirley Ardener, *The Incorporated Wife* (London, Croom Helm, 1984).

49 Nupur Chaudhury, 'Shawls, jewels, curry and rice in Victorian Britain', in Chaudhury and Strobel, *Western Women and Imperialism*, pp. 231–46.

50 Bernard S. Cohen, *Colonialism and its Forms of Knowledge: The British in India* (Princeton, Princeton University Press, 1996), p. 130.

51 Mrinalini Sinha, '"Chathams, Pitts and Gladstones on petticoats": the politics of gender and race in the Ilbert Bill controversy, 1883–1884', in Chaudhury and Strobel, *Western Women and Imperialism*, pp. 98–116.

52 Communication from Timothy Thomas, reader services curator at the India Office library and records department, London, Jun. 1989.

53 The most notorious case was that of Islam Bibi: a Hindu girl called Ram Kori made a runaway marriage with a Muslim in Mar. 1936 and converted to Islam. It aroused enormous passions and left a legacy of communal bitterness, especially as the colonial government intervened to restore her to the Hindu fold. There were several such runaway cases leading to rumours of Hindu girls being kidnapped by Muslims. See AICC Papers, F. no. 29, 1938, pp. 239–301.

54 Hindu communalists in Bengal, from the 1920s onwards, were increasingly giving a communal colour to similar 'abduction' cases. Many of these were runaway cases of low caste Hindu women and widows with Muslim men. Communication from Pradeep Kumar Dutta, New Delhi, Feb. 1997.

55 AICC Papers, F. no. 29, 1938, p. 241. The Congress report also indicates the complicity of British administrators with these raids. It argues that as British authorities were responsible for the granting of military contracts, they benefited most by operations in Waziristan, and the more Hindus were kidnapped, the greater chance there were of securing support for vigorous operations in the independent territory.

56 From Feb. 937 to Nov. 1938, there were 26 raids and an abnormally high number of kidnappings. A Congress fact-finding report of 1938, connected the raids with the British military operations in the NWFP and offered a very comprehensive explanation about how and why the Hindu minority came to be the prime targets of these raids.

57 Paola Bacchetta, 'The *sangh*, the *samiti* and the differential concepts of the Hindu nation', in Kumari Jayawardena and Malathi de Alwis (eds), *Embodied Violence: Communalising Women's Sexuality in South Asia* (New Delhi, Kali for Women, 1996), pp. 126–67.

58 In this connection a revealing observation of the British commissioner of police, Bombay, may be cited. In his letter no. 3916/A/207, dated 12 Sep. 1938, to the secretary of the home department government of Bombay, he maintained: 'The film has been produced by the United Artists Film Corporation, an American concern, which can have little or no interest in the British policy on the Frontier and appears to have endeavoured to produce a topical film which, it hopes, will produce adequate return as a result of its exhibition in this country. The agitation against it appears to be wholly artificial and sponsored by irresponsible youths who took at least a week to form the opinion that its exhibition in India was undesirable and objectionable.' On further inquiry, when he learnt that the film was indeed made by a British company, he had to withdraw these observations. His comments, however, point to the complicity of the colonial government and confirm the Indian audiences' reading of the film. MSA, Home-Poll, F. no. 237-I, pp. 57–71.

59 IOR, L/P&J/8/123, Coll. no. 104-A, 1939. See questions in the House of Commons put to the secretary of state for India regarding 'propaganda broadcasts being sent to various British dominions, colonies and mandated territories.'

60 *Ibid.,* Lt.-Comm. Fletcher, 23 Dec. 1937.

61 *Ibid.,* Arthur Henderson to the prime minister, 21 Nov. 1938.

62 *Ibid.,* telegram from Germany, dated 15 Nov. 1938.

63 IOR, L/I/1/777, information department, F. no. 462/22 , 1939–1947.

64 IOR, L/P&J/8/123, Coll. no. 104-A, 1939. See Arthur Henderson to the prime minister, 21 Nov. 1938. For a brief account of films from

Nazi Germany that showed Britain as ruthless exploiters of the colonies and a brutal enemy of order and civilisation, see Jeffery Richards, *Visions of Yesterday* (London, Routledge & Kegan Paul, 1984), pp. 347–57.

65 IOR, L/I/1/777, information department, F. no. 462/22, 1939–1947. See confidential report of the secretary of state for India, 17 Sep. 1939.

66 IOR, L/P&J/8/128, Coll. no. 105-A, pt. XIII, Apr. 1936–1939. See, for example, the *New York Times*, 12 Jan. 1935, which, while writing about *The Lives of a Bengal Lancer*, maintained: 'It is sympathetic in its discussion of England's colonial management and it ought to prove a great blessing to Downing street.' The *Picture Goer* (6 Feb. 1936) observed how 'Hollywood had glorified an British feat of arms and shown our soldiers in a eulogistic manner for which our native producers might have shrunk in modesty.' The *Evening Standard* commenting on *The Charge of the Light Brigade* observed: 'It is a good tale and the Union Jack is waved more flamboyantly than any British producing companies would ever dare wave it.' This film was also judged as the 'magnificent picture of the splendour of British rule in India.' The *Daily Express* (24 Feb. 1939) proclaimed in bold headlines: 'Hollywood glorifies the empire' and went on to conclude that 'the British empire need not worry for propaganda while Hollywood does its imperial publicity.'

67 IOR, L/P&J/8/128, Coll. no. 105-A, pt. XV, Feb.–Sep. 1939. See also foreign office to P&J department 12 Jun. 1936.

68 *Ibid.* See British consulate in Los Angeles to F. E. Evans, H.M. Consul, 26 Jan. 1939. Despite the instructions nothing really could be done about this matter. It had to await firmer steps, which were taken shortly afterwards.

69 IOR, L/P&J/8/131, Coll. no. 105-D, Jun. 1939–Apr. 1944. See extracts from *The Era* and *Cinematograph Times*, dated 15 Jun. 1939.

70 MSA, Home Poll, F. n. 81, 1939–41, p. 39.

71 *Ibid.*

72 *Film India* (Feb. 1939), p. 26.

73 *Bombay Chronicle* (12 Jan. 1939), p. 10.

74 *Hindu* (24 Dec. 1937), p. 5.

75 This film was previewed by Ram Bagai in Hollywood. See 'Anti-Muslim films' in *Film India* (Nov. 1939), p. 55.

76 *Hindu* (21 Sep. 1934), p. 5.

77 *Amrit Bazaar Patrika* (20 Apr. 1935), see editorial.

78 IOR, L/P&J/6/1995, 1930–38, p. 548.

79 Byron Farwell, *Armies of the Raj: From the Mutiny to Independence, 1858–1947* (London, Viking Press, 1990), p. 310. Among the Muslims, divisions made for recruitment were, Punjabi Muslim, Hindustani Muslim, Rajput Muslim, Madrasi Muslim and Baluchi Muslim.

80 IOR, L/P&J/8/123, Coll. no. 104-F, May 1937–Nov. 1941. Calcutta, Sylhet and Mymensingh had provided the major recruiting grounds for the crew of Indian-manned ships. Captain J. W. Doherty to the secretary of state for India, Nov. 1939.

81 In World War I, Britain's declaration of war on Turkey and the Sultan's declaration of *Jehad* against the Triple Entente had created a crisis of conscience among many Muslim soldiers in the British Indian army. As the Turkish Sultan was still the revered *khalifa* of Islam, many Muslims had 'qualms about making war on the Turkish co-religionists'. Consequently, the British had to make a conscious effort not to send Indian Muslims to Egypt, Sudan or Mesopotamia. They had a hard time fighting the rumour that Muslims were being sent to fight Muslims on the side of the non-believers. In fact, at Gallipoli, in May 1915, two battalions of Punjab Muslims had to be laid off as the commanding officer refused to take responsibility for the loyalty of his Muslim soldiers. Similar feelings among the soldiers erupted in the Singapore mutiny of the Fifth Indian Light Infantry when a single battalion refused to go to Turkey. See Farwell, *Armies of the Raj*, pp. 236–7. Also see David Omissi, *The Sepoy and the Raj: The Indian Army, 1860–1940* (London, Macmillan Press, 1994), pp. 129–52.

82 In 1914 many Pathans of the Baluch Battalion had refused to go on service. Of those who were sent to the Western Front during 1914–15, some Pathans had joined the enemy. In response the British had to disown the remaining 120 Pathans. Unlike other deserters who fled back to India and were quickly apprehended and court-martialled, Pathans escaped to the tribal areas that were not under British jurisdiction. Once there, these 'first rate soldiers' employed their knowledge of tactics learnt in the army in their struggle against the British. See J. G. Elliot, *The Frontier, 1939–47* (London, Cassell, 1968), p. 85; and Jeffrey Greenhut, 'The imperial reserve: the Indian corps on the Western Front, 1914–15', *The Journal of Imperial and Commonwealth History*, 12:1 (Oct. 1983), pp. 53–74.

83 MSA, Home-Poll, F. no. 69, 1932, pp. 3–11, 17–25, 39, 59–60; and F. no. 17, 1931, pp. 3–11. The inflammable nature of this propaganda can be evidenced in a play in Pushtu, *Dard*, by Amin Nawaz Jalya. In this, a character says, 'Is it not disgraceful and especially

for a Pathan that his mother is possessed by another man and not by his father?'

84 AICC Papers, F. no. 79, 1931, p. 33.

85 Amit Kumar Gupta, *North-West Frontier Province Legislature and Freedom Struggle, 1932–47* (New Delhi, Indian Council of Historical Research, 1976), pp. 24–61.

86 Ahmed, *Millennium*, p. 118.

87 Milan Hauner, 'One man against the empire: the Faqir of Ipi and the British in central Asia on the eve of and during the Second World War', *Journal of Contemporary History*, 16:1 (Jan. 1981), pp. 183–212.

88 AICC Papers, F. no. 29, 1938, pp. 59–61. Also see F. no. 16 (11), 1937, pp. 205–17.

89 Central Legislative Assembly Debates, vol. II, 20 Feb. 1936, pp. 1261–2; vol. IV, 26 Aug. 1937, p. 116; vol. IV, 27 Aug. 1937, pp. 664–7; and vol. V, 9 Sep. 1937, pp. 1380–1.

90 CLAD, vol. IV, 9 Aug. 1938, pp. 228–9.

91 *Hindu* (10 Feb. 1939), p. 7.

92 CLAD, 24 Aug. 1927. See Abdul Haye's question to J. Cerar.

93 ICC Evidence, 1927–28, vol. II. See written statement of Rao Sahib C. S. R. Rao, sub-editor of the *Statesman*, Calcutta, pp. 1019–22.

94 MSA, Home-Poll. F. no. 271, 1934–38.

95 MSA, Home Poll, F. no. 181, 1938, pp. 7–9.

96 *The Drum*, for example, was widely condemned. See the *Iqbal* (14 Sep. 1938), in MSA, Home-Poll. F. no. 271, 1934–38. Also important is the role played by the English-language film journal, *Film India*, which was pointedly 'Hindu' in its tone. Yet, in relation to the western films, its attacks were on anti-Muslim and anti-national grounds.

97 *Hindu* (7 Sept. 1934), p. 5; and *Hindu* (9 Aug. 1935), p. 5. Concerted demands had started to be made in this regard in 1922 itself. See S. B. Bannerjee, 'Crushing new taxation', *Hindu* (20 Apr. 1922), p. 5.

98 *Bombay Chronicle* (26 Feb. 1939), p. 8; *Hindu* (11 Aug. 1933), p. 12; and *Film India* (Oct. 1939), p. 3.

99 *Hindu* (14 Aug. 1936), p. 5. See the speech of G. V. Deshmukh, member of the Legislative Assembly of Bombay, to the executive council of the Motion Picture Society of India.

100 *Bombay Chronicle* (26 Feb. 1939), p. 8.

101 Low, *The History of the British Film*, p. 223.

102 *Film India* (Oct. 1938), p. 23.

103 Masters, *Bugles and a Tiger*, p.131.

104 A. E. W Mason cited in the *Bombay Chronicle* (15 Feb. 1939), p. 10.

105 *Film India* (Feb. 1939), pp. 26–7, 31.

106 AICC Papers: F. no. 29, 1938, pp. 45–6; F. no. P-16, 1939–40, pp. 99–101.

107 MSA, Home poll. F. no. 237-I, 1938, pp. 57–71. The details that follow, unless indicated to the contrary, have been taken from this source. For the media coverage of this agitation see *Bombay Chronicle* (9 Sep. 1938), p. 9; (10 Sep. 1938), pp. 7, 14; (13 Sep. 1938), pp. 1, 7; and *Film India* (Oct. 1938), pp. 25–7.

108 Not enough is known about the Muslim League criticism of the British policy in the NWFP. So far as this region was concerned, the Muslim League was conspicuous by its absence prior to 1936. In the 1937 elections the Muslim League was unable to win a single seat. In fact, it remained weak and disorganised until after World War II. During these years the Muslim League was attacking the Congress for dividing the Muslims, flouting Muslim opinion, destroying Muslim culture, interfering with their religious and social life and trampling upon their political and economic rights. These were the same objections which the Muslim League had been raising against the British colonial government. See Syed Waquar Ali Shah, *Muslim League in North West Frontier Province* (Royal Book Company, Karachi, 1992), pp. 22–92; and Stephen Alan Rittenberg, 'The independent movement in India's North West Frontier Province, 1901–1947' (Ph.D. thesis, Columbia University, 1977), pp. 194–267.

109 MSA, Home-Poll. F. no. 237-I, 1938. See handwritten remark for the attention of the home minister, dated 12 Sep. 1938. Only once was Aziz Mohammed Lalljee mistakenly identified as a Muslim League member in an English newspaper.

110 Other films like the 'devotional' and 'social', with their emphasis on social criticism, were the favoured genre of the middle class. Vasudevan, 'Addressing the spectator', pp. 305–24.

111 Other films of the same kind were *Gul Sanobar* (Homi Master, 1928), remade in Hindi in 1934; *Hatim Tai* (Prafulla Ghosh, 1929), remade in Hindi by G. R. Seth in 1931; *Diler Jigar* (*Gallant Heart*, G. D. Pawan, 1931); *Amar Jyoti* (V. Shantaram, Hindi , 1936); and *Jwala* (Master Vinayak, Marathi and Hindi, 1938).

112 National Film Archives of India, oral history project, J. B. H. Wadia, recorded interview, 6 Jul. 1984.

113 Kathryn Hansen, *Grounds for Play: The Nautanki Theatre of North India* (New Delhi, Manohar Publications, 1992), pp. 188–207.

114 *Ibid.*, pp. 194–5.

115 Some of the more notable films of *virangana* concept included *Sati Veermati* (S. N. Patukar, 1923); *Devi Ahalyabai* (B. P. Mishra, 1925); *Shoor Killedarin* (*Fair Warrior*, Vishnupant Anndhkar,

1927); *Lutaru Lalna* (*Dacoit Damsel*, Homi Master, 1929); *Shoornar Sharada* (*Galant Girl*, Homi Master, 1930); *Shri Sinha* (*Lioness*, Prafulla Ghosh, 1931); and *Stree Shakti* (*The Super Sex*, Hari Bhai Desai, 1932).

116 Wadia's *Hunterwali* with 'fearless Nadia', was a big hit. It led to the manufacture of *Hunterwali* match boxes, shoes and shirts on the Hollywood publicity pattern. *Hunterwali* was followed by a series of similar high-adventure stunt films.

117 IOR, L/P&J/6/1747, 1922–1930. See the newspaper cutting, 'In *swadeshi* film land', dated 4 Mar. 1926, p. 450.

118 Information given by Nasreen Fazalbhoy, 14 Oct. 1996. Also see Sharada Dwivedi and Rahul Mehrotra, *Bombay: The Cities Within* (Bombay, India Book House, 1995), pp. 226–7, 239.

119 Communication from Siddheshwar Dayal, whose family has been in the film exhibition business in Delhi since colonial days, Feb. 1997.

120 Frantz Fanon, *Black Skin, White Masks* (New York, Grove Press, 1967), pp. 52–3.

121 Kunj Patel, *Rural Labour in Industrial Bombay* (Bombay, Popular Prakashan, 1963), pp. 150, 153.

122 Radhika Ramasubban and Nigel Crook, 'Spatial patterns of health and morality', in Sujata Patel and Alice Thorner (eds), *Bombay: Metaphor for Modern India* (Bombay, Oxford University Press, 1995), pp. 143–69.

123 This hectic pace of construction in Bombay continued through the period of World War I, despite the shortages the war brought in its wake. See Dwivedi and Mehrotra, *Bombay*, pp. 223, 226.

124 Georges Kristoffel Lieten, *Colonialism, Class and Nation: The Confrontation in Bombay around 1930* (Calcutta, K. P. Bagchi & Co., 1984), pp. 56–7.

125 *Ibid.*

126 See Dwivedi and Mehrotra, *Bombay*, p. 223.

127 *Bombay Legislative Assembly Debates*, 1938, vol. III, pt. II. See debate on 27–30 Apr. 1938, pp. 2422–647. During the late 1930s the growing population had increased the pressure on land, leaving 50,000 people in the city with no accommodation.

128 1929: 2 riots (14 killed, 739 wounded, lasted for 36 days); 1930: 2 riots (no figures available); 1932: 2 riots (for one riot no figures available; for the second: 217 killed, 2713 wounded, lasted for 49 days); 1933: 2 riots (no figures available); 1936: 1 riot (94 killed, 632 wounded, lasted for 21 days); 1937: (11 killed, 85 wounded, lasted 21 days); 1938 (12 killed, over 100 wounded lasted two and a half hours). *Ibid.*, pp. 2474–5.

129 *Ibid.* See Jhabvala, 27 Apr. 1938, pp. 2464–5.

130 For an insightful analysis of the 1928–29 strike in which communalism was used to break the strike, leading to riots, see Sabyasachi Bhattacharya, 'Capital and labour in Bombay city, 1928–29', in D. N. Panigrahi (ed.), *Economy, Society and Politics in Modern India* (New Delhi, Vikas Publishing House, 1985), pp. 42–60.

131 Jim Masselos, 'Power in the Bombay "Mohalla" 1905–1915: an initial exploration into the world of the Indian urban Muslim', *South Asia*, 6 (Dec. 1976), pp. 75–95; and Jim Masselos, 'Bombay in the 1870: a study of changing patterns in urban politics', *South Asia*, 1 (Aug. 1971), pp. 29–35. On the political mobilisation of workers, see Rajnarayan Chandavarkar, 'Workers' politics and the mill districts in Bombay between the wars', *Modern Asian Studies*, 15:3 (1981), pp. 603–47.

132 Bhattacharya, 'Capital and labour in Bombay', pp. 42–60; and Lieten, *Colonialism, Class and Nation*, pp. 132–9.

133 MSA, Home-Poll, F. no. 237-I, 1939, pp. 3–7.

134 IOR, L/P&J/8/126, Coll. no. 105-A, pt. 1, Oct. 1935–May 1940. See questions raised by Jagadish Chandra Bannerjee on various anti-Indian films in the Council of State debates, 17 Sep. 1935. See also the questions raised by S. Satyamurthy in the Central Legislative Assembly between 17 Sep. 1938 and Mar. 1939 regarding such films, and the comments of A. Dibdin of the P&J department to F. H. Puckle, secretary to govt. of India home department, dated 25 May 1939.

135 The Congress was keen to have its programme and policies projected in newsreels and documentaries. Any ban on these provoked loud protest and condemnation. See MSA, Home-Poll, F. no. 8, 1932–33, pp. 121–9.

136 MSA, Home-Poll F. no. 137-I, 1938. See for example, Urdu newspapers like *Khilafat*, *Al Hilal* and *Hilal*.

137 Abdul Gaffar Khan had attacked British propaganda in Oct. 1938 in terms that reiterated the ideological message of *The Drum*. Speaking in Urdu the Pathan leader said: 'The British tell Muslims "there are 25 crores Hindus and if you will fight us and if we go away, then Hindu Raj will be established here." And to the Hindus they frighten by saying "if we go away from here, the Pathans will descend and swallow you."' [sic]. Speech cited in Tendulkar, *Abdul Gaffar Khan*, p. 187.

138 Claude Markovits, 'Indian business and the Congress provincial governments, 1937–1939', *Modern Asian Studies*, 15:3 (1981), pp. 487–526.

139 *Ibid.* There were 88 industrial disputes in Bombay in 1937, involving 1,09,858 workers, and 111 in 1938, involving 62,188 workers.

140 Rani Dhawan Shankerdass, *The First Congress Raj: Provincial Autonomy in Bombay* (Delhi, Macmillan, 1982), pp. 179–91.

141 MSA, Home-Poll, F. no. 237-I. See letter of commissioner of police to the secretary of the home department, government of Bombay, dated 12 Sep. 1938.

142 A Gujarati Bhargava Brahmin of about fifty years, Kanaiyalal Maneklal Munshi was a leading advocate of the Bombay High Court, with a practice said to be worth about Rs 10,000 a month, and director of a large number of companies.

143 Information given by Nasreen Fazalbhoy, 14 Oct. 1996.

144 MSA, Home-Poll, F. no. 237-I. pp. 179–81.

145 *Ibid.* See K. M. Munshi's orders, dated 20 Sep. 1938. Also see deputy commissioner of police to home department, 23 Sep. 1938.

146 *Ibid.* See Home-Poll DO. no. 1969, dated 7 Oct. 1938. These objections were first recorded by K. M. Munshi, in his own hand, on 27 Sep. 1938.

147 *Ibid.* See K. M. Munshi's statement to the Bombay Legislative Assembly, p. 247; see also pp. 35–7, 45. A revised version of the film, excising 1300 feet, leaving a length of 7,455 feet only, was certified in Bombay on 20 Oct. 1938.

148 *Film India* (May 1939), p. 25.

149 Lal Chand Navalraj, in the Central Legislative Assembly, cited in *Film India* (Apr. 1939), p. 34.

150 IOR, L/P&J/8/126, Coll. no. 105-A, pt. I, Oct. 1935–May 1940. See note to secretary of state for India, 15 Aug. 1939. See also *Bombay Chronicle* (8 May 1939), pp. 1, 9.

151 MSA, Home-Poll. F. no. 237-I, 1938. See notification no. 2060, Home Poll., dated 15 Oct. 1938, and the press note issued by the director of information in Bombay, dated 15 Oct. 1938.

152 In this brief period the excision of travelogue films was as follows: *Jaipur, the Pink City* (742 ft), *The Land of Shalimar* (660 ft), *Trade Winds* (6583 ft), and *Imperial Delhi* (765 ft).

1 *The Drum*. 'A dramatic moment' in the film: Marjorie Carruthers (Valerie Robson) safeguarding Azim (Sabu), neutralises the social exclusiveness of the British, and moves towards 'maternal imperialism'.

2 *The Drum*. British soldiers v. the rebel Pathans; a typical fighting scene, common to most empire films.

3 *The Drum.* A 'loyalist Pathan' with his 'natural friends': a happy Azim (Sabu), instrumental in the defeat of anti-British forces, with Col. and Mrs Carruthers.

4 *The Drum.* Symbolising British protection: Prince Azim (Sabu), after a violent suppression of an anti-British conspiracy.

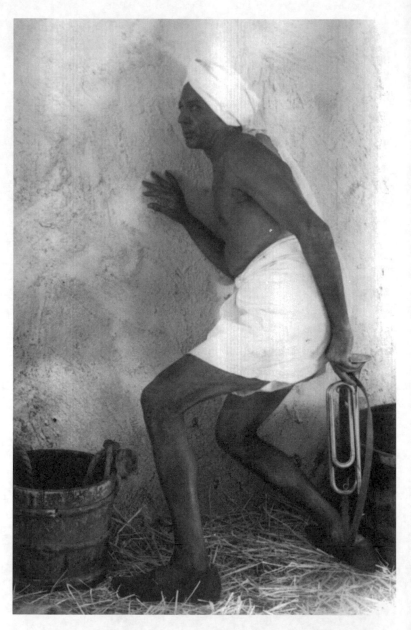

5 *Gunga Din*. Reiterating notions of how a 'native', a 'common man' of India looks and behaves: Sam Jaffe playing a cringing Gunga Din for the white western audience.

6 *Gunga Din.* 'Affectionate camaraderie' between Sergeant MacChesney (Victor MacLagan) and Gunga Din (Sam Jaffe), usually marked by extreme condescension and patronisation, but also disgust, bullying, insults and abuses.

7 *The Rains Came*. The attraction of the Other: first meeting of Rama Safti (Tyrone Power) and Edwina Esketh (Myrna Loy).

8 *The Rains Came*. Regression of the native: transformation of the anglicised Bengali *babu* into an orthodox Brahmin, in the wake of the rains and flood havoc. Edwina Esketh (Myrna Loy) and Ransome (George Brent) look on.

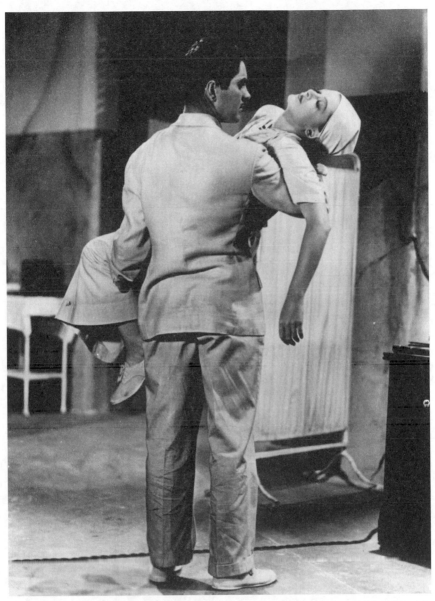

9 *The Rains Came*. Crossing the race and colour barriers: Rama Safti (Tyrone Power) and Edwina Esketh (Myrna Loy).

10 *The Rains Came.* Portraying 'Indian India': a resplendent Rama Safti (Tyrone Power) flanked by British officials, ascends the throne of a subordinate princely state.

3

Gunga Din (1939):
spectre of Hindu domination

At a crucial stage of Indian national independence, when a very serious challenge had been mounted against the British empire in India, the film, *Gunga Din*, gave a clarion call of 'All's well' – literally echoed from the rooftops in the film – for the benefit of the white audience. Greatly troubled by the notion of an independent India, it portrayed fears nurtured in the west about colonial empire. A reassurance was urgently needed, in view of the impending world war, that the colonials were more than adequately equipped to deal with the situation. The adoption of a comic mode in an adventure film, which made light of serious situations, communicated this confidence admirably. It helped generate an 'illusion of permanence'. On the one hand, such a portrayal appeased western fears and restored faith in their ability to deal with potentially dangerous situations. On the other hand, it belittled the danger itself by transforming and recasting Kipling's Gunga Din into a larger than life, ultra-loyal and ultra-heroic character, symbolising the existence of a vast pool of natives – the forgotten majority – who were ready to sacrifice all in order to defend the British empire. Gunga Din epitomises the affection, love, dependence and awesome loyalty of the 'common man' – the teeming multitudes of India – who wanted to maintain the colonial connection rather than sever it.

In delineating this preference, the film makes a comment on colonial society dominated by high-caste Hindus acting as a repressive and divisive force in Indian society. In projecting this, the film essentialised the character of Hinduism as inherently violent, stressed the extraordinary inegalitarianism of the caste system and focused on the plight and humiliation of the lowest of the low: the untouchables. This emphasis on the cultural diversity and heterogeneity of a socially-fragmented India underlined the difficulty of treating it as a single nation and, in view of the demand for independence, begged the question whether inhabitants of such a society were competent of governing themselves.

In portraying this, colonial nationalism was not ignored but played down. It was trivialised and treated as a minor development confined to a few isolated high-caste individuals – the demented freaks and religious fanatics – who represented none but themselves. More importantly, this nationalism was designated as Hindu nationalism in which the professedly saintly and pacifist figure of the Hindu villain had a hidden agenda to violently overthrow the British and impose Hindu rule. The film, in fact, plays up blatantly the spectre of Hindu domination of India to construct a threat from the inside rather than from the outside, by reinforcing the reigning communal ideology.

The Indian political leadership is opened not only to caricature and ridicule but more importantly to the subversion of its ideological programme, which is shown to be unacceptable to the great mass of India. This portrayal effectively establishes and justifies the white man's sense of responsibility towards India and its 'peoples'. The anxiety about the national leadership's assimilationist conception of the Indian nation, visualised as brotherhood or a confederation of communities, became in the film a vindication of the colonial masters' assumption of a paternalistic attitude towards the minority groups, especially the Muslims and the untouchables. In a highly fragmented India, they needed protection against domination by high-caste Hindus shaping the policy of the most important political party, the Indian National Congress.

As the film and the discourse embedded in it were polysemic, they evoked not merely the divisions within colonial society but also the difference between it and the imperial society. In making colonialism and its organisational apparatus attractive to the white audience, the film rearticulated colonial race relations that subverted rather than promoted the colonists' intent in the context of the non-white audience. This chapter highlights how in a very crucial way the ideological thrust of imperialism could be reversed to become subversive in intent. In this, I argue, the ability of the Indian cinema to articulate contemporary nationalist discourse in its own cultural way played a crucial role. Although the film, *Gunga Din*, was banned well before it could reach any category of this audience, it became significant for being the last of its genre that was produced during the British Raj.

Gunga Din was based upon a short poem by Rudyard Kipling, published in 1892, when he was twenty-seven years of age. Written in the rough barrack-room language of an infantry private, it tells of a low-caste *bhishti* (water-carrier) who, in the course of fulfilling his duty, lost his life while trying to quench the thirst of wounded soldiers in the British Indian army.[1] Extremely popular, this poem was said to be habitually recited in Hollywood by aspiring actors who wished to bring their talent to the attention of film directors.[2] Producers RKO in Hollywood acquired the rights of the Kipling poem *Gunga Din* in 1936. Directed by George Stevens, the film featured Cary Grant, Victor McLagan, Douglas Fairbanks, Jr, Sam Jaffe, Eduardo Ciannelli and Joan Fontaine. Released in the USA on 17 February 1939, it was rated one of the best and most popular of adventure films and went on to break box-office records in the USA and Great Britain.

A Kiplingesque scenario was developed around this short verse composition by the team of Ben Hatchet and Charles MacArthur. They made out of it a high-adventure fictional work located in the late nineteenth century, along the lines of the already very successful film, *The Lives of a Bengal Lancer*. In brief, the film shows a revival of *thuggee*, the ancient murderous cult, which had been eradicated from India under William Bentinck, the governor general of India from 1827–35. Fifty years later, under Queen Victoria, it was revived to threaten the already troubled North-West Frontier of India, where an outstation is attacked by the *thugs* and everyone killed. Out of the British troops stationed in this mountainous region of India, three of the toughest adventure-loving sergeants, MacChesney, Cutter and Ballantine, are sent to investigate. They reach the village to find the entire population missing. A few men are found by them hidden in a room who turn out to be the *thugs*. On a cue from one of them the sergeants are attacked. In the fight that follows the sergeants overpower and kill the *thugs* easily. The three of them return with evidence that the village was destroyed by the *thugs*. Close friends and a brawling threesome, they are constantly playing jokes on each other. Here a sub-plot takes over in which Ballantine plans to quit the service and marry, and consequently becomes a special target of attack and comedy. The other two use means fair and foul to keep this from happening. By the end of the film they are successful in breaking his engagement and retaining him in the army service.

Sergeant Cutter, the treasure-seeker, with the help of Gunga Din, both riding the friendly elephant Annie, set out to find the famed treasure said to be hidden in the hills. They end up by finding a Kali temple made of gold, which also turns out to be a *thug* hide-out. Here, the guru, the spiritual leader of the *thugs*, is making sinister plans to destroy the British troops. Cutter allows himself to be captured but sends back Gunga Din with information about the *thugs*. The other two friends follow Gunga Din on a rescue mission. They too are captured. The three sergeants and their native carrier, Gunga Din, are tortured by the *thugs*, but they succeed in outwitting the guru. They escape to the dome of the temple where, by holding the cult-leader prisoner, they are able to hold off his men. The guru sacrifices himself by leaping in a pit of snakes so that his followers will not be deterred from carrying out his plans to ambush British troops. A rescue battalion leads directly into the ambush. Gunga Din, whose heroics are not confined to water-carrying alone, as in Kipling's poem, now gets his big moment. With the three sergeants lying wounded and surrounded by *thugs*, Gunga Din, bleeding profusely, climbs to the topmost pinnacle of the temple and, while blowing a bugle-call to warn the troops, gets killed. His heroism averts the annihilation of the regiment, the sergeants are rescued and the uprising is stamped out. Gunga Din is suitably rewarded. His dream to become a soldier of Her Majesty the Queen of England is realised: he is posthumously made a corporal in the British Indian army in recognition of his loyalty.

Aura of authenticity: conflicting messages

Gunga Din, despite being a film primarily based on the antics of the three irrepressible British sergeants in the British Indian army, still sought to capitalise on the minor character of Gunga Din – an emphasis which accorded an element of authenticity to an otherwise improbable film. Declared to have 'inspired' this film, Gunga Din was projected as its hero. Bold banner headings proclaimed, 'water-carrier is the hero in *Gunga Din*'. Gunga Din, played by Sam Jaffe, was undoubtedly accorded a crucial role in the film, but he was not the star draw. Overshadowed in the star ranking, he was accorded far less footage than the three sergeants played by a trio of very popular and well-established Hollywood stars, Cary Grant, Victor Mclagen and Douglas Fairbanks, Jr. They had already featured in several hit films and had a vast fan following. Sam Jaffe, on the other hand, was only a second choice for this role after Sabu, star of *The Elephant Boy* (1937) and *The Drum* (1938), who was not available. Jaffe had previously played an Asian in *Horizon* (1937), and, lacking Sabu's star status, was able to portray the character of Gunga Din without imposing a pre-existing screen persona on it. This helped in providing an element of authenticity and acceptability that may not have been possible if a better known actor had played this role and immersed the character of Gunga Din with his own star status. Indeed, Jaffe was well-complimented by the film critics of both England and the USA for totally submerging his identity into that of Gunga Din and playing him so convincingly. In other words, Jaffe's performance conformed to preconceived notions of how a native ought to behave. The reception in India was very different as these claims had to be located in the social and cultural experience of the colonised people.

Greater authenticity, however, was imparted to the film by the creator of the character of Gunga Din, Rudyard Kipling (1865–1935). He was not only born in India in Bombay but he also spent much of his adult life in India. He worked as a journalist for seven years in Punjab, first on the *Civil and Military Gazette*, then on the *Pioneer*. His stories were widely-received as authentic, coming out of his experiences of India. He quickly achieved great fame, having been awarded the Nobel prize in 1907, and a large readership. Kipling was a favourite author of Hollywood film-makers in the 1930s, as witness the adaptations of *The Lives of a Bengal Lancer* (1935), *Clive of India* (1935), *The Charge of the Light Brigade* (1936), *The Elephant Boy, Wee Willie Winkie, Captains Courageous* and *The Light that Failed* (all 1937).

Kipling's Indian connection, his vast readership and the influence that his work had come to exert in the formation of British and Indian images and imperial myths was undeniable.[3] Literature about India had been accepted as one of the major sources of information for the British public. Kipling, through his novels and stories set in India, contributed very substantially towards building up this reservoir of imperial myths, which greatly influenced the way India and Indians were perceived by the British public.

Authenticity was further underlined by introducing Kipling as a character in the film. Played by Reginald Sheffield, Kipling is first shown riding with the British Indian army on the rescue mission of the three British sergeants. He is next shown sitting in his tent writing his famous poem supposedly inspired by the deeds of Gunga Din.[4] This poem is then recited by the commander over the dead body of Gunga Din. Such use of Kipling in the film creates an impression that he wrote this poem having witnessed a true incident involving a living flesh-and-blood character. Importantly, this characterisation established a continuum with the 1930s, rather than a break.

The most important addition to Kipling's poem was the introduction of the *thuggee* cult. This was the crucial peg around which the entire narrative was woven. The use of *thuggee* historicised the imagery, authenticated different aspects of its portrayal as well as established an essentialised Hinduism, imaging the Other India implied in *The Drum* – the Hindu India with its backward, inhuman and violent socio-religious ideology and practices. As the central adhesive of the film, this Hindu religious connection makes a socio-religious and political comment on contemporary India. In *Gunga Din*, then, the past was co-opted to inform the viewer about the present. The historical and literary merits of the picture, both the *thuggee* episode and the Kipling connection, were made special targets of publicity and instructions were issued to concentrate on them.

The film begins with a declaration in its credits: 'Those portions of the picture dealing with the worship of goddess Kali are based on historical facts.' This at once established a fundamentally unchanging Hinduism, which was not necessarily confined to the eighteenth century. The claims to authenticity underpinned the contemporaneity of the situation. This claim created such unease among British officials that not only was this ordered to be deleted for the empire audience, but a caption was inserted instead saying, 'The supposed story is entirely fictitious.'[5]

Nevertheless, the publicity drive of the film continued to

suggest the contemporary links of *thuggee* in a variety of ways. Huge posters of six-armed Kali sitting ferociously on the body of a male victim wearing double garlands of human heads was superimposed on a map of India with a huge pickaxe, the symbol of *thugs*, spreading from top to the bottom of this map. The caption read, '*Thuggee* the murder cult of India' and proclaimed 'one million human sacrifices by *thugs* on behalf of goddess Kali'. The imperial myth maintained that *thugs* were ritually obliged to use the pickaxes to dig the graves of their chosen victims in advance, as they were forbidden to spill blood and used 'strangling cloth'. The publicity write-up beneath the map read:

> Most dangerous of all the Asiatic criminal associations was that of *thuggee*, which spread through India in the eighteenth and part of the nineteenth centuries. The cult's origin is in the mists of antiquity. In its amazing career it is estimated to have stealthily snuffed out the lives of one million victims.
>
> The fatalism of Kali's devotees, added to their natural bravery and subtle battle strategies, made them as desperate adversaries as British soldiers ever encountered in moral struggles.
>
> Strange to say, the British Government was long in ignorance regarding the murderous activities of the worshippers of Kali.
>
> Lack of good roads and public conveyance until the latter part of the nineteenth century facilitated operations of the cult. With the coming of rail roads, and improved transportation, the task of rounding up the *thugs* became an easier problem to solve. By 1860, although some were still at large, they were practically eliminated as an organised body from the life of India.

Yet another prominent display read, 'The *thugs* of India, a group of professional assassins who strangled their victims according to secret religious rites, are depicted for the first time on the screen in *Gunga Din*.' In the film, a British colonel describes the *thuggee* as 'a murderer cult Colonel Sleemen crushed fifty years ago' and as a further elaboration mentions, 'There were at least ten thousand of them in India and they murdered thirty thousand people a year. *Thuggee* was practised from the Himalayas to Ceylon. The movement was religious and worshipped Kali, the goddess of blood. *Thugs* were stranglers and they dug the graves of their victims in advance.'

Thuggee, with its ritual blood thirst, religious sanction for acts of murder, cult status, and use of strangulation as the method of murder, had all a part in imperial folklore. Yet, for the Indian audience, the *thuggee* episode may well have recalled all the historical associations connected with the establishment of British paramountcy in India, its rapid expansion and the ruthless drive to achieve it. This expansion had led to declining service opportunities for Indian chiefs and rulers, who had to disband their militias all at once. The resultant great exodus had sent marauders on the roads as criminality formed a part of a range of subsistence options.[6] Moreover, the *thuggee* campaign had been part of authoritarian reforms that were established for the assertion of paramountcy in which British justice fell short of the professed aims as due process of law had to be bypassed. A policy of 'blood for blood' had been used by the British to eradicate *thuggee*. In fact, *thugs* had always been a threatening category for the British and their elimination had been a long and cruel one.

More importantly, a recall of *thuggee* and its association with the goddess Kali, the slayer of demons and all black forces, also highlighted recent waves of militancy and violence by revolutionary terrorists, particularly from Bengal, who were popularly known to draw their inspiration from Kali. With the Chittagong Armoury raid of April 1930, revolutionary terrorism entered its most energetic phase. By the end of 1931 it had surpassed all previous records with ninety-two incidents of violence and several murders, including those of the British magistrates of Midnapur and Tippera.[7] A frightened British government went in for draconian methods of repression. Highly romanticised in popular perception, these educated, youthful revolutionaries were widely admired and became household names not only in Bengal but in other provinces as well.

This overlapping of fiction with historical events infused the film with meanings different from those intended. This fact assumed yet greater significance because in the north, where *Gunga Din* was located, the revolutionaries and terrorists, unlike the early terrorists who were given to strong Hindu religiosity, were essentially secular and included members of different religious denominations. Among them, the leaders of the Hindustan Socialist Republican Army, founded in September 1928, were particularly marked by an increasingly deep commitment to Marxist socialism and militant atheism.[8] Perhaps sensing the possibilities of such connections with terrorism, brought to the surface through references to Kali, the officials recommended that all possible references to Kali should be cut out and if possible the idea of the resurrection of *thuggee* should disappear from the film.[9] However, since both permeated the entire film they could not be deleted.

Gunga Din implied that the cult had spread throughout India and beyond, extending from the Himalayas to Ceylon, although historically it had remained confined to certain regional pockets specially central India. The eradication of this 'scourge' from India, hailed as one of the most enlightened acts of the colonial British, legitimised imperial rule on civilisational grounds. From the British point of view, *thuggee* reflected those extremely backward and uncivilised barbarian characteristics of the Hindu religion and civilisation, which, despite their origins in the remote past, had remained unchanged.

Significantly, a counter-discourse to the western denigration of Hinduism and claims of historical authenticity was provided by the indigenous film industry. The Indian cinema – in different regional languages with *Hindustani* (a mixture of Hindi and Urdu) as its dominant component – situated as it was amidst the rising tide of nationalism showed, tended towards the mythological, drawing mainly upon the great Hindu myths. D. G. Phalke, the producer of the first Indian feature film, *Raja Harishchandra* (1913), privileged the mythological as a completely indigenous form of signification which may be taken, in the words of Sumita Chakravarti, as a 'bold decolonising gesture'.[10] Phalke, aware of the need to see 'Indian images on the screen',[11] used western technology and knowledge to create images drawn from Hinduism that had already come to signify certain values for the fairly large middle-class urban audience, associated with the articulation of Indian and nation. From the early twentieth century onwards the terms 'Indian' and 'national' as evaluating categories were used interchangeably. In fact, the nationalist programme had been marked by the political and ideological thrust seen in popular art forms like painting, theatre and literature,[12] all of which had a decided influence on the cinema.

In the cinema the mythological themes, very familiar to the Indian audience, came to be read politically as there was an accretion of newer meanings in the films. The Indian audience's ability to formulate their own meanings out of the films was not only possible because of their own experience of subjugation, but also because they had their own cultural codes to draw upon. The theatre in Bengal and Maharashtra, for example, was already making a frontal attack on British colonialism. A play like *Nil Darpan* (Dinabandhu Mitra, 1872) attacking the British indigo plantations, had proved so threatening to the British that the Dramatic Performance Control Act had to be passed soon afterwards. The *swang* or *sang* and *nautanki* theatres of northern India played on historical figures, both men and women, vanquishing 'aliens' as a common ploy to convey political messages. In Maharashtra themes of Hindu mythology was used in which characters like Keechaka, Kansa and others symbolised the evils of colonialism. In R. N. Mudaliar's *Keechaka Vadham* (1916) the audience identified in Bhima, the person of Lokmanya Tilak, and in Keechaka, the character of Curzon.

Consequently, when the cinema used these polysemous themes, its nationalist message could hardly be missed. For example, the silent-era Hindu mythological film *Kalia Mardan* (Dadasaheb Phalke, 1919), provoked a phenomenal audience response, with viewers reported to have reacted with shouts of *Vande Matram* when Kalia was killed or Kans was annihilated by the child Krishna – the incarnation of the god, Vishnu.[13]

Other films, like *Amrit Manthan* (V. Shantaram, 1934), drew on the reformist tradition in Hinduism, showing an enlightened Indian monarch purging practices like *pashu-bali* and *nar-bali* (animal and human sacrifice), considered essential to the Hindu religion by a handful of fanatical priests. An extremely popular film, it ran for twenty-five weeks in Bombay. It boldly contradicted western assumptions about Hinduism as an essentialised unchanging religion. It also debunked the layers of myth that the west continued to project, representing Hinduism as a fanatical religion.

Equally challenging were the historical recreations that closely followed the mythological. The historical films were not produced merely for reasons of easy identification and commercial gain. Like the stunt and adventure genre films discussed in the previous chapter, they also had nationalism on their agenda. In the heyday of nationalism they recalled and reconstructed historical memory, constructing an idealised national past. It was a

vivid and dramatic representation of the way in which people were reaching out to their colonial present, going into the past and projecting an idealised society, albeit highly romanticised and overriding its hierarchical organisation.

These were as selective in recreating historical memory for national purposes as the empire cinema was in denying any sense of nationalism among the colonised. Films of this genre represented popular attitudes concerning particular historical periods and historical personalities and thereby indirectly commented on the present.

As these films underlined popularly invoked values, suggesting general attitudes and concerns of the colonial period rather than the period they depicted, they stood to challenge, condemn and replace the dominant message of the empire films by exposing their hidden agenda. For example, *Pukar* (*Call for Justice*, 1939), the first in the line of Sohrab Modi's spectacular historical films, was already playing to full houses when *Gunga Din* sought to be released in India. It reconstructed the historical truth on celluloid for an Indian audience. Indian rulers are shown maintaining a single standard of morality – not one for themselves and one for the ruled. According to the producer-director, Sohrab Modi, it was a direct comparison with the British rule of law that placed the British above their own rule as well as above the colonised Indians.[14] Sohrab Modi's spirited speech in the role of an indomitable Rajput warrior who confronts the Mughal emperor Jehangir – popularly known to give unprejudiced and fair hearings to his people regardless of their status in life – brought crowds to the theatre halls over and over again. Enthusiastic viewers showered coins upon the screen, displaying a sign of audience approval and joy.

Similarly, the historical film *Sikander*, first made in 1923 in the silent era and remade in 1941 by Sohrab Modi, received the most enthusiastic response from the Indian audience. The verbal exchange between Sikander (Alexander) and Porus, an Indian ruler who stood out against foreign attack and questioned the moral and political ethics of the relationship between the victor and the vanquished, brought the house down with shouts and claps. Such scenes were popularly known to be greeted with national slogans.[15] Interestingly, *Sikander* was described as an 'Indian *Birth of a Nation*', on the lines of D. W. Griffith's famous epic, and a 'truly historic film', when it was dubbed in English and viewed in London in 1953.[16]

Communalising nationalism

The recall of historic truth in these historical genre films was as motivated as the recall and reconstruction of *thuggee* in *Gunga Din*. However, the latter went beyond constructing authenticity or historicity. These premises were used to offer a comment on colonial society in order to condemn rising nationalism. For example, *Gunga Din*'s emphasis on the religious symbolism of Kali evoked Hindu nationalism very powerfully to the exclusion of all else. The use of the map of India in *Gunga Din*, covered by the image of the Hindu goddess, projected a territoriality of India that was essentially Hindu at a time when territorial demands for a separate state, *Pakistan* (land of the pure), a loose acronym for Punjab, Afghanistan, Kashmir, Sindh and Baluchistan, had already been voiced (by Chaudhury Rehmat Ali on 18 January 1933) and was virulently propagated. The film, echoing the work of late-1930s writers like Edward Thompson suggested that 'it was more certain than ever that in the womb of the old India, struggling to be born were two nations tugging and fighting for mastery even before birth.'[17]

In this two nation imagery, that of the Hindu nation in a female form tended to dominate over the more generally held secular concept of mother nation that inspired people to a popular struggle against an imperial country identified as the national enemy. In the colonial period the concept of mother India had emerged as a powerful symbol in nationalist politics.[18] However, this female cultural representation of mother nation undoubtedly had a socio-cultural and religious origin in the form of the earthly mother, the mother goddess, the motherland and *Bharat mata*, all of which coalesced into the powerful mother goddess Durga/Kali – an important figure in the Hindu pantheon, at once nurturing and destructive.[19] In the militant discourse of Hindu nationalism this religious symbolism reigned supreme and mother India came to represent the holy land upon which *Ramraj* was to be constructed or founded. Communalist ideologues felt that her virtue and purity must be aggressively defended against alien men, whether Muslim or the British.[20] By contrast, the general conception of mother India was not concerned with communal issues.

The dominant images of nation and national popular practice in the indigenous film industry were also drawing upon Hindu mythology and images of women which were used as tropes for the nation. An engaging representative theme, taken from mythology, was that of Draupadi. Between 1916 and 1944, it was filmed eleven times. In the silent era its first version appeared as *Keechaka Vadham* (1916), which was followed by *Draupadi Vastaharan* (1920), *Sairandhari* (1920), *Draupadi Swayamwar* (1922), *Draupadi's Fate* (1924), *Draupadi Vastaharan* (1927 and 1928) and *Keechakvadh* (1928). As a talkie, *Draupadi* (1931) was followed by *Sairandhari* (1933) and yet another *Draupadi* (1944).[21] A mythological image, alluding to contemporary politics, Draupadi, as a helpless victim of illegal usurpation and contention, was clearly a trope for the nation.[22] As an 'object' of defence, Draupadi inspired action. This essential theme of *dharm yudh* (war of righteousness) and usurpation, at the centre of which stood the mother figure, had a clearly nationalist resonance culminating in claims of rightful inheritance and identity.

The centrality of the female form drawn from Hindu mythology in a symbolic representation of an Indian national identity, curiously overlapping with the powerful mother goddess Durga or Kali, was not unproblematic. This, in combination with a preponderance of Hindu imagery in nationalist propaganda, was to create uncertainty among Indian nationalists. For example, it was not necessarily acceptable to the Muslims, especially as at local levels the Congress and the Hindu communal organisations like Hindu Mahasabha often shared the same cadres till the late 1930s.[23] The Congress, in fact, recognised the reservations of the Muslims regarding the use of Hindu symbolism in relation to nationalism. In October 1937, for instance, the Congress working committee had significantly decided to keep only the first few stanzas of *Vande Mataram*, in view of the objections raised by their Muslim friends to certain parts of the song hailing Hinduism.[24]

By reiterating the danger of Hindu domination, the film *Gunga Din* reinforced the British efforts to communalise the nationalist movement, to intensify the growth of communal forces and to further the acknowledged antipathy to the Congress among the

Muslim masses.[25] It also sought to widen the growing differences between the Muslims and non-Muslims, especially in the NWFP, the one Muslim majority province, which had come under Congress rule in the 1937 elections. However, Khan Sahib's ministry, by 1938–39, had begun to lose support among Muslim peasants for failing to reduce rural indebtedness in the face of opposition from Hindu and Sikh traders and moneylenders.[26] Historically, the film's release at this juncture could well strengthen this alienation and opposition.

The likely communal impact of the film was well-recognised by the provincial governments, which had formed popular ministries in 1937. Bengal, for instance, banned *Gunga Din* on considerations of intercommunal relations.[27] Significantly, RKO, with the idea of counteracting any agitation against the film, had submitted *Gunga Din* to the Bengal Board of Film Censors rather than that of Bombay, for its first censoring in India, in the hope that it would get an easy passage due to the non-Congress complexion of the Bengal ministry. Much to their surprise, however, the film was banned.

The late 1930s were the years of consolidation of communal forces in India. The Hindu Mahasabha was gaining in strength during these years and its president, V. D. Savarkar, declared at the Nagpur session in December 1938 that 'We Hindus are a Nation by ourselves ... Hindu nationalists should not be apologetic to being called Hindu communalists.'[28] This was accompanied by the growth of the paramilitary communalist bodies of *Rashtriya Swayam Sevak Sangh* (RSS) with its highly disciplined cadres trained along military lines and its counterpart, the *Khaskars* among the Muslims. The expansion of the RSS was particularly rapid between 1937 and 1940, in the context of worsening Hindu–Muslim relations in northern India. For the Hindu communalists, both the British as well as the Muslims were the Other. The film, *Gunga Din*, recalled not only this sort of militant communal Hinduism but also the ideological thrust of the kind the Muslim League was propagating. The Muslim League in the NWFP, for instance, stressed that the nationalists in the Congress, being Hindus, were bent upon establishing 'Ram Raj', whom 'no true Muslim' could align with.[29]

This portrayal of Hindu nationalism in *Gunga Din* from which the Muslims were excluded, was not entirely without an echo in the popular Indian cinema of this period. Similarly, in the popular literature or theatre, larger notions of the nation rising above divisions of religion, region and language were projected along with narrow concept of the Indian nation which excluded Muslims from its fold and held them as aliens and enemies to be vanquished.[30] For the films, however, a great deal of research needs to be done, before any firm conclusions can be reached. The indigenous cinema in its development of various genres shows a far more complex picture. For example, the mythological films of this period like that of Phalke, who framed his nationalist vision for the cinema on the basis of Hindu mythological images, have been interpreted in a recent work as an act of constructing the 'Hindu', which created the Other.[31] However, these films, according to Ravi Vasudevan, can hardly be read as a self-conscious project that based itself on exclusionary imperatives.[32] Yet, a great deal depended on the context in which these films were screened and received. Phalke's mythologicals were extremely popular films and they were repeatedly screened well into the 1940s. The perception and reception of Hindu mythological films in a charged communal situation could well be different. The decline of this extremely popular genre in the immediate aftermath of independence may well be connected with such perceptions.

By and large, the Indian cinema showed a dual response to the escalating phenomenon of communalism. For example, Sohrab Modi's historicals explored the Mughal period, with a reading of history that reiterated amity in socio-political spaces and a sharing of syncratic traditions and culture rather than discord and inherent enmity. In the 1940s, a self-conscious effort was made to portray Hindu–Muslim amity in *Shejari/Padosi* filmed in 1941 by V. Shantaram. It addressed communal harmony directly and severely indicted the British attempts at divide and rule in relation to Hindus and Muslims. The film deals with an industrialist who wants to build a dam in a village. He is opposed by two senior guardians of the village, one Hindu the other Muslim. To achieve his objective the industrialist succeeds in causing a rift between the two friends. The film ends with the two friends eventually making up as the giant dam bursts and they die embracing each other.

Other films, such as those about the seventeenth-century Maratha ruler Shivaji, hailed the Hindu resurgence more directly by recreating the myth of medieval Muslim tyranny. For example,

Uday Kal (*Thunder of the Hills*, V. Shantaram, 1930), was claimed to be the first film which explicitly politicised the figure of Shivaji.[33] This was followed by the vastly popular films of Bhalchandra Gopal Pendharkar (Bhalji). A disciple of Savarkar and founder of the Kolhapur branch of Hindu Mahasabha, Pendharkar's commitment found expression in films that reconstructed Shivaji's exploits against the Muslim rulers, confirming him as a contemporary icon.[34] Yet, Ravi Vasudevan argues, the popular cinema was 'more expressive of a "Hindu" nationalist view-point' only after 1945.[35] According to Vasudevan films of this period were self-consciously creating an overarching 'Hindu nationalist identity,' effected through the types of cultural address, through narrational songs, gender idiom and modes of visual address. There may be a difference of opinion regarding the mid-1940s as a likely period from which Hindu nationalist expression in the popular cinema can be gleaned. Such a reading may well have been available in certain quarters in the late 1930s, depending upon the public reception and interpretation of the cinematic images.

This cinematic shaping of a symbolic Hindu identity helped inform Indian viewers' reading of *Gunga Din*. In it they saw an appropriation of Hindu nationalism and the strengthening of an ideological field seeking to reshape the image of India by keeping the Muslims out of it. The contradiction inherent in such a motivated portrayal came to the surface. For example, *Gunga Din* had deliberately substituted Islam, the dominant religion of this region, with Hinduism. In the association of Kali worship with the *thuggee* sect, the Muslims were also carefully excluded. This belied the well-known fact that *thugs* were drawn not only from Hindus of different caste groups but also from among the Muslims.[36] This substitution also reversed the hitherto maintained identity of the chief villains, who in all the other empire films of this genre had been Muslims. Shown to be the residents of the Frontier, they were depicted as a source of danger to the peace of India and to the British hold over India. It is not unlikely that this reversal was also connected with the official reports that such portrayals in the past had been the cause of protests among 'Muslim forces in India' as well as the 'Muslim community' in Britain.[37] Such protests had clearly grown over the years.

Gunga Din's representation of the NWFP as a region where the colonials faced the threat of Hindu rather than – as in so many previous films – Muslim attack, served to give the film a more contemporary angle. This shift was picked up on by the Indian media as a good reason for attacking the film.[38] Their attack clearly illustrates their understanding of the film's underlying message and the nuances of deliberate dissonance implicit in this distortion. This projection ultimately undermined the British position. It showed up the western knowledge of Indian religions and regions as motivated and deficient.

The film associated *thuggee* with Hindus and Hindus with nationalists. The Hindus emerge as the major threat to the British Raj. The film clearly established this connection when the arch villain, guru, the leader of the *thugs*, is made to articulate his anti-imperialism and nationalism. An important reason for this articulation was undoubtedly connected with the desire of the film-makers to keep the 'Indian susceptibilities' in view, in order to obviate any 'anti-Indian' charge from the critics of all the earlier empire films in India.[39] For this reason alone, the most riveting scenes from the point of view of the Indian audience may very well have been those with the guru sitting cross-legged in a saintly posture under the statue of Kali and inciting his followers by evoking the blessing of Kali and maintaining, 'Every man's hand is against us. We have been kicked, spat upon and driven to the hills like wild things.'

With his followers chanting Kali! Kali! in between, the guru further justifies his actions against the British:

My father was a *thug* and he was hanged. His father was blown from the cannon's mouth. And what of your kinsmen – your fathers and their fathers and their fathers' fathers before them ? Oh my brothers a new day is at hand. I have read the omens and they are good. Three nights ago a jackal screamed from the left; another answered from the right at once. What does that mean my brothers ? It means that mother Kali, with all her arms outstretched now hugs us to her bosom, welcoming us back as *thugs* – *thugs*, awakened from a sleep of fifty years.

For the Indian audience, this evoked the historical memory of the Mutiny, popularly acknowledged as the first war of independence, with its call for freedom from the conquerors. The British position, on the other hand, had always been that in brutally and severely putting down the Mutineers who had murdered Europeans, their actions were merely retaliatory. Consequently, the guru is made to mouth the senseless savagery of the colonised when he instructs the new recruits of *thugs*:

> Help them to be hard, to be cruel, to kill
> Kill lest you may be killed yourselves
> Kill for the love of killing
> Kill for the love of Kali
> Kill! Kill! Kill!

For the British audience, it was a superstitious, ritual-ridden, barbaric mind that dictated killing for the sake of killing. Its defeat established the ultimate superiority of a scientific mind that ignored the 'auspicious omens' of the *thugs*. A British sergeant single-handedly and defiantly marches in to a Hindu temple making a mockery of their superstitions, singing:

> Since mighty roast beef is the Englishman's food
> It accounts for the freedom that runs in his blood, tra! la! la!
> Oh! The roast beef of old
> Oh! England and Oh! For old England's roast beef.

The sergeant's insolent and disrespectful behaviour in the Kali temple, where he walks with his shoes on and calls it 'a *thug* temple', declaring its worshippers 'heathen', brought the approbation of the white viewers. But what of the native people? Moreover, the direct reference to beef as food for a superior race could prove explosive among an audience who held as part of their collective national consciousness the belief that the Mutiny broke out as a result of the widespread rumours of cartridges greased with the fat of cows (held sacred by Hindus) or pig's lard (held unclean by Muslims). Yet, there existed a larger social context to the meat-eating issue. It had become attached to the idea of cultural virility. Many Indians thought this food preference responsible for British imperialism, being the essence that made the Englishman strong.[40] The film drew upon some of these notions. Ideologically, for the white audience, it merely reflected the British explanation for the Mutiny, which had remained pegged to the superstitious suspicions of the Hindu and Muslim soldiers in the British Indian army that their cartridges for the Enfield rifle were greased with cow's and pig's fat.

In fact, there was an attempt at trivialisation of the Mutiny, held as a symbol of freedom and inspiration for the nationalists. Cutter, one of the sergeants, bored with the lack of action on the Frontier says, 'How can we get a nice little war going? What if I was to sneak out and blow up the Taj Mahal or one of their sacred tombs?' To which MacChesney replies 'No – what do you want to do, start the whole Indian Mutiny again?'

This jocular reference to the Mutiny was a way of denying or lulling the insecurity generated in the wake of the movement and to indicate the necessity of the British Indian army to the maintenance of imperial rule. Importantly, this show of over-whelming confidence is used in the film to belittle the guru's anti-imperialist, inflammatory speeches. Yet, the guru's diatribe against the British remains noteworthy. After capturing the three sergeants he pontificates, 'You may seem to think warfare an British invention. Have you ever heard of Chandergupta Maurya? He slaughtered all the armies left in India by Alexander the Great. India was a mighty nation then, while Englishmen still dwelt in caves and painted themselves blue.' Then mocking British Indian army officers he continues, 'Prime generals, friends, aren't made of jewelled swords and moustache wax. They are made of what is there [touches heart] and what is here [touches head].' When these utterances provoke Sergeant MacChesney to call him 'mad', the guru enlightens him:

> Mad! Mad! Hannibal was mad, Caesar was mad, and Napoleon surely was the maddest of the lot. Since time began they're called mad – all great soldiers in their world. Mad, eh ? We shall see what wisdom lies within my madness. For this is but the spring freshet that precedes the flood. From here we roll on – from village to town, from town to mighty city, ever mounting, ever widening until at last my wave engulfs all India.

When MacChesney threatens to kill the guru unless he orders his men to stop, the guru significantly says, 'What is my life to the life of our cause?' The scene climaxes with Guru sacrificing his life for his country by jumping into the snake-pit prepared for the three British sergeants. In his final speech, which could only be described as moving for an Indian audience, the guru says to the

British officers who try to stop him, 'You have sworn, as soldiers, if need be, to die for your faith, which is your country, your England. Well, India is my country and my faith, and I can die for my faith as readily as you can for yours. India farewell!'

This delineation of a different character from the stereotyped screen villain did not go unnoticed in the west. It was commented upon on behalf of the white audience by Jeanette Rex, in a preview of the film in Hollywood:

> The character of the villain as portrayed by Eduardo Cianelli, who plays the role of a Guru, the head of the *thugs*, has the strength and power of intellect. He gives the British soldiers a tongue-lashing which proves that he is far from the common ordinary low character desperado, herefore depicted ... *Gunga Din* goes a step ahead in portraying the Indian as a man of wisdom and strength of character.[41]

Some of the British officers had raised objections to the obvious pro-Indian articulations of the guru and termed them as 'revolutionary sentiments'.[42] These were brushed aside by the India Office as being insignificant in relation to the benefits conferred by the film. It was pointed out that films like *Gunga Din* offered many opportunities for the enhancement of prestige not only of the British and Indian troops, but of its followers such as the *bhishti*, Gunga Din. According to British officials, 'there seems to be nothing more politically oppressive in the whole story than has apparently been accepted in such pictures as *The Lives of a Bengal Lancer* and *The Drum* to which *Gunga Din* is closely comparable in composition.'[43]

Clearly, the vast underlying subversive potential of the film did not register with India Office officials because they read the film as a white imperial audience would. A tenuous equation of *thugs* with nationalists was not unattractive to them as the latter were demeaned to occupy no better status than the *thugs*; hence they deserved no compassion or justice and could be ruthlessly eradicated as they had been years earlier. The objections of Indians who found this equation unpardonable were brushed aside.[44]

Moreover, for the white imperial audience, the pro-India outpouring of the guru and the endorsement of Indian nationalist sentiments are complicated by certain ideological sentiments at play in the film. Apart from the blatant imperial jingoistic ideology, the other ideology given transcendent value by the narrative is religion. Religion, in the British discourse on India, was consistently opposed to a purely national interest. The guru, for instance, may mouth nationalism for the sake of British officials, yet the common denominator that binds him to his followers is shown to be religion. The guru evokes bonding on the basis of Hinduism. In fact, as a narrative it is religion which is privileged and not nationalism.

The guru, a Hindu, was cast in the stereotype mould of a 'mad Mullah', the favourite *bête noir* of all empire films to date. Like them, he placed emphasis on the central role of God and a reversion to fundamentalist ideology in order to ostensibly challenge the ideological tenets of the modern age as projected by the colonial government. The film cast their revolts as anti-western, anti-modern and fundamentalist and also against the legitimate authority, all of which deflected from the notion of nationhood.

Ultimately, the discourse that was shown to challenge the hegemony of the British was not a national one but a religious one. This was depicted in the film as deviant and non-national, turning the national discourse into a site of struggle. Positing the overpowering ideology of religion and superstition against imperialism and modernisation, the choice for the western audience was clearly made. For Indian audience the message was both ambiguous and contradictory with vast subversive potential.

At best, the idea of freedom – the political creed represented by the guru in the film – was presented in terms of its concrete impact on one character, a mere individual example of the whole concept of freedom. This spurious personalisation made him a social outcast in his own society, a *thug* hated by his own people. He is ultimately overthrown by the courage, honesty and fighting ability of white soldiers with whom the white audience is supposed to identify. The image of the guru and his anti-imperialist cry was effectively transcended by the all-pervasive successful justification of imperialism. His victory, in the eyes of a white audience would have been a defeat of a civilisation, of the rule of law and economic progress, all of them ably represented by the British Indian army. It was a dramatic juxtaposition of two entirely different worlds and civilisations: India with its extremes of mysticism, saintliness and roguery and the British with their superior organisation, their confidence in modern methods, their conviction in their ability to brush away like cobwebs native myths and beliefs – the former destined to disappear because of their inherent inferiority.

Indeed, the anti-imperialist ideological thrust adopted by the film had its own logic in film-making. In a curious way, the film sought to come to terms with the fact that India had a civilisation, however strange by European standards, which could not be written off. After all, it was this past that was evoked by the nationalists to rejuvenate India and motivate its people against the colonial rule. However, such a harking back to the past by Indian nationalists along with the concept of a 'golden age' was necessarily a Hindu one. This fact was not only underlined in the film but was also exploited to postulate a clear disjunction between India's past and its present. The civilised, military and masculinised India belonged to the bygone past. It no longer existed. The present India was only notionally connected to its once-civilised-self. Instead, the film asserted that a regeneration of India's past could only come about under colonial rule, which was fighting against existing irrational, oppressive and retrogressive elements.

Moreover, the guru's intelligent but treacherous and wily image had a lot to do with the media focus on the Indian national movement in the late 1930s, especially in the wake of the Round Table Conferences, held from 1931 onwards, which necessitated a more enlightened challenge to the British. Also, such a portrayal underlined the still greater resourcefulness, courage and intelligence of the colonial power in outwitting it. After all, the immense superiority of the British could be established only in relation to the diabolically clever and treacherous intelligence of the native. Outwitting of low intelligence and crude simplistic intrigue hardly underlined the extent of British superiority. Consequently, the guru was cast in a different mould.

Mahatma Gandhi: villain and saint

In a most significant display of contempt and cynicism the film cast the guru in the physical mould of Mahatma Gandhi. From his slight physique to his austere sartorial look wearing just a loin cloth and a *chaddar* (a large cotton shawl) draped over his shoulder or head, the demented villainous guru recalled the unmistakable figure of Mahatma Gandhi. Except for the head gear (turban), this was the dress which Gandhi wore during his visit to England for attending the Round Table Conference. Adopted from 1921 onwards, this dress contributed substantially in endearing him to the peasant masses of India. It was widely familiarised to the western public through the visual media.

Gunga Din collapses the actor and personality of Gandhi into one. For the white audience, this effected a closure between the real person and villain in the film, but for the Indian audience, it opened up the imperialist's motivated misrepresentation. Yet, this collapsing of the two identities made the identification of the Indian audience with the guru and what he stood for that much easier and more significant. The film had once again picked up, what a television critic was to point out much later, 'the worst nightmare of the British in India',[45] by making him the chief threat to the British Raj.

In the 1930s, Gandhi was a permanent nuisance to the British. By and large, he was considered and projected not as a saint in Britain but, as one official put it, 'as cunning as a cartload of monkeys', and his views on caste, the cow, Lancashire and women were made fun of.[46] Even sympathisers like Edward Thompson, who came to be a correspondent of Gandhi's and was a supporter of the Congress, found him deceitful. In his novels he offered serious doubts about Gandhi.[47] In fact, Gandhi was not treated particularly well in colonial fiction.

The portrayal of Gandhi as the chief villain highlighted the dichotomous perceptions of the two different audiences, western and Indian. For the western audience, the empire films confirmed the newsreel projection of Gandhi. According to Martin A. Jackson, these images of Gandhi were of 'a peculiar Oriental who had outlandish ideas about independence and who wore a loin cloth'.[48] Moreover, Gandhi 'being odd in appearance, full of surprises and engaged in the strangest activities, such as fasting or marching for independence', was a good subject for the news cameras. It was this image that was duplicated in the feature film. Hollywood's heavy reliance upon the British India Office for co-operation in the making of the film, along with Katherine Mayo and other British writers as a source of information, resulted in the particular propaganda thrust of *Gunga Din*. In this film especially, Hollywood gave shape to the British propaganda in the

USA, which depicted the Congress as fascist with its dictatorial leadership, its domination by a single race (Hindus), its standard uniform of *dhoti* and Gandhi cap (substituted by a turban in the film) and its veneration of Gandhi, which was projected to resemble that accorded Hitler by the Germans.[49] Yet, this film also allowed for alternative US perceptions. Ideologically, Gandhi had his following and admirers in the USA, which comprised a strong anti-imperialist lobby.

For the Indian audience, therefore, the resultant and essentially ambivalent cinematic portrayal provoked wide condemnatory comment in the media. The close resemblance of the villain in *Gunga Din* to Gandhi also reinforced the contemporaneity of the film. Writing about Gandhi's portrayal in this film, *Film India* recalled an earlier cinematic attempt in 1935, when RKO had produced a two-reel comedy, *Everybody Likes Music*, in which, 'Our revered leader Mahatma Gandhi was portrayed as an immoral drunkard with a low woman in a cheap saloon. His figure, his dress and all his peculiarities so sacred and dear to our nation were used to convey an exact identification, same as in *Gunga Din*, that could not be missed.'[50] For exhibition in India, the offensive portion in the film, *Everybody Likes Music,* was censored in 1935. Yet, this insult, it was pointed out, was 'broadcast all over the world and the white man laughed at the man who we worship as a God in our country.'

Such a reaction from the Indians was no surprise to the British. They were in fact aware of the annoyance in India caused by a German broadcast in which a Germanophile Indian student sneered at Mahatma Gandhi and other Indian leaders while denouncing the concept of non-violence.[51] *Gunga Din* went far beyond this: British army officers are shown to abuse the guru, repeatedly denigrating him as 'the dog', 'the filthy scum' and the 'maniac'. This abuse and ridicule directed at the Mahatma, could hardly fail to provoke an Indian audience.

At the same time, cinematically, this audience had Gandhi and his ideology amply projected in their own movies. A silent-era film *Sant Vidur* (or *Bhakta Vidur*), produced in 1921, provided a direct nationalist projection of Gandhi. In this Vidur was moulded on the personality of Mahatma Gandhi, played by Dwarka Das, an actor with a tall and lanky figure. His entire make up 'made him look like the Mahatma, including the *Dandi*

Danda in his hand'.[52] The film was banned initially because, as
J. B. H. Wadia observed, 'The innuendo was so clear.' The
censors maintained, 'We know what you are doing, it is not
Vidur, it is Gandhiji, we won't allow it.'[53] Later on, with several
cuts, the producer succeeded in showing the film in some of the
provinces, including Bombay. It did roaring business everywhere.
There were yet other films, like *Brahmchari* made in 1938, which
showed Gandhi's Wardha-like ashram run on nationalist lines of
self-help, hard work, the *khadi* (raw cotton) spinning and
weaving programme and other handicrafts. The *charkha* (spinning wheel), reminiscent of *sudarshan chakra* (the divine weapon
of the Hindu god, Vishnu, and a destroyer of all evil), and looked
upon as a potent icon of freedom movement, was popularly
perceived as a symbol of the annihilation of foreigners. This film
also ran into trouble with the censors because of its explicit
nationalist overtones and identification with Mahatma Gandhi.

An important landmark in early films incorporating the
contemporary nationalist discourse, especially in relation to
Mahatma Gandhi, was *Sant Tukaram* (1936). A vastly popular
film it ran continuously for a year in Bombay; in the countryside
people walked for miles to see its open-air screenings.[54] *Tukaram*,
as Geeta Kapur argues, has necessarily to be seen as a socially
symbolic narrative. It shows the cross-referencing between
cultural creation and political situation already conditioned by
the contemporary 'saint', Gandhi.[55] The film established a close
parallel between Tukaram and Gandhi in their message.

In the late 1930s the marketability of nationalism and its
viability were visible not merely in the films produced by Indians
– most of which became popular hits – but also in the way
producers, distributors and exhibitors advertised their products.
Mahatma Gandhi, for example, was a favourite for advertising
the films. Large size photographs of Gandhi adorned the film
advertisements along with much smaller photographs of the lead
hero or heroine. Yet other films were advertised as 'helper to the
cause of Mahatma Gandhi', or invited the viewers to see their
film, advertised as portraying 'the ideals of Mahatma Gandhi', or
claimed that 'Mahatma Gandhi's immortal words inspire a
picture'.[56] So much so that the distributors and exhibitors of a
Hollywood film also felt it commercially prudent to put in a sponsored advertisement claiming, 'Mahatma Gandhi sees the first

talking picture *Mission to Moscow*.' The report that followed suggested that Mahatma Gandhi considered this film to be of the 'right type'.

The British officials were aware of the public draw of the Mahatma's name in the film industry.[57] They had attempted to curb both advertisements and films that exploited the Mahatma's name. Yet, it is significant that despite this hyper-sensitive concern of the film censors in India – who saw in the title *Mahatma* (a Hindi feature film) 'a sinister association with Mahatma Gandhi' and pressurised the producers into changing it to *Dharmatama* – they failed to see or offer any comment on the allusion to Mahatma Gandhi in *Gunga Din*. One can speculate that perhaps they used this demeaning portrayal as a corrective to the one being projected in the indigenous film industry.[58]

The 1930s were also the years when Gandhi had emerged in the western world, especially in the USA, as enormously newsworthy. A large number of documentaries and newsreels were made of Gandhi's visit to England and his activities in India by foreign producers in keeping with the importance of Indian news in general and that of Gandhi in particular.[59] Consequently, a large number of documentaries and newsreels were made on Indian themes by foreigner producers. The Indian film-makers did not lag behind. For them it was an unlimited opportunity to project the national leadership and India's aspirations towards independence. For the British, however, these documentaries and newsreels, featuring Mahatma Gandhi, soon turned into 'propagandist films pure and simple', especially when the civil disobedience movement attained its height and had to be banned.[60] The Congress greatly publicised this ban in its newsletters and the national media subjected it to extensive comments.[61] The *Free Press Journal*, on 16 December 1932, declared the ban on account of danger posed to the British empire by the Gandhian ideas. The *Bombay Chronicle*, on 17 December 1932, asserted that the films could be prohibited but not Gandhism. Regional language dailies, *Gujarat Mitra* and *Gujarat Darpan*, on 18 December 1932, similarly declared that Gandhism could hardly be destroyed by such activities. The censorship of Indian films and documentaries during these years was so tight that even the framed photographs of national leaders in the background were edited out.[62] Similarly, between 1 August 1936 and

31 March 1937, several such films were banned on the grounds that they dealt with controversial politics and were likely to ferment social unrest and discontent in the country.[63]

The Congress ministries, after assuming office, relaxed such blanket bans. It is in such a climate of less stringent censorship of Gandhi and his ideology that the film *Gunga Din*, caricaturing Gandhi, has to be seen. The cross-currents of imperial arrogance and commercial considerations, in combination with the ideological compulsions of the film, made them ignore the likely impact of caricaturing Gandhi on an Indian audience. Ideologically, the film shows a complex handling of Gandhi as a character. Gandhi's semblance is in fact evoked to subvert his image and ideology. Gandhi is demystified as hypocritically spiritual while being shrewdly materialistic, violent and self-interested. This portrayal accepted the spiritual India of the past but reasserted the fall of Hinduism – into a ritualised violent cult going under the name of spiritualism – in the present context. This decadence is signified in the person of Gandhi, who, in certain sections of Indian society (among both Muslims and Sikhs) was seen as a Hindu fundamentalist, known to use religion and religious symbols as a rallying point for mobilising nationalist opinion against the British. His real agenda is shown to be a violent take-over of India and not a non-violent *satyagraha*, as professed.

It is here that a complete travesty of Gandhian philosophy and his political programme was effected. It is well known that the all-India movement of 1921–22 was abruptly and unilaterally called-off at the height of its popularity on 11 February 1922, at Gandhi's instance, following the news of the burning alive of twenty-two policemen by angry peasants at Chauri-Chaura in the Gorakhpur district of the United Provinces on 5 February. This decision was deeply resented by almost all the prominent Congress leaders, including his political heir, Jawaharlal Nehru, and even more so by the younger people.[64] Gandhi's own defence of this action as stated in his paper, *Young India*, on 16 February 1922, is revealing: 'I would suffer every humiliation, every torture, absolute ostracism and death itself to prevent the movement from becoming violent'. Gandhi's firm commitment against violence was to surface repeatedly as he continued to make effective use of the weapon of fast-unto-death to end riots and other forms of violence.

Putting an end to an effective, revolutionary and violent situation created widespread dissatisfaction and anger against Gandhi
and his methods, which produced a strong internal critique that
condemned his non-violent doctrine unequivocally and, at best,
made no pretence at understanding it. It also spurred fresh revolutionary terrorism, which climaxed in 1929–30, the year of a
whole series of terrorist actions in Punjab and United Provinces
towns. The Hindustan Socialist Republican Army, which played
havoc with British life and administration in northern India,
produced heroes and martyrs, who attained remarkable popularity. For example, Bhagat Singh, who was hanged for his terrorist
activities, outranked for a short time even Mahatma Gandhi 'as
the foremost political figure of the day in popularity'.[65]

The emergence of revolutionaries and terrorists as popular
heroes and martyrs enormously furthered the cause of Indian
nationalism. Yet, Gandhi's abhorrence of violence did not allow
him to speak or plead on behalf of political heroes like Bhagat
Singh. In fact, Gandhi condemned their violence. Durga Bhabhi,
the still-living widow of a compatriot of Bhagat Singh, spoke
recently of her own and widespread anger against Gandhi due to
his failure to save nationalists like Bhagat Singh from the gallows
by appealing to the viceroy for mercy.[66]

For Gandhi, the doctrine of *ahimsa* (non-violence) was not
only a personal credo and philosophy but was a deeply-felt and
worked-out philosophy. As a politician, he was aware that the
resultant perspective of controlled mass participation objectively
fitted in with the interests and sentiments of socially-divisive
sections of the Indian people. It could, for example, prove acceptable to business groups, as well as relatively better-off or locally-
dominant sections of the peasantry, all of whom stood to lose if
political struggle turned into uninhibited and violent social revolution. The concept of *ahimsa* and *satyagraha*, therefore, lay at
the heart of the essentially unifying umbrella type role assumed by
Gandhi and the Gandhian Congress.

The transformation of Gandhian work and ideology in *Gunga
Din* worked towards exposing Gandhian philosophy to generate
latent fears and reservations inherent in certain sections of colonial
society. The film, therefore, could well be seen by the different
Indian audiences as a deliberate travesty, which went beyond caricature and ridicule towards a motivated misrepresentation. The

violent repression of Ghandi's non-violent *satyagrahis* by the colonial state apparatus during the course of the national movement from the 1920s onwards was well known in India, as were General Dyer's orders to fire on a peaceful, unarmed crowd in Jallianwala Bagh in Amritsar in 1919. Stories of British violence against Indian nationalists had become part of nationalist folklore.

Rejecting these hard political realities about violence and the perpetrators of violence, the cinematic portrayal took off from the well-acknowledged scepticism of the British about Gandhi's non-violent programme and the militant and violent action perpetrated by certain social groups in northern India in the name of Gandhi and his ideology.[67] Even the revolutionaries, very far removed in methods from Gandhi, were known to celebrate their victories by evoking his name.[68]

The film, therefore, portrayed Gandhi (a real-life Vaishnavite and follower of *Bhakti*), as a worshipper of Kali, the goddess of violence, believing in the cult of violence and murder, to achieve his surreptitious agenda. The conspiracy to take over the whole of India is shown to be a Hindu conspiracy headed by Gandhi and as much against the British as the Muslims. In the days of the communalisation of Indian society and polity this could calculatedly generate great anxiety among the Muslims of India, especially those of the Frontier who had thrown in their lot with the Congress. Significantly, in the elections of 1937, the Congress, designated by the Muslim communalists as a Hindu association and projected by the British as such in the USA, had won an overwhelming majority in seven out of eleven states (and formed coalition governments in two others), which included the Muslim majority state of the NWFP. The Muslim League, which claimed to represent all Muslims, could not get a foothold in any state and was busy propagating the image of a Hindu-dominated India. *Gunga Din* greatly reinforced such a reading. The NWFP was especially troublesome for the British as it was Gandhi's influence on the Frontier leader, Abdul Gaffar Khan, which had led to the merging of his party, the Khudai Khidmadgar, with the Congress. The film's purely Hindu image of Gandhi and the latent violence of Hindus, not withstanding their minority position in this province, could be used to demystify and denounce his growing influence in the NWFP in particular and among the Muslims in India more generally.

Privileging religion and caste: categorising society

Curiously, the guru and Gunga Din are essentially the two faces of a single identity. The splitting of this one image and the resultant multiplicity of images, both overlapping and contradictory, introduces great ambivalence in its reading. The film emphasises an essential sameness in the image projection showing strong physical resemblances, particularly through the clothing they wear: loin cloth and a *chaddar*. The publicity material of the film concentrated on the 'everyday costume worn by the natives of India'. This costume was described as consisting of a loin cloth, a turban, and a *chaddar*, all of which comprised, in their opinion, 'of merely two pieces of cloth of varying lengths, wound around body and head'. The films made in the late 1930s greatly publicised this as the 'common man' image of India. Significantly, in 1942–43, Mahatma Gandhi was referred to as 'the Hindu Gunga Din in his loin cloth' by the viceroy of India.

Clearly, in using the Mahatma's image for the guru as well as Gunga Din, the film wished both to isolate the rebel and to incorporate the loyal. So, at the same time it sought to condemn and isolate the one and to reclaim and to retrieve the other. However, these categories became mirror-reversed in India, where the rebel was a nationalist and a loyal character a collaborator, and where the treacherous villain was the hero, especially in the case of the guru. In a situation of heightened national consciousness, to be an Indian would have meant to feel a natural solidarity with the victims of British reprisals, even though to the British it meant a victory and triumph of natural white superiority. Commenting in a similar vein, the *Film India* issue of February 1939 enquired of Hollywood:

> Is it any wonder that we, who are fighting for the freedom of our country do not like to be represented in this light? How would you have the British on the eve of your glorious war of independence, to have produced films generally depicting Americans as villains but glorifying a few licentious Indians who are loyal to Britain and then have exhibited them in American theatres? Exercise a little imagination Hollywood, you would know why *Gunga Din* can never be our favourite here.

Gunga Din and the guru are contrasting figures and yet there is also a curious merging of the two, with one having gone mad. The guru is, in fact, shown as an exceptional freak. As a native rebel, he grows out of a character disorder of ambitious individuals and remains a pervert; abnormality or madness does not question the normalcy of the status quo but reinforces it. Gunga Din, on the other hand, is also the 'lowest of the low' – an untouchable. As such, he is pitted against the high-caste Brahmin guru. On the one hand, this confrontation recalls the attempts made by high-caste Hindus in the *Sangathan* (consolidation) movement to integrate the untouchables into Hindu society through a *shuddhi* (purification) ceremony and the subsequent failure of such attempts. This confrontation also suggests that the untouchable and the common man in India needed protection from the domination of the high-caste Hindu Congress. This suggestion in the film allowed the British (themselves a foreign minority) to assume an attitude of responsibility towards the minority groups and potential victims, including the Muslims and untouchables, among others.

More importantly, such a claim sought to enlarge the loyal strata from that so far depicted in the empire films (namely, the army recruits) in a bid to incorporate the disadvantaged among the highly-hierarchised caste groups of India. The essentialised qualities of devotion, loyalty and obedience associated with the martial castes by British rulers were considered latent among the untouchables and were curiously echoed in traditional Indian society.

Indeed, the film portrays a cringing, subservient untouchable based upon a traditional Brahmanical model at odds with the reality of untouchables at this historical juncture. The most prominent leader of untouchables, B. R. Ambedkar, who hailed from a family whose male members had served in the British Indian army, was western-educated and highly articulate. He was eminently visible while making various demands from the colonial government, ranging from the creation of special regiments and facilities for recruitment for untouchables to special representation and reservations for them in the government. In a significant way this highly confident image of the untouchables, who had emerged as a force to be reckoned with, was ignored in favour of Gunga Din's stereotyped portrayal essentially as a servile, downtrodden but loyal caste type.

Much publicity was devoted to this caste factor in Hindu society of colonial India. After opining that 'the rules governing the conduct of the various castes are as peculiar to occidental eyes as they are injurious', the publicity drive of *Gunga Din* gave out the following details of the caste system:

> Among the regulations which have had to be observed in dealing with the Indians engaged to play fierce native tribesmen in the film were these: 'A Brahmin may eat sweetmeats or wheat with a man from the Kshatriya caste but not rice, for that would be admission of equality. Whenever money passes from high caste to low caste men, it is thrown on the ground to avoid defilement. They may not stand on the same carpet or enter the same room. Caste is even reflected in the jails, where prisoners of high caste are provided with their own cooks and water carriers. The only place where caste is dropped in India is the third class railway carriage where all castes are herded at a farthing a mile. But it is instantly resumed at the alighting station.'

More vivid descriptions especially of the low-caste 'teeming millions among the Indian population' followed. A press book of *Gunga Din* displayed the caption, 'Honours paid to *Gunga Din* jar caste system of India'. The write up which followed emphasised:

> In India the caste system exercises rigid rule. A low caste native is an underdog from the day of his birth, only in extremely rare cases does he arise above his fixed level in the social religious order of things. That is why peculiar interest attaches to the emerging from obscurity of a humble native hero in RKO Studio's new thrill-melodrama *Gunga Din*.

This was used in *Gunga Din* to make extensive comments upon colonial society riven with caste hierarchy and problems of untouchability. Such a propaganda reasserted that social differences combined with religious divisions would never allow India to become a composite nation.

The representation of the caste system as essential to Indian society and civilisation was also central to other empire films. *The Lives of a Bengal Lancer* and *The Drum*, which preceded *Gunga Din*, where both accompanied by long press notes and publicity material dealing with this 'essential reality' of India when, unlike

Gunga Din, the caste factor had no bearing on the narrative of either film. The notes for *The Lives of a Bengal Lancer* stressed the way high-caste men among 'hordes of Hindu actors recruited to play Afridi tribesmen treated their own countrymen by calling them swine and untouchables'. *The Drum*'s notes, in a like manner, stated in bold headlines, 'Caste causes woe' and 'Caste proves no aid to film-making'. They continued, 'Although in the eyes of an uninitiated westerner a Brahmin may look like a Vaisya and a Sudra resemble a pariah still to each other they are from totally different walks of life, enriched by invisible walls of caste and all must obey their caste rules of behaviour.' Korda, the producer of the British film, *The Drum*, was declared in the publicity drive to have successfully overcome these social difficulties by drawing caste-lines in the living quarters and even kitchens.

Perceived to determine all facets of Indian life from religion to politics and economics, this emphasis on the backward social practices in India could lay high claims to authenticity as there was an on-going parallel feeder discourse existing in various short films, newsreels and travelogues on native customs and religious rites. Some of the favourite themes included the bloody sacrifices to the goddess Kali, the tortures inflicted on the devotees during festivals, death rituals at burning *ghats*, images of *sati*, sex orgies of holy men, details of 'strange customs', the 'festival of conception' (Holi), the self-inflicted torture of pilgrims, and physical maiming perpetrated in the name of religion. The list continues to include 'indecent' dancing, caste rituals of both high-caste Brahmins and 'revolting' ones of low castes, details of caste system showing untouchables as being no better than animals juxtaposed to Brahmins known as 'sons of God', superstitions, enactment of 'indecent bestial scenes for public enjoyment', weird temples with 'copulating gods and goddesses' and 'primitive' methods of cultivation, irrigation and living still prevalent. 'Authentic' scenes of India, which had been photographed at different time periods during location-shooting on the sub-continent, were intercut with sequences shot in Hollywood.[69] These scenes were advertised as an 'authentic picture of conditions in India'. Their claims to authenticity was also derived from being non-fictional. The documentary style, based on the filming of facts and not fiction, confirmed this claim.[70]

One such film was *India Speaks* (1933), later renamed *Bride of the East*, which had to be withdrawn in view of vociferous objections in India in the national media and in the Central Legislative Assembly.[71] Subhash Chander Bose, in exile in Vienna, severely condemned it as being a 'libel and slander on India' and demanded its withdrawal from the western world.[72] Yet, it continued to be shown in the west in its unexpurgated version. Only for England certain cuts were effected, which were considered to 'offend Indian religious susceptibilities'. The exhibition of not merely this film but also many other publicity films on India that depicted 'baser elements in Indian life' confirmed the well-established orientalist image in the west.[73]

In fact, at a time when the two highly controversial films, *The Drum* and *Gunga Din*, were being shown in the west, another documentary film, *Sacred India*, made by Father Lhande, the author of *L'Inde Sacree*, was being screened as well. The *Kinematograph Weekly*, evaluating the film's potential selling points, established its close identity with the two other feature films:

> *Sacred India* is based on the travels in India of Father Lhande. The picture unfolds an authentic and vivid story of the grandeur and misery of India's vast population of 350 million people. It shows the implacable caste system from the pariah, hardly better than animal, whose very breadth contaminates, to the Brahmin, a strange being compounded of pride, intelligence and mysticism and known throughout the vast land as 'a son of the gods'.[74]

It also claimed to show a 'detailed picture of strange customs'. The viewers were guaranteed a 'spectacle that no European eye has ever seen'. The western press declared 'these tragically real pictures of India' to comprise 'an exceptional document'.

The propaganda claims, reviews, comments and images of these films, whether feature or documentary, were nevertheless reinforcing each other in the white world. Moreover, both were projecting the white man alone as the redeemer, the figure with a moral responsibility to civilise these 350 million people. In Lhande's documentary, it was the Christian missionary, in the feature films it was the British army officer, but in each case the aim was the same, the social situation faced identical. Clearly, both, the film and the perceived reality, merged for the western audience. This 'reality' of India was used to establish the illusion that the social world in the film story and its depiction were genuine. Moreover, as this confirmed the audiences' knowledge and expectations – already fairly well-fed by imperialist propaganda – the illusion was complete.

There is no denying that there were and continue to be rigid social barriers and pollution regulations in the caste system, especially in relation to lower caste groups, in different historical periods in India. Yet, in pre-British India, caste mobility had been facilitated by a fluid political system and a land surplus permitting easy migration.[75] The colonial period closed or reduced some of these avenues and promoted caste consciousness, solidarity and rivalry. The British mediated in Indian society and its caste system through a system of reckoning and evaluation, which centred on their own interests and specifications. Their system of classification of the native population had a profoundly interventionary impact in redirecting and reorienting existing group identities in India. In this, as with many types of internal tensions, whether of religion, region or class, imperialists made a skilful use of real grievances in fostering sectional consciousness to withstand the formation of social classes with any commonality of interest or unity of function.[76] In doing so, the British interests coincided with the top layer of the caste system in India, which was equally interested in maintaining caste distinctions and hierarchies. The combined efforts of these two forces undoubtedly provided one of the major reasons for its persistence.

Yet, the colonial period was not without its challenges to the system of caste in India. Many of the social reformers were critiquing, questioning and attacking the caste system. There were also socio-political movements that, at times, challenged the very basis of caste as in Maharashtra and Tamil Nadu.[77] The untouchable identity was also clearly at variance with traditional myths as it was being challenged by the untouchables themselves, who were refusing their caste status.[78]

An important and vastly popular area, co-terminus with the empire films, where untouchability was being challenged, was that of the indigenous films. The film producers of the 1930s and 1940s were making a conscious attempt to correlate their films with national efforts towards freedom and social problems.[79] As the national leadership at this historical juncture was emphasising social equality and focusing attention on problems like Hindu–Muslim unity, untouchability, literacy, questions relating to women and religious reforms, not merely as a part of their reformist agenda, but as part of the political campaign itself, these found a place in literature as well as in film. In fact, many of the social reform themes in these films were taken from novels written in different regional languages.

The Progressive Writers' Movement, which was formed in 1936, espoused the formation of a literature that thematised the downtrodden masses of India, social reforms and anti-British sentiments.[80] Many among this group of writers took to penning film scripts and screenplays. Among the themes chosen, untouchability and the removal of its disabilities, a reform close to Gandhi's heart, emerged as a favourite for writers and filmmakers. For example, films like the Bengali *Chandidas* (Debki Bose, 1932) and its 1934 Hindi remake showed a legendary fifteenth-century Bengali Vashnavite poet and his love for a low-caste woman; *Dharmatma* (V. Shantaram, 1935), in Marathi and Hindi, focused on sixteenth-century Sant Eknath's humanitarian defence of the untouchable castes; and the vastly popular Hindi *Achut Kanya* (*The Untouchable Girl*, Franz Osten, 1936), tackled the problem of untouchability through the ill-fated romance of a Brahmin youth and an untouchable girl. There were many others. The Tamil *Bala Yogini* (K. Subrahmanyam, 1936), one of the first reformist films of the Tamil cinema, infringed many caste taboos. It dealt with the story of a Brahmin widow thrown out of her own house who seeks shelter with her low-caste servant. *Lakshmi* (*Harijan Girl*, K. Subrahmanyam, 1937) and *Thyagabhoomi* (*The Land of Sacrifice*, K. Subrahmanyam, 1939), respectively dealt with the question of the conversion of untouchables to Christianity and attacked the caste system by exposing the hypocrisy of priesthood and pleading for better treatment of widows. All these were socially significant films which tackled the theme of untouchability in a major way through religion (that is, the way of *Bhakti*), love and courtship, social acceptance and directly by depicting Gandhian work among the untouchables.

In *Gunga Din*, on the other hand, the importance given to an untouchable as 'the hero' essentially emphasised the unbridgable stratification and discrimination of colonial society and reiterated that the British alone, standing at the apex of this society, could manage the inequitable and prejudiced power structure through their humane, progressive and superior handling and fair play. Unlike its highly romanticised treatment in the Indian cinema, which sought its solution within the Hindu social fold, Gunga Din's untouchability, elevated through loyalty, justified outside intervention and made a statement for the benefit of imperialism alone.

The British had long projected themselves as the protectors of millions of downtrodden untouchables in India not only in order to reinforce the vast social divisions of Indian society but also because they felt that the untouchables would make ideal 'loyal' subjects.[81] Yet, Gandhi had stolen a march over them. Because of his work among the scheduled castes (called *Harijans* by Gandhi), the Congress had won most scheduled caste seats in the elections of 1937, except in Bombay where Ambedkar's Independent Labour Party captured thirteen out of fifteen seats reserved for them. Significantly, it was Ambedkar who had tried to formalise this social division by demanding separate electorates for the scheduled castes and it was entirely because of Gandhi's intervention that this had not succeeded.[82] Ambedkar also had deep-seated reservations about joining the Congress. The film sought to strengthen such forces deepening splits within the national reformist agenda.

Loyalists and the army: surfacing contradictions

In underlining the various caste and community divisions of India, *Gunga Din* posited the British colonial rule as not only above Indian classifying categories, but also one which offered to the split native population – the 'Gunga Dins of India' – new opportunities in the British Indian army that would override their innumerable differences and insurmountable social barriers. Capitalising on this factor the publicity of the film emphasised:

> It offers its hero Gunga Din, a *bhishti* or water-carrier in the service of the British army, who despite his low caste, a tremendous handicap, the full significance of which can only be fully understood by those who know what the social divisions of the Orient meant to its inhabitants, rises from his humble estate to become a valiant fighting man.

Yet, as an untouchable, Gunga Din in the film could only occupy the lowly position of a menial in the British Indian army and could never become a soldier. Whatever the professed stand of *Gunga Din* and its publicity campaign, in reality, the colonial rule offered a very highly selective system of army recruitment along the lines of caste, religion, regional and linguistic affiliations.[83] In all this, the recruitment of the untouchables as soldiers had a chequered history. The British radically changed the base of recruitment in the nineteenth century and many caste groups, among them the untouchables, were no longer taken into the army. After the 1890s they were again recruited only to be once again dropped from the army list. There were concerted efforts from the untouchables and others to be recruited by the army, which was seen by many of them as a vehicle for upward mobility. This was a move that was aggressively opposed by the higher martial caste groups. Acknowledging the objections of caste Hindus, the untouchables, interestingly enough, offered to serve in segregated regiments or in Muslim regiments. It is not without significance, then, that the Muslim soldiers in the British Indian army are shown in the film to accept water from the hands of the untouchable, Gunga Din.

However, in view of the international situation and the rapidly growing movement for freedom in India, the British had to undertake not only limited Indianisation of the British Indian army but also open it to newer social forces, other than 'martial races', which by the time of the World War II recruitment drive had to be given up, having proved too narrow. These changes renewed among the master race fears of military contamination by nationalist and political forces. In fact, as units became more Indianised and political discussions became more frequent, those who were too vocal had to be eased out of the army[84] – indicating the deepening insecurity felt by the British in relation to the army at this crucial historical juncture. These changes had led the chief of staff in mid-1938 to issue a warning to the British cabinet that the steady progress of Indianisation would tend to increase the danger of disloyalty in the army units.[85] The attempt of *Gunga Din* to create a larger-than-life hero out of a loyal army man, therefore, has to be located in this reality and not in isolation or merely as part of adopting a popular well-tried and successful formula as a film story.

The film posited the loyal Gunga Din as a symbol of hope in a society not only riven with caste hierarchy and problems of untouchability, but by feelings of nationalism as well. In fact, it cinematically recreated loyalty, a highly estimable virtue in the west, and an over-arching category of the loyalist in an attempt to strengthen their own hands as well as those of the fictive loyalists. The category of loyalist reframed the context for the native, who alone was to be given an opportunity to transcend all the debilitating categories of Indian society and polity. In this, even the name *Gunga Din*, as a press hand-out of the film was to point out, incorporating *Gunga* the 'Hindustani name for river Ganges and *Din* an Arabic word meaning faith', was a composite one. With no discrete religious identity, this name symbolically drew the Hindus, Muslims and the downtrodden untouchables together in a united loyal fold under the British.

Gunga Din was the 'loyal humble servant of the empire' whose face and half-naked body in a loin cloth, depicted in a cringing supplicant posture, was most frequently used in the publicity drive of the film (illustration 5). Given a prominent place in the posters, his face and body also were used as book-markers, and a life sized cut-out of Gunga Din was propped up on an easel and displayed before a decorative backdrop in the lobby of the cinema houses in UK and USA. Placards invited passers-by to pose with the cut-out for a free picture with 'their favourite Gunga Din'. The publicity material and press books of the films highlighted 'The thrilling world-famed ballad of the native carrier's loyalty serving the British troops in India', and 'the devotion and loyalty of an elderly native water-carrier towards the British commanders during a campaign in India which forms the basis of the film *Gunga Din*.'

In this loyalty he was equated with the unquestioning, dumb, animal-like quality portrayed in the film by a female elephant called Annie. Indeed, Gunga Din – the *bhishti*, 'appropriately pronounced as beastie', as a US critic was to point out[86] – was closely identified with this animal. Such animal metaphors were used frequently by British officers to describe Indians in the army.[87]

The pronunciation of Gunga Din's name by the white races is also revealing. Pronounced as '*Goonga Deen*' (the dumb Din) in the film, it amply illuminates the concept of loyalty sought to be portrayed through him. This concept was deplored in the national media as not that of a friend – as an equal – but that of a 'faithful servant' portrayed 'to impress the world with the devotion of Indians and to teach the natives that the highest ambition of their lives must be the opportunity to serve their white masters.'[88] Commenting in a similar vein, the Indian film journals also hit out:

> All the British characters are honest, jolly souls while all the 'natives' are scheming, treacherous, unscrupulous devils. All but one, the solitary exception is Gunga Din, the faithful water-carrier loyal unto death despite the insults and curses that are invariably showered on him by his white masters. He is always cringing before them. The word 'cringing' occurs innumerable times in the scenario, for that is Gunga Din's consistent pattern of behaviour. That is how all loyal 'natives' must behave in the presence of their rulers.[89]

In the end Gunga Din, having met his 'glorious death' is suitably rewarded for his loyalty. The last scene shows a long shot of a line of natives moving towards a funeral pyre. Over this scene, the figure of Gunga Din appears in transparency. He is no longer half-naked, but in the full regimental attire of a corporal. A triumphant smile floods his face as he has achieved his life's ambition. Gunga Din had indeed paid a heavy price to be allowed to wear a corporal's uniform and be incorporated by the British rulers. Significantly, as there was a great deal of dissatisfaction at the promotional prospects of the natives in the British Indian army, this cinematic gesture could only reinforce this feeling among Indian audiences rather than register its denial or posit any hope.

A scene before this had shown the British colonel read the famous lines of the poem, *Gunga Din*, over his dead body:

> Though I've belted you and flayed you,
>   By the livin' Gawd that made you,
> You're a better man than I am, Gunga Din!

This appreciation of Gunga Din, pointed out as 'a respectful admiration of inferiority' in a press publicity of the book, was a reiteration of the special relationship that existed between British officers and natives in the army. The film celebrated this brotherhood between British officers, on the one hand, and the British officers as the father, brother and comrade of the native soldier, on the other.[90]

This strong male bonding, verging on homoeroticism among the former in the film, is shown to ultimately reject the odd female, although her appearance is essential to establish heterosexuality. This one female, in an overwhelmingly male film, is played by Joan Fontaine, suitably a little known actress (she achieved fame only after Alfred Hitchcock cast her in his first US film, *Rebecca*, in 1940), who is soon expelled from the narrative as inconsequential. But not before her presence and her desire to wed one of the sergeants is ridiculed. She is cast in a stereotypical image of a woman whose shopping spree for marriage effectively frames her activities and desires. She is considered a disruptive influence on the otherwise healthy, virile masculinity and bonding of British officers. Anyone succumbing to the charms of a woman declared a 'piece of dry goods' in the film, is not a soldier but is contemptuously dismissed by the fellow sergeants as a ladies' man, unfit to do a soldier's work.[91]

Among the British officers and the loyal native a curious blending of masculinity and camaraderie was forged. This portrayal owed much to the fact that the film was a Hollywood product. In keeping with certain traditions of portrayal, the emotional ties between the three sergeants and Gunga Din are suggestive of homoeroticism between white masters and a coloured servant, between the super-masculine and the emasculated male portrayed as effete and servile.[92] The rebels on the other hand, though militarised, are shown to be cruel and violent. They stand inferiorised and desexualised under the control of a man who procures his commands from a female goddess. These images directly contradict the self-image of Indians, deliberately created by the nationalists in Bengal, Maharashtra and Punjab, as virile, masculine and martial, harking back to the historical times of past glory.

The interpersonal relationship of such inferior humans with the colonisers could not possibly be unproblematic. The division between white and non-white is delineated as absolute. No amount of friendship and camaraderie could change the rudiments of racial difference; that cannot be questioned nor the white man's right to rule. Indeed, the interaction of the *bhishti*,

Gunga Din, with his superiors in the film is marked by extreme condescension and patronisation, and at worst by disgust, bullying, insults and abuses; a kind of behaviour which has been termed as 'affectionate camaraderie' between officers and their men[93] (illustration 6). This behaviour was more likely sharpened, in the wake of Indianisation of the British Indian army, by the superior ability of the Indian officers to handle and come close to their troops than the British officers.[94] From all the other standard terms of abuses used by British soldiers or officers for their Indian counterparts in real life – swine, nigger, wogs, Hindus, and black-bellied bastards – swine emerged as a great favourite for usage in the films.[95] Although deleted frequently in the versions that were sent to India, in deference to the religious susceptibilities of the Muslims, other derogatory remarks were kept intact. For example, in this film, MacChesney says to Gunga Din, 'I'll stuff you in this pistol and pull the trigger.' Balantine similarly says, 'I have a good mind to split you in two and stuff you up an elephant's trunk,' and proceeds to throttle him with his hands.

This behaviour could well be justified by the argument put across by Ashis Nandy that the 'overburdened white man with his civilising mission regressed into the savagery of the people he was ordained to rule'.[96] This puts the onus of degradation and dehumanisation of the colonisers squarely on the shoulders of the colonised. Yet, the white man's behaviour defied any sort of logic and transferred the use of such methods and the use of terror from means to end. It denied the existence of human feelings in the dominant colonising race. Notwithstanding the articulation of such derogatory race relations, the film very shrewdly promotes adjustment to humiliating conditions by presenting them as objectively comical and by giving a picture of a person who expresses himself even in his own inadequate position as an object of fun apparently free of any resentment.

This treatment meted out to Gunga Din was not unique. The inferiority of Gunga Din was the inferiority of all the Gunga Dins in the army. There was, indeed, no attempt to hide the racial and class overtones in the empire film package. In the eyes of the Indian audience, Gunga Din, as did other empire films, actually discredited the British armed forces, who are not shown observing any code of ethics. They are seen kicking Indians, desecrating their temples, foul-mouthing the colonised and looting them. For the Indian soldiers the film was an inevitable reference point to the reality of everyday life; it reinforced the racial and class discrimination that they faced in the army. In fact, when *Gunga Din* was seen by the military intelligence directorate, they confirmed the worst by observing:

> It shows the army in a ridiculous light. The troops from the commanding officers downwards commit the most elementary military mistakes, discipline is lamentably slack and, in general, the film is an excellent example of how things are *NOT* done in the British army. Some audiences (Allied troops for example) might use the film as a basis for criticism which, even if it were not intended to be taken seriously, might have unfortunate results.[97] (emphasis in original)

The interservice public relations directorate also confirmed the above observations and similarly commented that the film supported the suggestion that British soldiers were 'insidious or despoilers of Indian temples' and showed itself uncertain about the effects of portraying the British Indian army in the way attempted in the film.[98]

The experiential realm of the soldiers was repeatedly fore-grounded during the interwar period, when the British Indian army emerged as the focus of Indian nationalist criticism and attack. The Congress was very active in propagating against it. One of the major planks of its attack was the racial policy adopted in the recruitment of higher ranks of the armed forces. It was also a part of Congress policy to create disaffection in the British Indian army. From 1936 onwards the annual election manifestos of the Congress had taken to repeatedly declaring: 'opposition to the participation of India in an imperial war'.[99] The Congress was not prepared to view the defence of India from the angle of imperial interest. It was strongly opposed to the current British practice of sending Indian troops outside the country as an instrument of British imperialism.

At such a time the film's portrayal of interpersonal relation-ships between British officers and Indian recruits could well prove subversive to its intent. A feeling of uncertainty regarding the film among the British officials in India emanated from the fact that Indian army personnel provided a large and very important segment of the cinema audience for western films.

The British were acutely nervous about Punjab due to its links with the army, proximity to the Frontier province, where the Khudai Khidmadgar were a serious problem, and the existence of a radical fringe – the Navjawan Bharat Sabha and the Kirti Kisan group – operating on the border line of terrorism and Marxism. With World War II looming large on the horizon, the army personnel formed a particularly vulnerable group as their loyalty, applauded by the empire films, was already under attack from nationalist forces. These loyalists were condemned as collaborators and traitors. The contradiction inherent in the aforementioned portrayal, therefore, increased the vulnerability of the army personnel. The behaviour of army officers shown in *Gunga Din* was to militate against the traditional reverence which Indians had for the army; army service stood discredited in the eyes of the Indian audience and Indian soldiers in particular. Intelligence reports confirmed that the portrayal of the British Indian troops in this film was used by 'certain sections of [the Indian] public to exacerbate the relations between troops and civilians'.[100]

Yet, in the context of the late 1930s, this rearticulation of the interpersonal relations between such loyal Indians and the British officers has a certain validity and justification in relation to the white audience. Those scenes that were causing such anxiety among British officials in India were not only attractive to the white British audience but were also the need of the hour. In the wake of World War II, Britain had to cope vigorously with the problems of recruitment at home.[101] In fact, the shortage of officers for the British Indian army turned out to be a handicap that was never completely overcome.[102] One of the major reasons for this lay in the devaluation faced by the British Indian army in the aftermath of World War I, when its Indianisation, which had been stemmed for political reasons, had to be partially lifted (in October 1932), although the pace was kept deliberately slow and the British component was not compromised.

The greatest objection to Indianisation, which was proving an obstruction to recruitment in England, was the racial prejudice of British officers who were unwilling to serve under Indians. The *Morning Post* of 20 February 1923 put this feeling bluntly: 'To many of the most open minded soldiers the idea of being under the command of an Asiatic is insufferable.'[103] Senior officers feared that if Indian officers holding the King's commission were allowed to enter the service on an equal footing, the supply of suitable officers willing to serve would dwindle. Lord Rawlinson, similarly observed, 'Old officers say that they won't send their sons to serve under natives.' Quite clearly even this extremely limited Indianisation devalued the British Indian army, making those already in, reluctant and unwilling to serve in the Indianised units.

The colonial administration was faced with the daunting task of accommodating a growing number of Indians within the existing military structure that threatened the exclusive rights and privileges to which generations of colonial officers had grown accustomed. The assertion of white masculinity in the films served to appease any such fears by making a straightforward defence of racial exclusivity. It challenged and belied the unarticulated shift in colonial military policy. It reconstructed a certain view point about India, its army and the exercise of imperial power, which had a generative impact on the recruitment drive in appeasing anxieties about the changed nature of the army, the position of the white man in it and interracial relations.

The film portrayed that in India the sword was mightier than the pen, for it was ultimately responsible for law and order as well as for peace – the basis of all development. This projection reiterated the belief among British army officers that their profession was more important in India than in England.[104] In this connection Edward Thompson, who was the special correspondent for the *Manchester Guardian* in India from January–March 1931, wrote about the considerable latitude of action allowed to the British administrators and army officers in the NWFP. He aptly described this province as an autocracy, seeing it as 'the militarised section of India,' and he commented that '"the sahib is a sahib" doctrine shaken every where in India, was erect and strong [in this region], the army approving it'.[105]

Such issues were prioritised in *Gunga Din* and in other films of this genre. One might add that this portrayal of the British Indian army was true of a certain aspect of colonial penetration in India that did not necessarily share in the rapidly changing interpersonal relationships between the coloniser and the colonised. Indeed, changes relating to the British Indian army were largely ignored and the films tended to eulogise British soldiers and glorify the British empire and imperialism.

Reception of the film: national and imperial

Gunga Din was obviously serving the purposes of British imperialists. In this peddling of imperialism, Hollywood had its own reasons. For colonial India, the cinematic images projected a multiplicity of meanings simultaneously ambiguous, subversive and reaffirmative. For example, the predominant image of British officers had severe racial and class resonances. Offence was taken, however, not so much against the representation of a white, invincible male who single-handedly made mincemeat out of several thousand Indians, as against this notion of the heroism of loyalist Indians like Gunga Din. For Indian nationalists, loyalists were little more than collaborators with the British Raj; Gunga Din's 'heroism', which led to the dealh of so many Indians, was a bitter pill for an Indian audience to swallow.

As an active participant and recipient of the nationalist discourse the heterogeneous Indian audience, with all its segments highly politicised, was in a position to subvert the notions of patriotism as depicted in the empire cinema. This subversion, effected by Indian audiences can be visualised in the testimony of Bertold Brecht who spoke of the effect of the film *Gunga Din*:

> In the film *Gunga Din* ... I saw British occupation forces fighting a native population. An Indian tribe ... attacked a body of British troops stationed in India. The Indians were primitive creatures either comic or wicked. Comic when loyal to the British and wicked when hostile. The British soldiers were honest, good humoured chaps and when they used their fists on the mob and 'knocked some sense' into them the audience laughed. One of the Indians betrayed his compatriots to the British, sacrificed his life so that his fellow countrymen should be defeated, and earned the audience's heartfelt applause. My heart was touched too. I felt like applauding and laughed at all the right places. Despite the fact that I knew all the time that this was something wrong, that the Indians are not primitive and uncultured people but have a magnificent age-old culture, and this Gunga Din could also be seen in a very different light i.e. as a traitor to his people. I was amused and touched because this utterly distorted account was an artistic success and considerable resources in talent and ingenuity had been applied in making it.[106]

This insightful comment signifies Brecht's notion of conscious political criticism and its applicability in relation to the so-called dominant cinema and highlights multiple viewing positions for a western white male spectator. It may be noted that a large number of British and US critics were cavilling at the empire cinema propounding British imperialism at the cost of the colonies. Yet, these critics, though radical in their own social milieu, were still unable to see this thrust of imperialism from the native's point of view as was done by Brecht, who spoke from the position of the native. The radical critics were progressive and full of admirable sentiments, but not so when it came to what was being done in the name of imperialism in the colonies.

Commenting upon Brecht's observations on *Gunga Din*, Jeffrey Richards maintains, 'the propaganda had no effect on Brecht, whose views on imperialism were already formed and developed. But its effects on those who had no previous view must have been immense.'[107] It is clear that Richards is referring to the white imperial audience to the total exclusion of an Indian audience. How, for example, was the Indian audience expected to respond to the frequent projections on the screen of the Union Jack or expected to behave in moments when the screen showed only a Union Jack in close-up. The British audience were seen to be 'proudly applauding those moments'.[108] But did the Indian audience also cheer? The evidence suggests to the contrary. The emphasis upon hard work, sportsmanship and hypermasculinity of the white in the film was not only to impress the white audience but also the colonised by display of this conspicuous machismo. There was no way in which the film could persuade Indian viewers to enter the structure of attitudes and judgement by inviting them to see themselves as British army officers. This inevitable failure to incorporate them meant a failure to identify them with the political and social status quo.

The impact of *Gunga Din* on young impressionable minds of the 'master' race was undisputed. Russell Ferguson, the well-known British critic, in a highly perceptive first person account of a twelve-year-old schoolboy wrote:

> When I grow up I am going to join the Indian army as an officer, and fight for the Queen, and do all the things I saw in *Gunga Din*. I will have a revolver and a horse and a lot of men under me, and

a white uniform with plenty of bandoleers and straps and buckles and a white helmet ... I will always be going as a strong detachment to places where there is a lot of danger ... I will not get killed ... because they can fire at me as much as they like, they will never hit me because I am white.[109]

Ferguson succinctly underlined the fact that in films such as *Gunga Din* certain characters served as surrogates for the audience, especially in dealing with high adventure. The western audience, which identified fully with the heroes, imagined themselves entering this space to conquer and subjugate the colonial, uncivilised world. This helped to unite the nation behind imperialism by perpetuating a national myth of invincibility. The films played upon xenophobic and racist beliefs prevalent in Britain.

That these two audiences – imperial/white and colonised/coloured – drew upon very different cultural references when they decoded the film and constructed contradictory, even hostile, meanings needs to be emphasised. By the late 1930s, the film projections, as pointed out by the *Bombay Chronicle*, had finally become one of imperialism versus nationalism.[110] Protests were made at 'insults wantonly flung at our prestige and nationalism', wrote this national daily. The empire films were thought to be 'attacking the present awakening for nationalism' and 'trade in a nation's prestige and revile its patriotism'.[111] A warning was also issued that 'those days when India took everything lying down are now gone'. It was also noted that the 'foreigners have not yet realised the exact temper in which our nation is at present'. *Film India* put its finger on the pulse when it wrote that it was the portrayal of Indian sentiments 'wedded to British imperialism' that was proving objectionable to the Indian audiences.[112] The *Bombay Chronicle* also maintained that even if seventy-five per cent of this film was excised, it would still remain, in substance, 'a slander on India'.[113]

Even before the film was released, the national media were busy building up educated middle-class opinion against *Gunga Din*. Eminent US and British film critics were frequently cited to build up pressure upon the colonial government regarding such films. The *Bombay Chronicle* in its issue of 19 April 1939, while quoting James Dugan's opinion on the film as 'a bad joke, a dirty snivelling joke on the Indian people', commented that 'these words were not uttered by an Indian but an eminent American film critic'. British author Ethel Mannin was also quoted: 'Every Indian with any self-respect and nationalist spirit must protest vehemently and insistently against such degrading and blatantly imperialist propaganda films such as *Gunga Din*'. The *Bombay Chronicle* added: 'If an American critic and a British author have thought it fit to protest against this film, is it not our duty to stop this slander by every means possible.' The editorial of the *Bombay Chronicle* went on to highlight that 'even impartial and fair-minded foreigners have given expression to their utter disgust at such an atrocious misrepresentation of the Indian people'.[114]

The film journals followed suit by extensively quoting criticism from outside to bring the point home. *Film India*, for example, cited the *Motion Herald of America*, which declared *Gunga Din* as a 'blunt hard statement of the imperial policy that was and may yet be England's ... The picture depicts the heroics of those who fought, screamed and slugged back India into submission.'[115] The *Irish Press* was also quoted: 'The picture is based on a poem by Kipling, the arch-imperialist jingler of catchy and famous lines – a rotten theme.'[116] Indian media expressed great delight and supreme satisfaction when the film, *Wee Willie Winkie*, was banned in Oslo, Norway, for 'depicting British domination in India'. The ban imposed by Japan on *Gunga Din*, on the grounds that it 'injures the sentiments of a friendly nation – the Indians', also was widely publicised.[117]

Attempts at mobilisation of public opinion in India were followed by similar attempts in Europe. At a conference held at Zurich in June 1939, this issue was successfully raised by K. B. Hirlekar, founder member of the Motion Picture Society of India. *Today Cinema*, in its issue of 1 July 1939, proclaimed, 'Huge Indian Market'. It continued, 'India protests against feature films which offend Indian susceptibilities which were not taken notice of.' Calling for severe restrictions on such films, it further added, 'It is not apparently realised here how strongly India feels on this matter.'

In India, the highly successful popular agitation against the release of *The Drum* in September 1938 had already cleared the ground for the reception of *Gunga Din*. The Congress and non-Congress ministries established under the scheme of provincial autonomy moved swiftly. *Gunga Din* was quickly banned in

Bengal and in Bombay, followed by other provinces as soon as moves were made to release it in April 1939.[118] The successive banning of these two films acted as the proverbial last straw for many studios in the USA, where similar projects were abandoned. The producers were afraid to put money into ventures that would not be allowed in the country about which the film was made. The risk of losing the Indian market was a considerable deterrent.[119] By May 1939, *Gunga Din* and its predecessor, *The Drum*, were publicly affirmed by British officials to have caused 'disturbances to Indian opinion'.[120] The British and Hollywood producers were sternly warned and told to desist from making such films; a warning which brought the production of empire films located in India to a virtual halt.

Gunga Din brought to a close the highly-lucrative empire package of adventure genre films, with the British Indian army at their centre, made during the decade 1929–39. All these films have been so far accepted as stressing 'fundamentally mythic and unreal or historical rather than contemporary and potentially contentious setting'.[121] In attempting to elaborate this, Jeffrey Richards, the leading film historian on empire cinema, emphasises the view that the empire films regarding India, although made in the late 1930s, evoked late nineteenth-century ideas and not contemporary ones; the attitudes, the political situation all belonged to the latter part of the previous century. According to him this explains why the constitutional development which had taken place in the interwar years in India finds no place in the cinema of the empire. They did not draw upon any contemporary reality and remained at the level of imperial propaganda. These films also showed no indication of the flux that the empire actually found itself in during the interwar years. This is the interpretation that subsequently has been accepted by the film historians who followed Jeffrey Richards in this field.[122]

My analysis of *Gunga Din* argues that even though this film and those of its kind are set in the late nineteenth century, the frame of issues surrounding them relates to the contemporary concerns of the late 1930s. This contemporaneity is established in locating the film in its historical contexts (national, international and colonial), in analysing the ideological thrust of the film, in assessing the press and publicity material of the film and in evaluating its reception among different audiences, both white and non-white. In other words, this contemporaneity has to be evaluated not necessarily in terms suggested by Jeffrey Richards, but in terms of socio-political developments that form the background to certain vital issues relating to the rise of Indian nationalism. These were of primary concern to the British both in India as well as in their home country. Britain was forced to recognise the emerging nationalism in order to condemn and denigrate it. Consequently, the film *Gunga Din*, did not ignore this contemporary state of affairs but offered a comment by firmly denying its validity. It emphasised the lack of unity in India, propounded the idea that the nationalists were not facing the reality of the Indian situation and suggested that India was not a unified nation ripe for independence.

In the 1930s, the future of India was still visualised as being well within the British empire and not outside it. During this period the impact of the peace movement and unprecedented economic crisis, unemployment, disarmament, rearmament, fascism, the growing anti-fascist front and the Spanish civil war rendered the question of Indian self-determination futile. For the major political parties, the idea of severing links with Britain did not arise.[123] The film that followed *Gunga Din* had to actively foster this near unanimity of dominant British public opinion about India's continuing relationship with Britain, even though the colonial reality challenged and denied it vehemently. *The Rains Came*, which broke with the set formula of the adventure genre films made so far on colonial subjects, tried to portray a different reality of India, without compromising the essential colonial interests, in a most dramatic way.

Notes

1 T. S. Eliot (ed.), *A Choice of Kipling's Verse* (Suffolk, Great Britain, Methuen & Macmillan, 1983 [1941]), pp. 179–81.
2 IOR, L/P&J/ 8/ 128, Coll. no. 105-A, pt. XV, Feb.–Sep. 1939. See *The Times* (27 Feb. 1939).
3 Edmund Candler, who later became a well-known writer of fiction dealing with India, recounts how before he went out to India as a teacher he had read all about that country from the point of view of authors like Kipling. Indian army officers similarly vouched for such an influence before they came over to India. In addition, the British in India often tended to take fictional types as their ideal. One

author writes, regarding 'the cult of the strong silent man', that when he came out of Punjab at the turn of the century this cult was worshipped in all the clubs and messes. For details see Allen J. Greenberger, *The British Image of India: A Study of the Literature of Imperialism, 1880–1960* (London, Oxford University Press, 1969), pp. 1–3.

4 Kipling's family had raised objections to Kipling being used as a character in the film. Consequently, a wagon was superimposed over the tent, effectively blocking Kipling from view. Both versions of the scene still exist. See *American Cinematographer*, 63:9 (Sep. 1982), p. 895.

5 IOR, L/P&J/ 8/ 128, Coll. no. 105-A, pt. XV, Feb.–Sep. 1939.

6 For an insightful analysis of this phenomenon see Radhika Singha, '"Providential" circumstances: the *thuggee* campaign of the 1830s and legal innovations', *Modern Asian Studies*, 27:1 (1993), pp. 83–146.

7 For details see Sumit Sarkar, *Modern India, 1885–1947* (Delhi, Macmillan, 1983), pp. 144–9, 251–2, 287–8, 302, 314–5.

8 Bhagat Singh, one of the founders and main pillars of the Hindustan Socialist Republican Army, wrote the famous tract, '*Why I am an Atheist*', defending his total rejection of all religions on grounds of human dignity and rationalist logic.

9 IOR, L/P&J/8/128, Coll. no. 105-A, pt. XV, Feb.–Sep. 1939.

10 Sumita S. Chakravarty, *National Identity in Indian Popular Cinema, 1947–1987* (Delhi, Oxford University Press, 1996), p. 36.

11 In Phalke's words: 'While the life of Christ was rolling fast before my eyes I was mentally visualising the gods Sri Krishna, Sri Ramchandra, their Gokul and Ayodhaya ... Could we, the sons of India, ever be able to see Indian images on the screen?' Dadasaheb Phalke cited in Ashish Rajadhyalsha, 'The Phalke era: conflict of traditional form and modern technology', *Journal of Arts and Ideas*, 14–15 (Jul.–Dec. 1987), pp. 44–77.

12 The paintings of Raja Ravi Verma with their mythological themes, for example, created an 'Indian identity' based upon a cultural synthesis which provided the hegemonic image as an image of national unity. See Geeta Kapur, 'Ravi Verma: representational dilemmas of a nineteenth-century Indian painter', *Journal of Arts and Ideas*, 17–18 (Jun. 1989), pp. 59–80; Tapati Guha-Thakurta, *The Making of New 'Indian' Art: Artists, Aesthetics and Nationalism in Bengal, 1880–1920* (Cambridge, Cambridge University Press, 1992); Ratnabali Chattopadhyay, 'Nationalism and form in Indian painting: a study of the Bengal school', *Journal of Arts and Ideas*, 14–15 (Jul.–Dec. 1987), pp. 5–45; Anuradha

Kapur, 'The representation of gods and heroes: Parsi mythological arena of the early twentieth century', *Journal of Arts and Ideas*, 23–24 (Jan. 1993), pp. 85–107; Tanika Sarkar, 'Bengali middle class nationalism and literature: a study of Sarat Chandra's *Pather Dabi* and Rabindranath's *Char Adhay'*, paper presented at NMML, 15–18 Dec. 1980; Tanika Sarkar, 'Bankim Chandra and the impossibility of a political agenda: a predicament for nineteenth-century Bengal', NMML, Occasional Papers, second series, no. 40; Sumit Sarkar, '*Kaliyuga, chakri and bhakti*: Ramakrishna and his times', *Economic and Political Weekly*, 27:29 (18 Jul. 1992), pp. 1543–66; Kathryn Hansen, *Grounds for Play: The Nautanki Theatre of North India* (New Delhi, Manohar Publications, 1992), pp. 106–43; and Sudhir Chandra, *The Oppressive Present: Literature and Social Consciousness in Colonial India* (Delhi, Oxford University Press, 1992), pp. 17–70, 116–54.

13 Personal interview with Suresh Chabbria, director of the FTII, 12 Jun. 1992.

14 Sohrab Modi in conversation with P. K. Nair made these comments. Personal interview with P. K. Nair, former director of the FTII, 12 Jun. 1992.

15 Communication from Vidya Vati, 9 Apr. 1997.

16 *Manchester Guardian* (12 Sep. 1953). This film was taken by the Asian Film Society for screening. Although it was considered 'over played' by European standards of acting and direction, its battle scenes were highly acclaimed and considered comparable to those of a D. W. Griffith's epic.

17 Edward Thompson, *An End of the Hour* (London, Macmillan, 1938), p. 175.

18 For literature in recent years on the identification of the nation with the female body (the national) see Joseph S. Alter, 'Celibacy, sexuality and the transformation of gender into nationalism in north India', *Journal of Asian Studies*, 53:1 (1994), pp. 45–66.

19 Ashis Nandy, 'Woman versus womanliness: an essay in cultural and political psychology', in Ashis Nandy, *At the Edge of Psychology: Essays in Politics and Culture* (Delhi, Oxford University Press, 1980), pp. 32–46. Also see Somnath Zutshi, 'Women, nation and the outsider in contemporary Hindi cinema', in Tejaswini Niranjana, P. Sudhir and Vivek Dhareshwar (eds), *Interrogating Modernity: Culture and Colonialism in India* (Calcutta, Seagull, 1993), pp. 93–142.

20 This image was and remains, as pointed out by Joseph S. Alter, at radical odds with the kind of xenophobic chauvinism that the popular militant/communal usage conveys. See Joseph S. Alter,

'Celibate wrestler: sexual chaos, embodied balance and competitive politics in north India', in Patricia Uberoi (ed.), *Social Reform, Sexuality and the State* (New Delhi, Sage Publications, 1996), pp. 109–31.

21 *Seventy Five Glorious Years of Indian Cinema, 1913–88* (Bombay, Screen World Publications, 1988).

22 Draupadi is a central female character in the epic Mahabharata. Wife of the five Pandavas she is first coveted by the Kaurvas, thrown out of her kingdom and later, when in exile masquerading as Sairindhari, the maid under the protection of King Virat, she has Keechak lusting after her. In the grand war that followed between the Pandavas and Kaurvas, her honour is ultimately redeemed by her husbands and the country wrested from its enemies.

23 High-ranking Congress leaders like Madan Mohan Malaviya and Lala Lajpat Rai were also active in the Hindu Mahasabha.

24 Sisir Kumar Das, *An Artist in Chains* (New Delhi, The New Statesman, 1984), p. 222.

25 In October 1939 Nehru admitted to Rajendera Prasad, 'there is no doubt that we have been unable to check the growth of communalisation and anti-Congress feeling among Muslim masses.' Uma Kaura, *Muslims and Indian Nationalism: The Emergence of the Demand for India's Partition, 1928–40* (Delhi, Manohar Publications, 1977), pp. 127–8.

26 Amit Kumar Gupta, *North-West Frontier Province Legislature and Freedom Struggle, 1932–47* (New Delhi, Indian Council of Historical Research, 1976), p. 93.

27 *Hindu* (10 Mar. 1939), p. 7. See also *Film India* (Apr. 1939), p. 25.

28 Sarkar, *Modern India*, pp. 356–7.

29 Stephen Alan Rittenberg, 'The independent movement in India's North West Frontier Province, 1901–1947' (Ph.D. thesis, Columbia University, 1977), p. 263.

30 Chandra, *The Oppressive Present*, pp. 17–70, 116–54. See also Hansen, *Grounds for Play*, pp. 128–37.

31 Zutshi, 'Women, nation and outsider', pp. 83–142.

32 Ravi S. Vasudevan, 'Film studies: the new cultural history and the experience of modernity', NMML, Research-in-Progress Papers, second series, no. 105.

33 *Encyclopaedia of Indian Cinema*, compiled by Ashish Rajadhyaksha and Paul Willemen (New Delhi, Oxford University Press, 1995), p. 234.

34 Communication from Hema Raikar, 8 Jan. 1998. Pendharkar's *Vande Mataram Asharam*, made in 1926, was a major silent film

influenced by Lala Lajpat Rai and Madan Mohan Malaviya. It was banned by the British and triggered a major censorship case in 1927–28. See *Encyclopaedia*, p. 231.

35 Ravi S. Vasudevan, 'Addressing the spectator of a "third world" national cinema: the Bombay "social" film of the 1940s and 1950s', *Screen*, 35:4 (Winter 1995), pp. 305–24.

36 For the Muslim followers of the *Thuggee* cult, despite divinities, rites and beliefs in omens associated with Hinduism, see Singha, 'Providential circumstances', pp. 83–146.

37 IOR, L/P&J/7/831, 1935. See R. T. Peel to J. Brooke-Wilkinson, secretary of the BBFC, 6 Jun. 1935. See also the telegram from government of India to secretary of state for India, 1 Jun. 1935.

38 This substitution played havoc with the use of a dress, which establishes a link between the preferred practices of attire and a geographical location. *Film India* indicated the 'ridicule' heaped on the Frontier people in the film by showing them as Kali worshippers who wore loin cloths instead of *salwar* (baggy trousers, tied with a draw-string), which everyone, Hindu or Muslim wore in the NWFP. See *Film India* (Feb. 1939), p. 27.

39 IOR, L/P&J/8/126, Coll. no. 105-A, pt. 1. Oct. 1935–Aug. 1940. See minute paper of P&J department 16 Aug. 1939.

40 A ditty of Gandhi's school days runs as follows: 'Behold the mighty British / He rules the Indian small / because being a meat eater / he is five cubits tall.' Cited in Susanne Hoeber Rudolph, 'The new courage: an essay on Gandhi's psychology', in Thomas R. Metcalf (ed.), *Modern India: An Interpretative Anthology* (New Delhi, Sterling Publishers, 1990), pp. 323–41.

41 *Hindu* (5 Mar. 1939), p.11.

42 IOR, L/P&J/8/128, Coll. no. 105-A, pt. XV, Feb.–Sep. 1939. See F. E. Evans, British counsel in Los Angeles, to information officer at the India Office, London, 26 Jan. 1939.

43 *Ibid.*

44 *Film India* (Feb. 1939), p. 28.

45 *Voice* (2 Apr. 1985), p. 36.

46 Cited in Suhash Chakravarti, *The Raj Syndrome: A Study in Imperial Perceptions* (Delhi, Chanakya Publications, 1989), pp. 126–7, 132.

47 See, for example, Edward Thompson, *A Letter From India* (London, Faber & Faber, 1932), pp. 37–8, 40. Thompson was somewhat friendlier towards Gandhi in his earlier novels, but by 1931 he was writing, 'Mr Gandhi was living by instinct and passion and not by reason any longer.' See his *A Farewell to India* (London, Faber & Faber, 1931, pp. 141, 144.

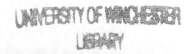

48 Martin A. Jackson, 'Film and the historian', *Culture*, 11:1 (1974) pp. 223–40.
49 Garry R. Hess, *America Encounters India, 1941–1947* (Baltimore & London, Johns Hopkins Press, 1971), p. 120.
50 *Film India* (Mar. 1939), p. 4.
51 IOR, L/P&J/8/123, Coll. no. 104-F, May 1937–Nov. 1941. See *Daily Express* (20 Jun. 1939).
52 NFAI, Oral History Project. J. B. H. Wadia, recorded interview, 6 Jul. 1984.
53 *Ibid.*
54 For the first time an Indian film won an international award. This film was rated as one of the three best films at the prestigious Venice film festival in 1937.
55 For an insightful essay on this theme see Geeta Kapur, 'Mythical material in Indian cinema', *Journal of Arts and Ideas*, 14–15 (Jul.–Dec. 1987), pp. 79–108.
56 MSA, Home Poll. F. no. 225, 1938, p. 5. Also see *Film India* (Jul. 1939), pp. 29–30; (Mar. 1940), p. 25; (Jun. 1944), p. 5.
57 MSA, Home Poll, F. no. 271, 1934–38, pp. 69–70, 111–12.
58 It is interesting to note in this connection that Col. Hanna had raised severe objection to Gaumont British's synopsis of a film called *Black Land* in 1934, which came too close to some of the recent events in South Africa, having identifiable British officials under a thin disguise. See Jeffrey Richards, *The Age of the Dream Palace: Cinema and Society in Britain, 1930–1970* (London, Basil Blackwell, 1983), pp. 147–8.
59 The newsworthiness of India can be seen in the fact that the British Movietone News kept a crew permanently in India during these years with a view to securing a 'constant supply of Indian pictures'. Moreover, because these films were widely exhibited in the USA, it was considered 'highly desirable that their subject matter and method of presentation should be carefully considered' with an eye to the effect they were likely to produce abroad. Therefore, a close British superintendence was placed over the filming crews. This 'close co-operation' was of 'mutual advantage', as certain aspects like the Round Table Conference, authenticating 'honest intentions of the British' came to be projected, on the one hand, and the film-makers were able to cater to the growing demands of their market on the other, by acquiring a facilitated entry in India. MSA, Home Poll. F. no. 230, 1930, pp. 73–91.
60 These films were *Gandhi in England, Gandhi Sees the King, Gandhi's Activities in England, Forty-fifth Indian National Congress at Karachi, Mahatma Gandhi after his Release, Mahatma*

Gandhi after the Truce, National Flag Hoisting and Salutation Ceremony, Epoch Making Voyage of Mahatma Gandhi to London, Gandhi News, Mahatma Gandhi in London, Gandhi and Charlie and *Arrival of Mahatma Gandhi in London.*

61 MSA, Home Poll. F. no. 8, 1932–33, pp. 121–9.

62 *Film India* (Dec. 1945), p. 3.

63 IOR, L/P&J/6/1995, 1937–1939, pp. 332, 350.

64 Jawaharlal Nehru, *An Autobiography* (New Delhi, Jawaharlal Nehru Memorial Fund, 1982 [1936]), p. 82.

65 Confidential intelligence bureau account of terrorism in India (1917–1936) cited in Sarkar, *Modern India*, p. 269. Bhagat Singh's actions had included the murder of a much-hated British official, Saunders, in Lahore in Dec. 1928 in revenge for the police assault on the unarmed Lajpat Rai during a peaceful demonstration, which had led to his death.

66 Communication from Uma Chakravarti, Jul. 1997.

67 Shahid Amin, 'Gandhi as Mahatma: Gorakhpur district, eastern UP, 1921–22', in Ranajit Guha (ed.), *Subaltern Studies III: Writings on South Asian History and Society* (Delhi, Oxford University Press, 1984), pp. 1–55.

68 The Chittagong group of revolutionaries headed by Surjya Sen brought off the most spectacular coup in the entire history of Indian terrorism on 18 Apr. 1930 by seizing the local armoury and celebrated it with a cry of 'Gandhiji's Raj has come'. See Sarkar, *Modern India*, p. 287.

69 IOR, L/P&J/ 8/127, Coll. no. 105-A, pt. II, Feb. 1933–Mar. 1936. See letter from H. T. Cowling, New York, 28 Jan. 1933.

70 After World War I there was a great deal of official encouragement for 'the factual film' in England, as cinema's propaganda potential was realised. See Nicholas Reeves 'Film propaganda and the audience: the example of Britain's official films during the first World War', *Journal of Contemporary History*, 18:13 (Jul. 1983), pp. 463–94.

71 IOR, L/P&J/8/127, Coll. no. 105-A, pt. 11, Feb. 1933–Mar. 1936. See objections regarding the film, *India Speaks*, raised by Seth Govind Das and Lal Chand Navalraj in the Assembly, 3–11 May 1935. A very large number of Indian newspapers, both in English and regional languages, wrote extensively against the film reviving memories of agitation against Katherine Mayo's book, *Mother India*. For details see MSA, Home Poll, F. no. 71, 1935–38.

72 MSA, Home Poll, F. no. 71, 1935–38. See Subhash Chander Bose's condemnatory references to this film, expansively covered by the

Bombay Chronicle (13 Mar. 1935; 23 Mar. 1935; and 30 Apr. 1935); and *Times of India* (28 Mar. 1935).

73 Mayo's book, *Mother India* (New York, Harcourt Brace, 1927), emphasised the most backward and primitive aspects of Hindu life and culture: the horrors of the child marriage system, the universality of sexual vice in its most extravagant form, the monstrously absurd brutalities of the caste system, the 'filthy personal habits' of the most highly-educated classes, the total degradation of the Hindu woman, universal cruelty to animals, and the prevalence of laziness, untruthfulness, cowardice and personal corruption. This frontal attack upon the entire social system of India made for the most powerful defence of the British Raj and made all the claims of *swaraj* (self-rule) seem absurd. This book was widely debated in newspaper columns, journals, articles and in public in India, Britain and the USA. Over twenty different books, a dozen pamphlets and at least one Broadway musical appeared in direct response to *Mother India*. It appeared on best sellers' lists in the USA during 1927 and 1928, and undoubtedly influenced the attitudes of many Americans towards India. It also generated a huge controversy owing to its claims of authenticity. See MSA, Home (special) F. no. 715, 1927, pp. 15–275.

74 IOR, L/P&J/8/128, Coll. no. 105-A, pt. XV, Feb.–Sep. 1939. See *Kinematograph Weekly* (15 Dec. 1939).

75 The Sadgops of medieval Bengal, for instance, migrated to virgin lands along the Bengal-Bihar border and sometimes also carved out local principalities. See Sarkar, *Modern India*, p. 55

76 Various scholars of modern India have demonstrated the manipulation of caste by the imperialists. In the colonial period, mobilisation of caste became essential for social recognition, jobs, political favours, etc. A direct contribution to this came in the 1901 census, when castes came to be classified every ten years on the basis of social precedence as recognised by 'native public opinion'. This immediately encouraged a flood of claims and counter-claims among different caste groups, galvanised caste associations and caste movements. See for example, Joan P. Mechner, 'On being an untouchable in India: a materialist perspective', in Eric B. Ross (ed.), *Beyond the Myth of Culture: Essays in Cultural Materialism* (New York & London, Academic Press, 1980), pp. 261–94; Arjun Appadurai, 'Number in the colonial imagination' in Carol A. Breckenridge and P. van der Veer (eds), *Orientalism and the Post-Colonial Predicament* (Delhi, Oxford University Press, 1994), pp. 314–40; Nicholas Dirks, 'Caste of mind', *Representations*, 37 (Winter 1992), pp. 56–78; Arjun Appadurai, 'Putting hierarchy in

its place', *Current Anthropology*, 3:1 (Feb. 1988), pp. 36–49; Rashmi Pant, 'The cognitive status of caste in colonial ethnography', *Indian Economic and Social History Review*, 24 (1987), pp. 145–62; and C. J. Fuller (ed.), *Caste Today* (Delhi, Oxford University Press, 1996).

77 For example, the 1930 Self-Respect movement in Tamil Nadu, under E. V. Ramaswami Naicker and Satya Shodhak, in Maharashtra. See Gail Omvedt, *Cultural Revolt in Colonial Society: The Non-Brahmin Movement in Western India, 1873–1930* (Bombay, Scientific Socialist Education Trust, 1976), pp. 137–62; 295–9.

78 Mechner, 'On being an untouchable in India', pp. 261–94.

79 P. K. Nair's observations are based upon his extensive talks with several producers of the 1930s and 1940s.

80 This movement was started by Sajjad Zaheer and Mulk Raj Anand, and included others such as Munshi Premchand, Sadat Hasan Manto, Rajinder Singh Bedi and Ismat Chugtai.

81 This was especially felt in certain sections of the army. See Henry Lawrence writing in the *Calcutta Review* in 1840s cited in Sarkar, *Modern India*, p. 34.

82 At the end of second Round Table Conference itself, Gandhi had indicated his determination to risk his life in order to keep the untouchables part of the Hindu community.

83 For details see David Omissi, '"Martial race": ethnicity and security in colonial India, 1858–1939', *War and Society*, 9:1 (May 1991), pp. 1–27.

84 General K. S. Thimayya cited in Steven P. Cohen, *The Indian Army: Its Contribution to the Development of a Nation* (Delhi, Oxford University Press, 1990), p. 123.

85 Milan Hauner, *India in Axis Strategy: Germany, Japan and Indian Nationalists in the Second World War* (London, German Historical Institute, 1981), p. 127.

86 George E. Turner, 'The making of *Gunga Din*', *American Cinematograph*, 63:9 (Sep. 1982), pp. 895–9, 958, 964.

87 Lionel Caplan, 'Bravest of the brave: representations of "the Gurkha" in British military writings', *Modern Asian Studies*, 25:3 (1991), pp. 571–97.

88 *Bombay Chronicle* (15 Sep. 1939), p. 10.

89 *Film India* (Feb. 1939), pp. 26–7.

90 This feature has been described by John Masters in several novels and the two volumes of autobiography, *Bugles and the Tiger* (New York, Viking Press, 1956) and *The Road Past Mandalay* (London, Michael Joseph, 1961). Also see Cohen, *The Indian Army*, p. 50; and Caplan, 'Bravest of the brave', pp. 571–97.

91 Russell Ferguson, writing from the point of view of a twelve-year old schoolboy wrote: '[There] was a silly bit, all the same, where Douglas Fairbanks nearly got married – no wonder the other boys all laughed at him … He should have had more sense. When I get to India I am not going to get married or engaged or anything, the girls can make love to me as much as they like, I won't pay any attention to them, I will just stay in the army fighting all the enemy and killing them all. When I get wounded I will crawl about shooting black fellows harder than ever, especially those who are just going to kill my chums'. *Sight and Sound*, 8:29 (Spring 1939), pp. 4–5.

92 Shohat and Stam argue that in Hollywood films the subtext of inter-racial homoeroticism forms part of a long tradition that runs from *Robinson Crusoe* and *Huckleberry Finn* to *Around the World in 80 Days* (in the figures of Phileas Fogg and his dark servant Passepartout). The film, *Trader Horn* (1930), glorifying British imperialism in Africa, develops a strong homoerotic subtext in the relations between white adventurer protagonist and his black servant, whom he verbally abused throughout the film but whom he carries and caresses when the servant is wounded. The film's emotional paroxysm comes in a tearful homage after the death of the black 'boy', not unlike the tribute paid to Gunga Din after his death. See Ella Shohat and Robert Stam, *Unthinking Eurocentrism: Multiculturalism and the Media* (London & New York, Routledge, 1994), p. 168.

93 The abusive behaviour of officers towards their subordinates in the army is widely accepted in the army circles as a form of practice prevalent under the British and followed to this day. The Indian army officers opine that this behaviour is not only expected of them by their men but is something which the *Jawans* (soldiers) do not mind.

94 Cohen, *The Indian Army*, p. 145.

95 See John Master's account in his autobiography, *Bugles and a Tiger*, p. 75.

96 Ashis Nandy, *The Intimate Enemy: Loss and Recovery of Self under Colonialism* (Delhi, Oxford University Press, 1988), pp. 32–79.

97 MSA, Home Poll. F. no. 81, 1939–41. See confidential information from general staff branch, military intelligence directorate, dated 20 Jan. 1944. This information was given when a second attempt was made to release this film in its re-edited version in India, during the war.

98 *Ibid*. See note of the interservice public relations directorate, dated 29 Feb. 1944. The re-edited version, after drastic cuts, was declared 'rather incomprehensible even for a European audience'.

99 AICC Papers, F. no. P–16, 1939–40, pp. 99–101.

100 MSA, Home Poll. F. no. 81, 1939–41. Cited in a report dated 20 Jan. 1944, regarding the screening of this film in India in 1939.

101 The strong reaction against militarism produced by World War I, leading to a dismantling of the great military machine, along with overwhelming pacifist sentiment, in Britain, had meant that by the 1930s the British army was stagnating as an instrument of war. The British government's decision to rearm could not obliterate the pacifist sentiment in Britain nor raise the prestige of the army. These factors were to prove a great hindrance to the recruitment drive of the British in the wake of the growing militarisation of Germany. See Correlli Barnet, *Britain and Her Army, 1509–1970: A Military, Political and Social Survey* (London, Helen Lane, Penguin Press, 1970), pp. 84, 410–2; and Brian Bond, *British Military Policy Between the Two World Wars* (Oxford, Clarendon Press, 1980), pp. 35–6.

102 For a variety of reasons why India was not popular with British recruits to the British Indian army see Bond, *British Military Policy*, pp. 98–126. It was perhaps not unintentional that these films of army life showed a highly romanticised colonial army service. A display of pageantry, dances, processions, parades, banquets, linked with personal dramas, made army service a highly attractive and adventurous one. As a film critic pointed out, 'The glitter of lowered lancers, the scudding thunder of hoof and heavy gun, the rally, the revenge, the silver mutiny of trumpets – all were sufficient to persuade the most ardent pacifist, of war's undoubted glamour.' BFi, see a review of *The Charge of the Light Brigade*, dated 27 Dec. 1936.

103 Cited in Byron Farwell, *Armies of the Raj: From the Mutiny to Independence, 1858–1947* (London, Viking Press, 1990), pp. 207–8. For a similar opinion of the British Indian army officers see Cohen, *The Indian Army*, pp. 116–17.

104 Cohen, *The Indian army*, p. 125.

105 Thompson, *A Letter from India*, pp. 80–1.

106 Cited in Jeffrey Richards, 'Boys own Empire: feature films and imperialism in the 1930s', in John M. Mackenzie (ed.), *Imperialism and Popular Culture* (Manchester, Manchester University Press, 1986), p. 144.

107 *Ibid.*

108 *Screen Picture* (Mar. 1937).

109 *Sight and Sound*, 8:29 (Spring 1939), pp. 4–5.

110 *Bombay Chronicle* (15 Feb. 1939), p. 10.

111 *Bombay Chronicle* (8 Feb. 1939), p. 10.

112 *Film India* (Apr. 1939), pp. 3–5.

113 *Bombay Chronicle* (19 Apr. 1939), p. 10.

114 *Bombay Chronicle* (20 Apr. 1939), p. 10.

115 *Film India* (Apr. 1939), p. 26; (May 1939), p. 9.

116 *Ibid.* Also cited in *Bombay Chronicle* (19 Apr. 1939), p. 10.

117 *Bombay Chronicle* (17 Dec. 1939), p. 23.

118 *Film India* (Apr. 1939), p. 25; (May 1939), p. 25.

119 *Film India* (Apr. 1939). See Sir Reginald Maxwell, the home member in the Central Legislative Assembly, replying to the question of S. Satyamurthy, cited on p. 34.

120 IOR, L/P&J/8/126, Coll. no. 105-A, pt. 1, Oct. 1935–May 1940. See J. W. P. Chidwell of the P&J department to R. W. A. Leeper of the foreign office, London, 10 May 1939.

121 Richards, *Dream Palace*, p. 152.

122 See, for example, Roy Armes, *A Critical History of the British Cinema* (London, Secker and Warburg, 1978), p. 125; and Clive Coultass, 'British feature films and the Second World War', *Journal of Contemporary History*, 19:1 (Jan. 1984), pp. 7–22. Coultass calls this phenomenon 'nostalgia for the period of expansion'.

123 Suhash Chakravarty argues that the hold of imperial consciousness on the British psyche was very strong even in the 1930s and 1940s. Despite heightened anti-imperialist consciousness, it even permeated the perceptions of the liberals and the declared friends and sympathisers of India, as also the British left, particularly its intellectual representatives. See Suhash Chakravarti, *The Raj Syndrome: A Study in Imperial Perceptions* (Delhi, Chanakya Publications, 1989). Hutchins has called this 'the illusion of permanence' – the idea that whatever may be said about the progress towards ultimate independence, the British in fact expected and believed that their empire was timeless and eternal. See Francis Hutchins, *The Illusion of Permanence* (Princeton, Princeton University Press, 1967).

4

The Rains Came (1940): imperialism, racism and gender relations

The changing imperatives in the strategies of colonial rule in the late 1930s, as well as the altered conditions in India and the world over, demanded a kind of image and message production in the cinema, which could feed into the discourse of imperialism and colonialism. This was exemplified in the film, *The Rains Came*. Made in late 1939 and released in India in 1940 by Twentieth-Century Fox, it focused attention on indirect rather than direct rule in British India and showed the emergence of a 'new India' under British colonial domination. Produced by Darryl F. Zanuck and directed by Clarence Brown, it was based on a novel written by Louis Bromfield. The main leads were Myrna Loy, George Brent and Tyrone Power.

Set in the British India of 1938 it contradictorily emphasised the developmental side of British rule under moralistic paternalism and projected a new image of the empire as partnership. Widely publicised as the 'true face of modern India', the film produced a grand narrative of social progress, exploring the evolution of imperial relationships and focusing on developments in Indian society. The film reinforced the myth of 'two Indias' and the fast disappearing personal traditions of governance. In creating princely India as 'Indian India' the film lent itself to a highly complex reading which shed fresh light on imperial strategy and the British colonial ideological premise. The film conceived the Indian princes as potential sources of political leadership and support. The partnership so visualised called upon the traditional world of the states to bulwark the 'democratic' world of the provinces. The British, fenced in as they were by the demands of nationalists, depended more and more on the conservative interest groups and ideologues. The reinforcement of communal and casteist forces, on the one hand, and the cultivation and politicisation of Indian princes, on the other, were two sides of the same imperialist coin. In consolidating the Indian princes as the last vestige of Indian sovereign power, the film sought to use them as a valuable propaganda vehicle. This chapter emphasises how it was part of British imperial strategy to project princes favourably at this time in an obvious attempt to consolidate loyal conservative opinion. The film has to be seen as a part of London's last propaganda effort to hold India within the empire.

The Rains Came is located within its historical frames in order to demonstrate that changed ethnic and gender images, reflecting on racism and imperialism, were made to surface at a strategic moment. Curiously, at the heart of this film lay the inflammable theme of miscegenation in the shape of an interracial romance between an enlightened western-educated Indian prince and an English woman. As such, The Rains Came projected a complex configuration of gender, race and class to articulate a fresh understanding of the British empire in India. It sought to show how this film used the ambiguous role represented by western women in a colonial setting to promote imperialism and its ideology of the innate superiority of the British race. The earlier emphasis on the masculine nature of colonialism, with its essential components of domination, control and structures of unequal power was to be partially reversed. It rejected the notion of empire solely as a male proponent and introduced the white female as the central catalytic agent. This emphasis on the non-threatening feminine nature of imperialism opened up the possibilities of negotiating a different agenda within the colonial setting. Depicted as an agent of civilisation and a conduit for a better, more civilised and modern society, the white woman allowed Britain the more progressive role of developer, which not merely brought social and economic development of the colony, but also afforded training to the native to stand on his own feet.

Endorsement and justification of imperial notions of superiority are subverted by an equivocal treatment of the colonised male. The historical juncture changed the production-thrust of knowledge about India and Indians in British orientalist discourse. The notion of colonial and colonised identity itself was problematised. The transcendence of racial and cultural differences in gender relationships offer an alternative reading of imperialist, racist and masculine ideology, highlighted in other empire films offering an insight into the working of race and class ideologies. Thus, in a significant way, the film both subverts as well as reinforces the western notions of race, culture and gender to allow for a more textured understanding of their dynamics.

Images and accentuation: old and new

The Rains Came with its emphasis on gender along with race and class was totally different from the films that antedated it. It marked a decisive break with the high-adventure genre of films made during the decade 1929–39, with India as its central theme. Thematically, the high-adventure films located in the Frontier revolved around the revolt of some tribal chief who planned to oust the British from India with the help of outside foreign powers. The British Indian army crushes this revolt ruthlessly and brings about peace and order for the inhabitants of India.

By the late 1930s, this political stance in the films was to prove highly embarrassing to the British in India. The adventure genre films were drawing attention to the NWFP, the British policy followed in this region and the British Indian army at a time when these had come under severe attack in India and abroad. The Frontier was undergoing its most active anti-imperialist and nationalist phase. This movement was greatly strengthened by prolonged tribal insurrections in the non-tribal territories of this region, which could not be controlled despite extensive and ruthless operations by the British Indian army. This was under attack from the nationalists in India for its racial and imperialist underpinning and showed severe disaffection among its lower ranks. The concentrated focus of the empire films on the British Indian army could well find its most vulnerable spectator group among the Indian soldiers as they provided a significant sector of the Indian audience for western films.

The years 1937–38 also saw an escalation of anti-British propaganda by Italy and Germany, especially in relation to India's NWFP. They propagated the negative aspects of British colonialism under which Indians showed no progress. The empire cinema was seen as proof of this. Sections of the US media were also highly critical of British imperialism. Its criticism of the empire films was picked up by the Indian media to reinforce its own attacks of the British. Protests in India against the empire cinema voiced through petitions, in the press and State and Central Legislative assemblies had grown over the years.

In such a sensitive political situation, the release of *The Drum* in September 1938, justifying the British Frontier policy, and recreating communal stereotypes among the Muslims, was to create opposition among different sections in India and nervousness among British officials. The wide-scale agitation against it proved the proverbial last straw. *The Drum* had to be banned, as also *Gunga Din,* which had followed it in quick succession. It was realised that the adventure genre package of films, by concentrating on the exotic, oriental or backward side of India for consumption by the white audience, were actually proving counter-productive and playing into the hands of Britain's antagonists.

Consequently, the need to replace the image of India created by the Gunga Din stereotype was urgently required so as to underline the modern progressive nature of British achievements in India and to counteract the themes of colonial oppression and India's backwardness under British colonialism. This clearly meant that the high-adventure military drama films, which had shown conquest and subjugation requiring a masculine capacity, had to be dropped as a central theme. In addition, the management of the empire was shown in these films as a distinctly British prerogative that denied any representation of the local people. Foregrounding military action also automatically showed up the exploitation and use of force in the colony. The colonial service was presented as a male domain with its masculine ideology and military organisation, processes and rituals of power and hierarchy. This need for a reversal in the empire cinema was finally implemented in *The Rains Came.* The film sought to suggest a constructive partnership under British rule, playing down both the glorification of the British and the negative image of Indian life and customs.[1]

The most constructive prop in the British opinion lay in their partnership with the Indian princes. Consequently, the film, *The Rains Came,* based on a vastly popular book written by the US author, Louis Bromfield, in 1937, was given the go-ahead by the BBFC. The board with its greatly tightened hold over the production of films, its pre- and post-censorship practices, and its effective threat of banning a given film throughout the British empire, was in a position to dictate to the film-makers both of Britain and Hollywood. This close surveillance of films extended from the choice of the subject to its ideological content. The end- product, therefore, always had the stamp of approval of the British authorities.

Regarding filming of *The Rains Came*, several proposals had been made to the BBFC by different Hollywood companies. These had been firmly rejected at least on three different occasions. Its theme had at first been resolutely dismissed as an 'unsuitable subject' for the production of a film.[2] It was only in 1938–39 that the board reversed its earlier decision after eliciting the views of the India Office. This film came to be given a closer scrutiny and a far greater supervision than any other film by the British censors and the India Office authorities, in consultation with British colonial officials in India. The BBFC deleted from the film script 'practically all the immorality which was so flagrant in the book'.[3] Copies of the revised script of the film were sent to seek clearance from the India Office and the BBFC. Detailed instructions were sent by the India Office not only to delineate British characters in the film in a fine manner but also to portray favourably the Indian characters and to avoid any difference of opinion between the British and Indians.[4] In view of the reservations of British officials in India the story was greatly modified according to the dictates of the board.

Throughout the making of this film, a close contact with British authorities was maintained and care was taken to implement any suggestions emanating from them. In return they were assured that everything possible would be done to help get this film through. F. L. Harley, the managing director of Twentieth-Century Fox in a most revealing remark to Lt.-Col. A. F. Rawson Lumby of the military department in the India Office, London, declared *The Rains Came* to be 'a great tribute to India and one which would be helpful under existing conditions'.[5] Some of the highest India Office officials like the under-secretary of state for India, as well as military officials, even viewed the film before it was released to determine the way 'new India' was projected.[6] This cinematic change brought into the empire cinema those aspects of India that had not been considered suitable earlier.[7]

The officially approved scenario of *The Rains Came* is as follows:

In Rajputana, a district in the north west of India, is the native state of Ranchipur, ruled wisely by an ageing Maharaja and his Maharani. Tom Ransome, an artist who had lived well, having drifted to Ranchipur, is settled there. Mrs. Simon, the snobbish wife of an American missionary, invites Ransome to a tea party where he meets Fern Simon, young and pretty and utterly discontented with her life at home. She tries to enlist Ransome's sympathies to help her escape. Lord and Lady Esketh arrive to stay at the palace and Ransome is invited to meet them. He finds lady Esketh to be Edwina, an old love of his and an unrepentant gold digger. She is married to a common millionaire, whom she despises.

Fern arrives at night at Ransome's bungalow, wishing to stay and damage her reputation. Ransome persuades her to go to Smileys', Americans who run a mission school, and whose house is kept by Aunt Phoebe Smiley, a thoroughly homely and understanding person. Edwina meets Major Rama Safti, a young Indian *adopted and educated by the Maharaja, who is in charge of the hospital and has fine ideals for the welfare of India.* She starts to vamp him and Ransome tries to intervene with no success. The overdue rains come, there is an earthquake, *the dam* bursts and terrible floods ensue. Lord Esketh has taken ill and dies in this earthquake. The Simons are killed too and Fern goes to Ransome's bungalow in a boat to rescue him. Edwina is with him, they having dined together with friends. Ransome takes Edwina to the Smileys and returns for Fern. The Maharaja dies and *the Maharani takes control of the organisation, forming a council. Communications are cut,* and there is an outbreak of plague. Ransome is given work to do and he gets Fern to help him. The Smileys' house is full of rescued children. *Edwina volunteers to work at the hospital to be near Safti. An airplane arrives with messages from the Viceroy and news that food was being sent in more planes.* There is room for one more passenger to return to safety; the Maharani decides Edwina must go as she intends to hand over the ruling of Ranchipur to Safti and *he must marry an Indian.* Edwina believes she is really in love, and *Safti, infatuated, declares he will renounce*

Ranchipur and follow her. However, Edwina is tired and careless, and drinks from a glass used by a dying patient, she contracts plague and dies. *Before her death, she tells Ransome that she has left 100,000 pounds to be used for the state of Ranchipur.* Ransome marries Fern. *Safti becomes Maharaja and with the help of Edwina's legacy, Ranchipur is rebuilt.*[8] (emphasis added)

This changed imagery, emphasising the developmental side of British colonialism, located in princely India, sought to produce an aura of liberal constitutionalism by stressing the practice of indirect rule through loyal native chiefs and councils. From the 1920s onwards the loyal Indian prince had a new focus in the literary imagination.[9] Up to this point, on the rare occasions when depicted, the Indian princes were shown in negative terms as proof that direct British rule was beneficial. The popular images and ideologies of the princes showed them to be indolent, corrupt, sexually depraved, buffoons, worthless figures and, by and large, puppets in the hands of British administrators.[10] A similar celluloid portrayal of the oriental rulers was also made.[11]

Politically, this opinion regarding princely states was far from unanimous. Since the first half of the nineteenth century there was an on-going debate concerning the relative merits of British and Indian rule.[12] But little heed was paid to these opinions. Now, the more politically conscious writers in the period after World War I were stressing their loyalty. Maud Diver, for example, in her book published in 1938, makes reference to the aristocratic nature of Indian society which could only be properly reorganised through a federation of princes rather than any democratic government.[13]

The Rains Came was a part of the same drive. It used the cultural identification of India – in which kings and kingship were a part of India's image abroad, and thus easily identifiable to the western public – to extend recognition of the worth and contribution of the princes to the British colonial empire. It attempted to cash in on the political legitimacy enjoyed by the Indian rulers, based on the immense reservoir of loyalty which the rulers commanded, their deification by their subjects and the respect and veneration offered to them by many Indians in British provinces.[14] This meant a reversal in a substantial way of the hitherto held and popularised images and ideologies associated with princes. The reasons for this image and ideological reversal, crucial to the making of *The Rains Came*, need to be historically located and understood.

Historical complexity: princely states and development

In imperial politics, the princely states had come to dominate more and more London's strategic thinking about the subcontinent. In the early twentieth century they served as an important break-water not only against armed rebellion (as in the nineteenth century) but also against the menacing political consciousness that threatened a move towards democracy in British-administered India. They were used repeatedly by the British at every stage of political concession as a counterpoint to the growing nationalist demands.[15] The relationship between the crown and the princes had been so close that a retired British official unblushingly described them in 1929 as 'our sheet anchor in India'.[16] Compelled to make political concessions in the form of the Government of India Act of 1935, the British effectively used the princes to counteract their offer of responsible government – the federal structure was to come into effect only after fifty per cent of the princes had formally acceded to it. Although the federal part of the act was never implemented, the British had created for the Central Legislative Assembly a powerful princely bloc, forming one-third of the total members of the proposed federal legislature, to checkmate nationalist pressures.

With the establishment of popular governments in the provinces, the British and the princely states came to face a far graver challenge to their established authorities. The two years of provincial autonomy (1937–39) stand out as years of great turmoil in the Indian states, witness to a large number of movements demanding responsible governments and reforms. The local organisations or the States' People's Conferences (*Praja Mandals*), which had sprouted in many of the states in the first and second decades of the twentieth century, multiplied greatly in number spreading during this period, extending into states that had earlier had no such organisations. Major struggles broke out in Jaipur, Kashmir, Rajkot, Patiala, Hyderabad, Mysore, Travancore and the Orissa states. As the states' peoples movement against princely autocracy gathered momentum, the

Congress was forced to change its stand regarding princely states. So far the Congress had hesitated in giving open support to agitators, which, in the context of the near total lack of political rights and rampant feudal oppression characteristic of many states, had considerable socially radical potential. In February 1938, for the first time, the Congress declared the *Purna Swaraj* (full independence) ideal to cover the states. This shift endorsed by Gandhi was formalised by the Congress resolution at Tripuri in the States' Peoples Conference in March 1939.

The pressure of this link-up and the mounting apprehensions of the British and their most dependable allies – the princes – forced the British Raj to contain the popular movements that had broken out in the princely states, in order to subvert the charge of despotism and corruption. Most of the princely states were run as unmitigated autocracies and stood in direct contrast to the limited democracy operative in the provinces at this time.

This made the British position particularly shaky. The British were unnerved by the ability shown by the Indians in the post-1935 phase in tackling democracy and the escalation of their democratic aspirations and hopes. The Indian politicians could hardly be told that they lacked the ability or the experience to govern themselves; the records of the Indian provincial ministries proved otherwise. It, therefore, became essential that India's other face be shown, which, in British perception, could be found among the vast multitudes in the princely states who did not want democracy and were not familiar with the concept of democracy or self-rule. An attempt was made to suggest that democracy had no roots in India. William Barton, a senior British officer in the colonial political service catering to the Indian states, stressed this fact in relation to the states in the 1930s and asserted that the states were capable of giving their people good government without an 'injection of democracy'.[17]

In fact, the British projected what Rosita Forbes, a freelance journalist and author, taking the British official line, professed in 1939: if the British were to withdraw altogether 'India would revert from most of the western democratic institutions imposed on her to forms of autocracy more or less benevolent. For India will always follow the man rather than the cause.'[18] She goes on to quote an Indian ruler as saying: 'What is this talk of democracy? Were the British to leave India there would not be a

Province left. We would come back into our own.' Another prince, in a more revealing commentary, pontificated: 'India cannot altogether break away from her past. Her development and her progress must be a logical result of what she has been.'[19]

In redrawing the political map of India and concentrating on two-fifths of India (712,000 square miles), with nearly one-quarter of the Indian population (81 million) outside direct British control and its concept of democracy, the film sought to emphasise and evoke an entire governing order with roots going back to antiquity. On the one hand, it suggested that, historically, an enlightened princely order, albeit under British protection, was there to stay. It also confirmed the imperial attitude that the princes required external assistance as their governments would face extinction should the Congress come to power.[20] On the other hand, this 'Indian India' was posed as a problem in new India. This led to a subtle suggestion that, for democracy to survive in India, the forestalling of the princes was necessary, which the British alone could do. In any reading, whether from the point of view of the princely states or the nationalists, the subtle suggestion was that the British were needed for a longer time.

Therefore, in this portrayal, the princes are not shown on the decline but in a modernising, ascending order. The propaganda in the 1930s concentrated on projecting the 'Indian India' as it had been spoken of by the Indian nationalists in the late nineteenth and early twentieth centuries. Although nationalists had displayed a wide variety of attitudes, the princes and their states had also been glorified by them as examples of how well Indians were able to govern themselves in order to refute arguments about the necessity for British trusteeship.[21] Every instance of political and social reform in the Indian states had been magnified, partly to inflate the image of Indian rulership and partly to obliquely criticise British politics. However, by the late 1930s there was a radical change of opinion among the nationalists regarding the princes and their role in independent India, as I shall discuss presently. The British chose to ignore this changed opinion.

Due to political exigencies and the great need to use the princely states against the rising tide of nationalism and democracy, the British political service officials reiterated the following point of view, also hinted at in *The Rains Came*: 'In the context

of the time, a well-ruled Indian state was a better form of administration than anything we had in British India, because it was an
Indian ruling his own people – not just a Governor, but a man
whose dynasty had always ruled, so that *ma-baap*, the mother
and father of his people, was what he was.'[22]

This well-ruled state was significantly possible only under
British overall paramountcy. British opinion held that democracy
would cause chaos for princely India, just as it had done for
British India.[23] The film uses the rains and their havoc as
symbolic of this anarchy, and the princes are shown to guide
India towards an ordered development as signified by the British
connection.

In fact, many British officials in the political service saw the
princes as the last survivors of 'Indian India', which they claimed
governed in trusteeship in order to raise it to western standards of
civilised life,[24] as shown in the film. Yet, even the most enthusiastic British officials were reluctant to press for reforms, if such
activity would jeopardise broader imperial concerns. In fact,
many a potential reformer among the rulers was gradually
drained of initiative by the constant surveillance and interference
exercised by the British government through their appointed residents in the states. There were exceptions, however, and some
states, like Baroda and Mysore succeeded in promoting partial
industrial and agricultural development, administration and
political reforms and education to a limited degree. In this, the
basic logic underlying British rule in India, direct or indirect, was
the same. Although the states were not annexed by the British,
they were nevertheless controlled, used or exploited by them. As
Bharati Ray argues, 'Imperial and pragmatic considerations and
no ideology or zest for modernisation, dictated British action in
each state and in each case. By siding with the forces of modernisation, if possible, by supporting reactionary elements when
necessary, British paramountcy was steadily maintained.'[25]

This film, on the other hand, revealingly highlighted developmental aspects of the princely states as part of the new thrust in
British propaganda, which characterised overall British colonial
rule in India. Colonial domination was shown as a powerful agent
of modernisation, as an entry into the modern, industrial age. The
concept of development and modernisation had made a significant appearance in the interwar period.[26] This was the time when

'the civilising mission' of the west had come under sustained and skilful attack.[27] The civilising mission, located in biologically based racism, had emphasised the colonised as beyond the preview of the coloniser's civilising efforts. The colonised were identified by their racial characterisation and were often regarded as mentally inferior in the fields of technology, science, art, religion and morals. Racial difference and inferior ability were presented as a descriptive reflection of reality. By the 1930s this had been firmly rejected. The new eugenics did not hold the inherited qualities of a specimen to be fixed, but accepted that these were changeable and there was a moral duty to improve the human stock.[28] The concept of development incorporating this thrust of racism envisioned the colonised as the main agents of the transformation of their society, albeit under the guidance of the colonial masters. This concept of development justified white dominance and its continuation in a new way.

Yet, the portrayal of the colonial masters, as development workers, employed in ridding India of its social stagnation, backwardness, and massive poverty caused by cultural ineptitude, could well be read as a version of the same racial theme as before. This paternalistic policy, on the converse side, showed the deeply rooted mistrust of the native will and ability. That development was offered from the outside by the colonisers smacked of patronage – a boon from the top that not only ignored any demand from the colonised people for independence but also refused to consider colonial policies in relation to that demand. Such a position would have minimised the concept of bestowed bounty and shown it merely as an additional advantage for themselves and for keeping their position intact in the colonies – a direct necessity for survival. In fact, the interwar period for the British was a critical one, during which it had become difficult for the Raj to sustain itself in India. Consequently, they had to grant more and more concessions. The film effectively reversed this reality.

The developmental ideological thrust certainly meant that the image of the lazy, dull, mentally deficient native was changed. He was promoted from underling to fellow, still inferior but available to moral and intellectual improvement under white guidance. Yet, cinematically, this fine distinction could hardly by maintained; there was many a slippage in the non-white characterisation, as I shall show presently. Ultimately, the paternalism of *The Rains Came* was reminiscent of the same racist stereotype about defective human material, which had survived in the popular discourse and had been used in earlier films to explain the contrast between superior and inferior.

As desired by British authorities, the US publicity and film reviews, followed closely by those of Britain, concentrated on the developmental and modernising effects of the imperial rule in India.[29] In this, stress was placed on 'real service', that is, philanthropy rendered through 'selfless' women. This changed focus on women – reconstituted as agents of reform of colonial subjects – cinematically acknowledged a process that began in the nineteenth century, when there was a widespread induction of white women in diverse and complex ways – as missionaries, educationalists, social reformers and doctors – into the otherwise largely male enterprise of empire building. This restructuring was needed to shift the accent from the basic legitimisation of conquest over natives for economic and military superiority to moral superiority.

The Rains Came represented this new face of British imperialism. It replaced the masculine ethos by feminine modes that at once projected sympathetic understanding, with a move towards egalitarian rather than authoritarian relations. The covert homoerotic bond of the earlier films between loyal Indians in the army and British officers was replaced with different sexual and symbolic suggestions regarding interpersonal relationships between the colonists and the colonised. Although the central Indian figure still remained the loyal male Indian, the dominating love affair was now heterosexual with a female representing the developmental mission of the British rather than conquest and subjugation. Yet, the power equations were to remain the same, with a superior and inferior bonded together in loyalty and love. The heart of the film lay in a cross-racial liaison, which not only lent itself to a highly ambiguous reading but also offered a valuable comment on imperialism, racism and gender relations.

Miscegenation: resolving contradictions

The crucial plot on which the film hinges deals with the hitherto taboo theme in the films: miscegenation. An earlier British film on this theme, *The Chinese Bungalow* (1926), was refused certification in India because it introduced 'the vexed question of marriages between western women and Orientals'.[30] Miscegenation nevertheless was, and remained, a popular melo-dramatic theme in the west calculated to provoke among white viewers latent desire and a sense of possession for the Other. In view of the attraction of this theme, a few attempts to produce films centred on miscegenation were made in 1931 and 1932; these were rejected at the synopsis stage itself. In 1933, however, Frank Capra filmed *The Bitter Tea of General Yen*, dealing with the love of a Chinese warlord for an American girl. This film, although screened in the west, was banned throughout the British empire.

The official acceptance of this theme and imagery in *The Rains Came* in 1939, therefore, has enormous significance. The images of a cross-colour interlude between Lady Edwina Esketh and Crown Prince Rama Safti have to be understood in terms of the sexual and racial construction of the colonial female and native male and their friendship across the colonial divide. This friendship seeks to foreclose the physical and psychological distancing of the colonisers and the colonised (illustration 7). All earlier films had emphasised this distance, which symbolised the relationship of the colony with its master. The high-adventure films had shown the colonists separated from the indigenous people in segregated residential and recreational areas, thus rationalising spatial segregation in military terms. Racial exclusivity of the white women was necessary as her relations with native men and women were considered subversive to the colonial order. In fact, the most virulent objections to the empire films were on racial grounds.

This portrayal needed to be corrected, especially as opposition to racist practices, a common focus of the nationalist campaign, was one thing that united competing nationalist groups. Indeed, the declared government policy was against racial discrimination. Yet, all the earlier films, with their focus on the British Indian army (under constant nationalist attack for denying Indianisation), had highlighted colonial racial discrimination rather than denying it. *The Rains Came* sought to neutralise the social exclusiveness of the British towards their non-white subjects. Consequently, the erection of insurmountable barriers against contact with native people were breached in the film. *The*

Rains Came tried to portray the trust and confidence built over the years, and show an admirable feature of British imperialism in India: namely, that there was virtually no race prejudice of any kind that prevailed. It showed physical and emotional intimacy to be not only possible between the coloniser and the colonised but also to be beneficial to the latter (illustration 9).

Importantly, it is the white woman who extends her hand and initiates the relationship. The film endows the white woman with initiative in going beyond the constraints of the colonial hierarchy to cross racial boundaries. It was a deliberate recasting of a white woman from the position of stereotypical, marginal figure to central character that helped redefine gender and racial relations in empire cinema. A display of sexuality subverts the image of white woman as vulnerable and passive. Edwina is an active agent in making overtures to the coloured man. In this, she openly challenges the reigning ideology concerning womanhood, sexuality and morality. The outcome of this transgression, however, was in the mould of several other similar transgressions in the colonial fiction – the woman dies as punishment for breaking social conventions. Moreover, Hollywood's production code of 1930–34 explicitly forbade miscegenation and allowed it to be screened only on the condition that it be severely punished at the film's end.[31]

Yet, Edwina's death by plague is not quite the same thing as the Victorian punishment of female transgression. In stories dealing with the theme of miscegenation there is the continued belief that nothing but evil can come from such a relationship because of the enormous difference between ways of life. In *The Rains Came*, the reverse is repeatedly highlighted. In a number of ways, the film delineates the benefits of such a relationship, which accrue to the colonised.

This transgression also challenges the whole system of racist and masculinist domination and subverts the concept of racial superiority. An alliance or contact between the native male and European female went against the notions of male and superior white racial domination. It recreated fears of loss of race, class and status. In colonial scholarship it has been observed that sexual domination has figured as a social metaphor of European supremacy. Thus, in Edward Said's treatment of orientalist discourse, the sexual submission and possession of oriental women by European men 'stands for the pattern of relative strength between east and west'.[32] In this 'male power-fantasy', the orient is 'penetrated, silenced and possessed'. *The Rains Came*, however, reversed this order. In doing so it also eliminated the binary opposition of the nationalist enterprise versus imperialism and its homogenised orientalism. Orientalism itself was made more complex.

The Rains Came demonstrated a greater diversity and complexity of experience that underlay the discourse of imperialism, racism, sexism and gender reconstruction. For example, this reversal may be seen as reviving the ultimate fear and fantasies of miscegenation – that is, the rape of a white woman by a coloured man – and recapturing the entire backlog of 'racial memory' of Mutiny days and the sexual threat Indian men posed to the white women.[33] Recent scholarship has very convincingly argued that this sexual fear of the native was used as a trope to depict covert challenges to the colonial order, even as outright expression of nationalist resistance.[34] If rape was used, as Jenny Sharpe argues, as 'a concept metaphor for imperialism',[35] what does a sympathetic treatment of miscegenation – especially between a coloured male and white female – indicate? *The Rains Came* goes beyond rape and portrays this alliance as love. In doing so, it introduces several fresh dimensions to the nature of its imperial domination in India.

Located in historical frames of reference, *The Rains Came* demonstrates that miscegenation, considered fearful by the colonists, was made to surface at this strategic moment to produce value for colonialism. On the one hand, it breaks the taboo of racial segregation at a very crucial time – allegorically, Edwina is Britain who loves India (Rama). This is an image of a British–Indian relationship in which Britain is the giver and India is the receiver. On the other hand, by incorporating this cross-racial alliance and accepting it as a 'non-threatening', even desirable, deliberately denies a challenge to its authority. This redefinition of sexual access and morality in the film emerged during a crisis of colonial control precisely because British rule in the late 1930s was being questioned and challenged as never before. By denying this fear it sought to reassert its confidence. The theme of miscegenation was used to reformulate or re-express imperial domination in India.

However, the miscegenation in *The Rains Came* has also to be located in relation to the actual experience of those who lived in colonial societies in order to give a more complex view of the social relations that the film was opting to portray. In the 1930s there was substance to such interracial alliances: several such unions existed, especially where white women (both British and non-British) had married Indian men. A noticeable number were married to Indian civil servants and army officers and yet others to private individuals.[36] A person of no less stature than Khan Saheb, the Congress premier of the NWFP, had an English wife.[37] Considered a dangerous threat to colonial rule, these legally married white women could not be deported out of India, even during politically sensitive periods.

There were other prominent white women who had become close collaborators of leading sages and political leaders and had achieved acceptance and even reverence at the hands of the nationalists.[38] These western women presented extreme cases of the subversion of imperialism, having crossed sensitive race and gender barriers. Considered 'traitors' by the British, their treachery compounded by their betrayal of 'white womanhood', they were considered to undermine the system in the colony. A distinct embarrassment to the British, the film incorporated women like them, by presenting them as nurturants – a 'gift' – to the colony. What the film sought to cash in on was their acceptance by the colonised and their ability to collaborate across racial categories. It is significant that in the late nineteenth century some prominent Indian men, notably Rammohan Roy and Keshab Chandra Sen, had indeed sought the assistance of British women. The film seems to be capitalising on this fact.

Yet, as Ann Stoler argues, 'miscegenation signalled neither the absence nor presence of racial prejudice in itself; hierarchies of privilege and power were written into the condoning of inter-racial unions, as well as into their condemnation.'[39] Indeed, a possible real life breach of racial barriers was qualified in the film, by replacing racial superiority as a source of power with a sense of shared class superiority. Rama Safti, for example, is royalty with an identifiable western standard of living, dress and life style. A medical doctor, he is also not inferior in the field of technology or science. The film makes it a point to emphasise this class similarity among natives, complete with kings, councillors and those whose style of life was analogous with their own. The racial difference stood blurred at a class level. Hereditary, environmental factors and education determine the new colonial subject, who is no longer wholly determined by racial factors or characteristics.

This erasure of racial difference was also achieved in the film by casting Tyrone Power, a top star of the late 1930s in the USA, as the Indian prince. Well known for his romantic portrayals, Power's star ranking both subsumed the role he played in the film as well as made it more acceptable to his vast fan following among the white audience.[40] His playing the Indian prince made it easier for the film to gratify western female desire for an exotic oriental lover. The film uses the contradiction inherent in racism by acknowledging the attraction it felt for the inferior Other. The attraction felt by Edwina for Rama in preference to the men of her own race is located in the suggested 'difference' between the races, which renders the inferiorised Other attractive in the eyes of a woman. The film effectively explores the possibilities of transgression and fantasises their interracial, cross-colour sexual desires from the point of view of the viewer, before allowing the normative to take over.

This portrayal of miscegenation leaves the image of the white man and his masculinity untouched – an image linked to his ownership both of the white woman and the colony. It is certainly left to the white woman to negotiate the ideology of imperialism but, ultimately, the white woman is treated as a gift of the masculine white world to the colony. She is offered as a civilising agent.

Transgressor as the 'giver': symbolising relationships

Recent feminist writing has argued that women have been used by the empire in a variety of ways leading to an ambiguous position in the colony. They have been both subordinate in colonial hierarchies and served as active agents of imperial enterprise in their own right. *The Rains Came* portrayed this ambiguity to an ideological advantage. Through the character of Edwina, the film focused on what Barbara Ramusack has called 'maternal imperialism'.[41] This focus emphasised the gentler side of imperialism, which nurtured its colony with compassion and understanding, keeping it together as one big imperial family. There is also a suggestion of this in the British-produced film, *The Drum*. Edwina's characterisation in *The Rains Came,* however, was far more clearly and consciously delineated. In fact, her role of 'refined British motherhood', was well in keeping with the traditional view of imperial motherhood symbolised by Queen Victoria. A gigantic statue of Queen Victoria is repeatedly imaged to drive home this point. She represented far greater warmth and sympathy towards Indian people than the white man, who similarly served as civilising agent but also was equated with aggression, masculinity and power. In the symbolic matrices, the physical nature of men translates readily into metaphors of power and effectiveness, whereas that of women does not. This shift not only validated pre-existing structures of colonial authority (with its violent military past) on new grounds, but laid the foundation for the institution of a new imperial order.

Edwina with her devalued life still bestows extraordinary value upon British womanhood and reproduces a developmental discourse of colonialism. A transgressor, she is also the ultimate giver in this relationship. She not only leaves all her inheritance to be used for the building up of Ranchipur, she also renounces her love of a man and bequeaths him to Ranchipur, which has a greater need for him. This transposition of sexuality into the sphere of social action and communication is important, for despite the transgression she shows herself as a responsible imperial citizen. In this she emerges, in the words of Ella Shohat, 'as the vehicle less for a sexual gaze than a colonial gaze'.[42] In this final 'sacrificial' gesture, Edwina symbolises the essence of the relationship which the British in India shared with its colony. Edwina emerges as a martyr, not unlike the missionaries who were popularly perceived in the west as sacrificing their lives for the good of humanity. Edwina uses the ruling class prerogative of power and wealth while using the rhetoric of paternalistic responsibilities. She underlines the unselfish nature of her devotion to the colonial empire and imperial cause by enhancing the reputation of the empire builders as developers.

The Indian experience of Raj, however, was bound to read the transgression differently – as the sexual norms of the 'decadent west' had come under popular attack in the nineteenth century. According to Partha Chatterjee such women came to be parodied and ridiculed in virtually every form of written, oral and visual communication – from the essays of nineteenth-century moralists, to novels, farces, skits, jingles and the paintings of the *patua* (scroll paintings) – and were considered 'brazen, avaricious, irreligious, and sexually promiscuous', like the common women of the lowest social rung.[43]

An enormous reinforcement of these attacks occurred in the aftermath of Katherine Mayo's publication of *Mother India* in 1927, which, by 1937, had undergone forty-two reprints. Highly racist, even the title of her work, *Mother India*, denigrated Indian women by referring to the popular iconography of the nation as mother (*Bharat Mata*) and mother goddess in the nationalist discourse of India.[44] The popular reaction to her attack was to defend Indian womanhood, on the one hand, and to denounce the white woman, on the other, by contrasting Indian women's 'purity' and white women's 'licentiousness'.[45] The general stereotype of the white women in British colonies was that she was not much better than a prostitute – immodest in dress and indulging in drinking, smoking, dancing and promiscuous behaviour. The Indian media was vociferous in condemning this 'licentious image and living'.[46]

Edwina fitted this image fully. The fear of such representations in western cinema had been one of the basic concerns of the British government in 1927–28, when they canvassed the opinion of select Indians and Europeans about the cinema.[47] The responses had indeed confirmed their worst fears. Throughout this period the British remained deeply concerned about the display of western norms of sexuality and especially the portrayal of western women before an Indian audience.[48]

In the Indian cinema, westernisation, as well as modernity, had a contentious relationship to women.[49] The stereotyping characteristic of the popular cinema reduced the modern, western woman to a series of superficial attributes indicated by dress, sexual licence and morality. The 'white', westernised, Anglo-Indian actresses had been the foremost entrants to the world of Indian cinema. In the role of heroines, argues Kathryn Hansen, they had enabled the male Indian spectator, through the exercise of the gaze, to possess the 'English beauty', and in so doing enact a reversal of the power relations that prevailed in British-dominated colonial society.[50] In their role of Indian women these actresses had represented the epitome of perfection and set ideal feminine standards of behaviour and dress. However, the 'possession' of a white, westernised woman (Edwina, for example) in her representation as a white woman, may have, because of the pejorative associations of the white woman's image, not been so enthusiastically received by the male Indian audience. The latter was in a position to both consume the image of the white woman and reject her simultaneously as in the case of the sexually-charged Anglo-Indian heroine played by Ava Gardner in *Bhowani Junction*.

The white, westernised woman remained an object of denigration and was later to dominate the Indian screen in the full blown character of a vamp. The vamp has remained a staple in Indian cinema because it enabled the male audience to consume her without breaching his preference for the loyal, good woman portrayed by the heroine. Even a subtle and ambiguously coded film, like *Andaz* (Mehboob Khan, 1949), introduced the highly westernised heroine ultimately to condemn and penalise her for her 'un-Indian', westernised conduct, and valorised her only in her motherhood.[51] Populist cultural nationalism echoed the familiar patriarchal reconstruction of feminine identity which valorised motherhood and linked it literally and metaphysically with nationalist ideals.

This concept of nationalism defined the European woman as the Other in national, cultural and class terms. Considered very threatening, these European women robbed Indian women (and by implication, the Indian nation) of their own men, and were the potential cause of divided loyalties in their off-spring.[52] From the colonised point of view, therefore, a woman like Edwina subverted the potential of an enlightened educated Indian male. In a fight against imperialism, such a temptress was nothing but an agent of imperialism.

For the west, however, her giving up the love of her life symbolised a supreme gift to India. Significant here is the fact that if the white woman were to appropriate the male for herself, then the whole structure of India, as depicted, would collapse. This role of the British as givers and Indians as receivers decries the exploitative nature of the British rule in India and permits claims of development and modernisation. Such a role was in direct contrast to the earlier portrayals, which showed Britain as determined takers, resolute to retain their hold on India in the face of repeated opposition and rebellions. *The Rains Came* showed an India well contented with Britain, being nurtured and endowed with all modern conveniences. In this, it effects a reversal of the drain theory and represents the British as givers on a higher ethical and material plane, without asking anything in return. In fact, reciprocity is totally denied in the film, suggesting the dependency of India on the 'gift' of Britain.

Edwina's death also indicates the willingness of the colony to advance along its own lines in terms of its institutional social structures, which had not been eradicated by the colonial state but transformed with modernisation. Yet, although not spelt out explicitly, it remained an alien structure, comprising a form of social organisation in which there was an ambiguous acceptance of the right of royalty to govern, but with the real power residing elsewhere. The film highlighted this aspect by eliminating the novel's natural, though minor, heir of the Maharaja and turning Rama into an adopted heir. This deliberate substitution underlined the overwhelming power of the British, who reserved the right to recognise the adopted heir of the ruler of a protected State. Consequently, in case the ruler of a protected state died without a natural heir, his state was not to pass to the adopted heir sanctioned by the age-old traditions of the country but to one selected by the British. This was effected by Lord Dalhousie, governor general of India (1848–56), under the doctrine of lapse, which became the chief instrument through which he implemented his policy of annexation in India. In seven years his government annexed seven states. This policy became one of the major causes of the popular uprising in 1857–58.

This right to determine the question of succession was one of the most blatant and ruthless interventions of the colonial government in Indian society. Making Rama Safti an adopted heir of the Maharaja thus created an anomalous situation where the legitimacy and claim of Rama was questioned, the outcome lying in its recognition by the colonial masters. The film, therefore, emphasised that the succession of Rama to the throne was dependent on the British colonial structure and control. The end finds Rama, resplendent as the Maharaja of Ranchipur, flanked by British officials underlining British protection and the dependent status of the state (illustration 10). The film seemed to confirm the imperial attitude that the princes required external assistance. Their governments were subject to extinction if democracy was to take over or should the Congress come to power.

Similarly, in the evolution of colonies towards responsible government and dominion status, the ideological thrust of the film was that the colony, whether under the princes or directly governed by the British, could be prepared and trained towards this end and Britain would have nothing to fear. Though allusion to autonomy is made in the indefinite future, there is no indication in the film that empire is moving towards the promised land of self-government.

The colonised male is, in fact, shown reluctant to move towards self-government or break this alliance symbolised in the film as interracial heterosexual alliance. In this portrayal Rama is denied rationality. Edwina, on the other hand, has the requisite knowledge and maturity to make this supreme sacrifice. Edwina's knowledge and maturity is symbolic of the colonising country. This is brought home in an interesting comment made by Ransome to the Indian Maharani, which uses the feminine metaphor to validate imperialism and colonial domination. While equating the qualities of the Maharani and Edwina, he reverses their ages. Complementing the Maharani as 'young' and depicting Edwina as 'old', he reintroduces India not as a country with an old civilisation and culture, but in relation to England as young and inexperienced, which has still to learn from the older experienced England. Ultimately, the portrayed similarities between white and non-white are all negated. Rama is shown as lacking maturity, taking up a child-like stance, and Edwina as more powerful and secure in her relationship.

Constructing femininity in a colonial setting: class dimension

The interaction between race, class and gender and the way femininity is constructed in the film offers a more complex view of social relations. For example, as a woman, Edwina is shown to yield to her irrational lust, unable to control her desires. Being 'a self-confirmed society whore', as an indignant letter to the secretary of state for India pointed out, she is shown to be lusting after the Indian doctor, on whom she makes no impression until she 'turns saint' by cleaning the floor of the native hospital.[53] In one scene, the letter went on, 'she all but threw herself in the dust at his feet to make him come to her'.

In the deeply class-conscious society of Britain, Edwina, a member of the gentry, albeit a greatly impoverished one, had married well beneath her class with a *nouveau riche* trader-turned millionaire, who had purchased his peerage. This major social transgression makes her second transgression more acceptable to the white audience. The film shows class prejudice in Edwina's portrayal because of her ambiguous status. She does not show the kind of self-restraint and discipline that was perceived to characterise the 'true blue' gentry. With her marriage into a lower social class she also adopts the behaviour of that class. Her 'sluttish' behaviour and reference to her innumerable affairs in the film, makes the Indian doctor just one more in the series of her lovers. Her succumbing to the charms of a native is thus far more understandable and acceptable by white standards in a woman of loose character than some one who was pure and chaste. Edwina's behaviour was certainly reprehensible by the standards of the privileged class of the white in the colony, but in projecting moral inferiority, and a lack of discipline characteristic of the lower classes, the film aptly projected the derogatory and discriminating attitude held by the British elite for those of their kind who intermixed with their social inferiors and blurred the class lines.

The dominant ideological thrust of the film places such a female as inherently inferior, uncivilised, primitive and lacking in self-control in contrast to the male. Yet, in the context of imperialism, white women were placed firmly in the civilised camp, in opposition not only to non-European women but also to the non-white native male of any class. This meant that white women could occupy both sides of a binary opposition. Edwina, therefore, is a degenerate in relation to white men but an enlightened virtuous soul in relation to non-white men and women.

This also made the incorporation of Edwina's character easy, as, ultimately, it was that of an inferior. In a colonial situation of structural hierarchy by race and class, the white woman was ultimately a member of a sex considered inferior within a race that held itself to be superior. This left the ultimate white male superiority intact. The centrality of gender in the film, based on the notion of incorporation, therefore furthered the colonial enterprise. The film does not disturb the fixed hierarchy of domination and subordination, superiority and inferiority inscribed upon a racially marked colonial body.

The Rains Came provided an ideological space in which different meanings of femininity could be explored and contested. The white woman abroad could be at once a many-faceted figure, from an intrepid adventuress, a go-getter, a social climber, defying social and sexual boundaries to a heroic mother responsible for the imperial family and for superior social and moral action. The film uses the prominent and well-acknowledged images in the west, of female missionaries and nurses involved in the selfless work of uplifting and caring for coloured souls and bodies, in an attempt to foreground the non-political, non-economic stakes in the colony, presenting the women as nurturants and mother figures. Women, in the role of missionary or nurse, were considered to be endowed with unquestionable moral superiority rooted in purity and nurturing. Yet, as Kumari Jayawardena reasons, these images were not read in the same way in the colonies. In south Asia, missionaries, both men and women, were regarded as agents of imperialism, who were trying to win over the 'heathens' through material inducements ranging from trinkets and food to education and health facilities.[54] Moreover, carrying the 'Christian burden' in relation to the colonies, many among them believed that 'premature independence for India would be ... an abdication of the ordained exercise of Christian rule'.[55]

In the film, this altruism of the colonists is essentially highlighted by the fact that Ranchipur is shown as an isolated small state: a place where nothing happens; where life is very dull, prone to stagnation and exposed to elemental wrath like rains and floods. The climate is shown to be extremely hot with attendant rampant disease. It portrayed admirably the selflessness and philanthropy of those British and Americans who came to India with or without their families despite their knowledge that they were facing an environment likely to result in speedy death.

India, despite its vast size, is shown to have a claustrophobic effect especially on white women, creating abnormality in their behaviour. This is brought home in the film in relation to the young eighteen-year-old daughter of the US missionary and the nurse. The former is shown to be desperate to get out even at the cost of compromising her reputation and the latter, as the lone white nurse serving under the Indian doctor, is shown to desire him, just like Edwina. The nurse shows suppressed sexual frustration, which comes through in a menacing way, taking into account her mature years, spinsterhood and less attractive appearance. Here the ambivalent attitudes held by dominant white men towards white women in the colonial situation are revealed in relation to nursing. The female members of this hallowed profession based in the colonies were known to exploit opportunities of sensual and sexual freedom.[56]

As opposed to these deviants, and their 'dishonourable' and 'abnormal' sexuality, the film posits the 'honourable' and 'normal' sexuality of a white eligible couple. Within the norms of white society it is sanctioned with great approval. The sexuality of the eighteen year old, on open display to Ransome (much in the same way as that of Edwina to Rama), is sanctified in marriage. Unlike Edwina, Fern is vulnerable but, in relation to a white man, is very much his companion. This companionship is denied to the cross-colour lead. These varied images of white women and femininity obviously had implications for relationships between men and women, but they also worked as part of the racial dynamics between white and non-white.

As opposed to the images of white women and projection of complex subjectivities involving their femininity and sexuality, the images of Indian women were largely left unattended. Rama Safti is shown to be central to the desire of two sets of women: Edwina and the hospital nurse, on the one hand, and Edwina and the Maharani, on the other. In the former both are white. If one of them had been an Indian, an entirely new dimension would have been imparted to the film, as, ultimately, Rama Safti, signifying the new India, is claimed by England and Edwina and not left to the Indians. So, although by the end of the film, England and Edwina are removed from Rama's life, he does not belong to an Indian.

The latter situation is complex in its implications. What the Indian Maharani and Edwina share is a discourse of power and territoriality over Rama Safti. In the consequent rivalry between the two women, one Indian and the other European, the latter has an edge as Rama is willing to relinquish all, even abandoning the Maharani for Edwina, who has far greater power over him. Significantly, this power was not exercised by men over men but by a woman over a man, reasserting the ground rule of colonial domination and subordination. Rama, on the other hand, a product of the west and western knowledge, is shown to belong more to the west than to the east. His 'need' of Edwina overrides all other sentiments and rationalities. This marks the Maharani as a resister of the civilisational thrust of Britain. Implicit in this is the question of which relationship – that with a Briton or an Indian – works best for Rama and, by extension, India. Edwina's withdrawal, despite her love for Rama and India, silences the Maharani and others of her ilk, but not before it is fully asserted that Edwina's self-sacrifice, duty and devotion extend the social mission of colonialism. Ultimately, Edwina's love and sacrifice is in keeping with the moralistic paternalism by which she clearly scores over his foster mother, the Maharani, in her relationship with Rama. The ideology that she presents legitimates the form of power exercised over the colonised people.

In a curious way, both the Maharani and Edwina are endowed with agency and both negotiate for power within gender roles that constitute the cultural norm. Yet, Edwina's emancipation is grounded in the moral superiority of the British as an enlightened race engaged in raising natives into humanity. Consequently, her agency has racial superiority over the Indian Maharani. The Maharani is portrayed in the well-known historical tradition of female regents in different parts of India but with a difference. Women, such as Razia Sultana, Kurma Devi, Dayavati, Tarabai, Ahalyabai and Lakshmibai (Rani of Jhansi), assumed power as queen regents and were perceived as warrior women.[57] Representing a more positive female agency, these women were popularly depicted in the theatre not only in the role of military leadership but also as wise, just and generous rulers. The agency of the Maharani in the film, on the other hand, is set within certain constraints. She is not an agent of her own will like the *viranganas* (or even like Edwina). Representing a surrogate agency on behalf of her husband she is shown to only be committed to extending her husband's death wish, ensuring a peaceful succession to the throne. Having fulfilled this limited role of a regent and instrument in making way for the adopted male successor she retreats into the background.

As a point of comparison, the Indian Maharani can be contrasted with the old Maharani Victoria. Played by the German actress Maria Ouspenskaya, the Maharani is diminutive, below five feet in height, wrinkled and flat-chested in direct contrast to the ample bosomed motherly figure of Victoria who even physically symbolises the 'imperial motherhood'. Moreover, the Indian Maharani shows a major deviation from the novel where she is the mother of a minor son. In the film, her barrenness (Rama is the adopted heir) contrasts with the well-known fecundity of Victoria, who as the mother not only gives to her own children but to Other children as well. This role is significantly denied to the Indian Maharani. Interestingly, both Edwina and the nurse are also 'barren'. The nurse happens to be a 'spinster' and Edwina is certainly childless if not literally barren. In a socially unequal marriage between the gentry and the trading class, childlessness is not only accepted but also preferred to fecundity. The eugenics argument regarding limiting the number of 'unfit' holds true for the ambiguous class status for the offspring of such a union. It is, therefore, the barrenness of the Maharani that is condemned and held symbolic of infertility in other fields as well.

As an individual, the Indian Maharani is endowed with many noteworthy 'qualities': she is shown to be wise in reaching out to the British for help and in knowing their 'superior ability' and the 'weak national character' of her fellow Indians; efficient in organising through the British the control of a disaster situation caused by rains and flood; benevolent in keeping the interest of her people and her state paramount, by insuring the rightful succession to the throne. Moreover, the authority with which she speaks is a sign of her class-standing and not race. Racially she is denigrated as a savage, uncivilised and thus inferior. She is conceived in the mould of an oriental despot who is autocratic and cruel. She is ready to eliminate Edwina to keep the purity of her royal family and caste intact. In this one gesture the entire violent history of colonial interaction is not only denied, it is replaced with the violence of Indian society and its ruling classes.

This depiction also shifts the emphasis away from the colonists' obsession with regarding white women as the guardians of the purity of their race. In reality, the British in India found such marriages among the royalty unsettling as they 'confused the racial, sexual and class hierarchies of empire'.[58] The official wishes and the policy adopted showed a strong disapproval of mixed marriages, especially those of the royalty in India. Declared to be against 'people's custom', these marriages were denied official recognition, and the children were treated as illegitimate by the British until the very end of the Raj.[59]

Moreover, by transferring to the Indians this opposition to a cross-racial alliance, the colonial government is absolved of any racist attitude. The onus of this failure is placed on the caste consciousness existing in India, underlining its social backwardness. However, apart from caste and community objections there could be far stronger objections to this alliance on nationalist grounds. Objections to a threatened breach of 'home', considered undominated and sovereign, by a white woman, an agent of the colonial state which dominated the 'outside', was certain to be on the nationalist agenda. In the 'outside' world, as argued by Partha Chatterjee, the imitation of and adaptation to western norms was a necessity; at 'home' they were tantamount to 'annihilation of one's very own identity'.[60] This interracial alliance could well symbolise for an Indian audience, this annihilation, underlined in the film by Rama, who is shown willing to renounce all, even his patrimony, in order to marry Edwina.

Central to this interracial projection is the conceptualisation of gender relations of the colonised by the white dominant races, which is not directly portrayed but exists in the film by default. There is no other Indian female, apart from the Maharani, who makes an appearance in the film. The high-caste woman whom Rama is to marry in a match arranged by the Maharani is only referred to, she is not shown in the film. The absence of images leaves the visualisation of Indian women to the western viewers' imagination, conditioned by demands of caste and culture voiced in this film, along with the images of colonised women popularised in other empire films, in which they were either closeted in harems to control them, veiled and invisiblised in public, or presented as reserved objects awaiting male desire and sexuality. This off-screen characterisation of coloured femininity made an implicit comment on the modernised progressive Indian men, such as Rama, who remain socially located in feudal notions of gender relations. These covert gender relations were posited in the centre of an ideological evaluation of Indian masculinity, civilisation and culture and used to denigrate it as socially backward.

Coloured masculinity: the emasculated male

The images of Indian men and their masculinity work as counter-points to reinforce the dominant ideological thrust of the film. The Indian male, recipient of the assiduous attention of two white females, is essentially effeminate. In this, the choice of a slender, delicately featured actor like Tyrone Power, as opposed to the 'manly physique' reserved for the white character, played by robust and rugged George Brent, is visually very powerful in dividing masculinity into physical stereotypes. The film certainly broke away from earlier depictions of the coloured man as villain, but did not go so far as to make the coloured hero assertive or virile – qualities reserved for the parallel white lead.

Moreover, when compared to earlier films, this portrayal was not without its contradictions. Previous films had suggested the physical 'unmanliness' of those who defied or opposed the rulers. The stately, well-built physicality of Indian recruits in the British Indian army of the adventure films was reserved for the loyal. The masculinity of the Indian male was, therefore, synonymous with loyalty. The rebels, on the other hand, were depicted as physically effeminate, as witness the character of the guru, in *Gunga Din* or Gul Khan in *The Drum*. The latter also represented wanton sexuality. Effeminacy, with its deviant and ambiguous sexuality, not to mention association with the feminine attributes of deceit, treachery and falsehood, all genderised attributes, made its own statement.

The Rains Came introduced a further contradiction in this imagery. The maleness of a loyal Rama had to appear inferior to the white female to project what Mrinalini Sinha has called a 'bastardised or incomplete form' of masculinity.[61] This was done not only by a neat reversal of the physical, stereotypical projection but also in characterisation. Rama has many 'white' or western attributes, yet a sharp distinction is made between 'being white' and 'assuming whiteness'. Rama, for example, who has successfully assumed whiteness through education, dress and behaviour, nevertheless breaks down under emotional stress. Confronted with a crisis he remains a victim of self-doubt revealed in the following comment: 'We are different, deep down where it matters. I am an Indian, I can't remain calm and emotionless. I want to tear my clothes and wail like Banerjee.' He can only compose himself when told by Ransome, 'You are not Banerjee. Do not betray all. We have faith in you. You are a man, a doctor.'

In fact, Ransome's relationship with Rama Safti suggests shades of sexual ambivalence in the latter thus inferiorising him further. Ransome shows concern for Safti because of Edwina's designs on him and does not want her 'philandering around the hospital' and 'meddling up the life of the major'. It may be noted that the film avoids giving any impression of Ransome's reservations about miscegenation. He is also not shown as sexually possessive of Edwina, who was an old flame of his. Ransome shows his apprehensions about the major whom he says he loves and respects. In this triangle it is Ransome and Edwina who are competing for Rama, with whom the former has established an unconscious homo-eroticised bonding. In this bonding, it is Ransome who occupies the dominant superior male role to the effeminate Rama, who has to be reminded that he is a man and should not cry and wail like a woman.

Rama's identity has to be seen as born out of the conflict between two cultures: the rational educated western element and the highly emotional one, lacking in self-control, that stems from the east. The triumph of the former is the triumph of the superior, which alone is posited as valuable and capable of overcoming danger and difficulty. A man who is so highly emotional and incapable of conducting himself in a disciplined manner can only be inferior.

Clearly, despite ostensibly rejecting the stifling, biologically-based, 'scientific racism', the film suggests a slide back to it before accepting that the colonised might be raised to acceptable British standards under their guiding hand. Yet, this did not necessarily resolve the bias of biological racism; it only class-based it with certain reservations. In a critical situation – where even a European-trained medical doctor is unable to apply his scientific training – a core ideology was exposed belonging to an inherently inferior, emasculated race. In the film, Rama is brought to his senses by the superior reasoning of the white character who purges his passion, which would have otherwise led to certain ruin. Being both royal and loyal, Rama comes out of his natural self to 'assume whiteness' once again.

Underlying the premise of 'assuming whiteness' by the

coloured hero is the fact that he is *allowed* to assume it. It is the colonial intervention that makes it possible for Rama, a child of 'oriental exoticism', to be so transformed as to be labelled the 'symbol of modern India' by the white heroine. As such, he remains a gift of the British colonial masters to India, on a par with other civilisational gifts such as hospitals, railways, public works, the post and telegraph services, and the modern communication network, all of them graphically shown in the film.

As a gift of the west to India, Rama displays all the symptoms of cultural dependence and looks at his society and people through the prism of colonial culture. It is this concept of masculinity that operates in the relationship between the colonised and the coloniser, between men and women, and between coloured and white. Such a masculinity could hardly be threatening for the British in India. Lest it be overlooked, the Indian Maharani is made to voice the emasculation of Indians as follows: 'The weakness of our national character has been that we are inclined to blame the gods for our catastrophe and fail in our duty. I don't purpose to allow that.'

A further dimension is added to the working out of masculinity in relation to the educated Indians in the characterisation of Banerjee in the film. Banerjee, a high-caste Brahmin, symbolises a mix of others of his ilk in Bengal, Maharashtra and Madras, who were among the first Indians to master the new language and imbibe the modes of behaviour necessary for dealing with British officers. They struggled desperately to maintain their status in a situation in which the right to assign status was no longer theirs. On the whole, education had disturbed the traditional social hierarchies, especially of the Brahmins, and, in the British perception, created deep resentment among them against the British. As such, Banerjee also symbolises all the insecurities that the British were feeling in relation to the educated minority of Indians, the spearhead of the national movement. Greatly ridiculed and despised, their image had come to be concentrated in the person of Bengali *babu*, the most active recipient of British education, but shown as totally untrustworthy.

It was really this Bengali *babu*, a section of the Indian middle class in Bengal, as pointed out by Mrinalini Sinha, which was stereotyped as 'effeminate' by the second half of the nineteenth century. According to Sinha:

Over time, effeminacy had evolved from a loosely defined attribute associated with the entire population of Bengal, and sometimes by extension of all of India, to an attribute associated very specifically with western-educated Indians, a large majority of whom were Bengali Hindus. On the other hand, the concept of Bengali effeminacy was also greatly expanded to include the politically discontented middle class 'natives' from all over India.[62]

This emasculation of Indians and homology between sexual and political dominance that the British imposed in India, in conjunction with its acceptance by the colonised, became the basis of resisting colonialism and challenging specific colonial policies, resulting in some of the most effective forms of protest against colonialism. In Ashis Nandy's opinion, the origin of the new stress on Ksatriyahood, on 'martial Indianness', leading to the terrorist movement in Bengal, Maharashtra and Punjab led by semi-westernised, middle-class, urban youth can be traced to this politics of masculinity.[63] In the 1920s and 1930s, there was a marked change in the British attitude towards the educated middle class and its able leadership of an increasingly mass-based national movement. The terrorist movement furthered this perception. Together it resulted in an entirely different view of Indian masculinity that was essentially at odds with the mid-nineteenth-century stereotypical visualisation of the British.[64] In *The Rains Came*, it is the nineteenth-century viewpoint of Indian masculinity that gets transported into the 1930s, indicating the eclectic adaptation of several strands of ideologies in the empire cinema.

In *The Rains Came*, the middle-class Banerjee and the upper-class Rama Safti typify the colonial stereotype of 'effeminate Indians'. In this respect, two important classes of Indian society are joined together. The other common factor that joins the two is their access to western education and knowledge. Significantly, by the interwar period a large number of Indians had received a university education in India and elsewhere and were practising in a variety of modern professions. Yet, in the film, this educational identity has to be foregrounded in an identity drawn from birth and personal wealth. A western-educated identity, which is outside the social structure of birth and wealth, as is the case with the Bengali *babu*, is condemned as false, considered inauthentic and severely limiting.

In other words, Banerjee's 'limited knowledge' was the one equated with this class, and could not be accepted as representing any larger interests or people. Reception of 'true' western knowledge meant discipline and moral improvement as signified by Rama's behaviour. It was this difference which divided those with a 'true' education from those who, despite formal education and affectation of western dress and behaviour, remained without real knowledge, as ignorant and backward as the uneducated.

In the film, Banerjee is turned into a caricature of a highly anglicised, middle-class Bengali who wears a monocle and dinner jacket and mouths 'awfully good to see you' and 'jolly good show' in imitation of the British. He is shown to be an upstart and pretentious, with no 'class' background to sustain his education. The superficiality of his education is shown up by his underlying superstition, conservatism and irrationality, which come to the fore at the first hint of disaster. He is shown to view this disaster as the vengeance of the gods, puts on a loin cloth, shaves his head and resorts to ritualised worship of the gods, chanting the *mantra*, '*om swaha*' (illustration 8). He also drops his affected British speech, takes to Hindi, calls Ransome a '*melacha papi*', translated in the film by Edwina as 'impious barbarian' and, when offered help by the Englishman, refuses it by saying, '*papi ke sath nahin jaaenge*' (I will not go with a sinner). The transgression of the social code of 'proper conduct' is illustrative of the racism inherent in the colonial situation. Such stereotyping also hid class prejudice. There were clearly no 'white qualities' in this specimen of the middle classes.

It is interesting that Banerjee, at a crucial juncture of alienation from the British, whom he has been aping successfully in clothes, manners and speech, lapses into a native tongue (not Bengali but Hindi) and does not use the master's language to abuse them. This is unlike the colonial masters who invariably use the native language to abuse the native as portrayed in all the earlier adventure films. Portrayed with an eye to the sensibilities of the western audiences, it had wider ramifications. The use of language is undoubtedly fraught with questions of power and authority. Implicit in this is why people learn languages and how they use them. In the colonial situation, when the white man learns the native language he does so to dominate, subjugate, command, threaten, abuse and denigrate. It is a language best understood by the native – a use of his own language to subjugate him. The reverse, however, is not true in the case of the native. Despite learning and speaking the master's language he never achieves parity with them, but remains subordinate and subjugated, the reversal of the power exercised by the white man through the use of a native language.

The knowledge of language remains inhibiting for the native. It offers him a space only if he articulates what the ruler wants to hear. Any other articulation must be made in his own language. This articulation, however, confirms his true identity and inferiorises him. It also reiterates the fact that a white man could colour his face and become one with Indians (as in *The Drum*), but an Indian could not do the reverse. Even if accepted socially at a certain level because of the 'white attributes' he had imbibed, he couldn't change the colour of his skin; he remained a coloured person. This was true both of Banerjee and Rama Safti. Banerjee reverted at the time of crisis into a simpering, praying idiot, and Rama Safti suffered his own moments of doubt during the crisis.

In contrast to the Indians, Ransome, an English wastrel and philanderer living in India, shows his 'true blood' in a crisis. He emerges as a 'true' Englishman and a gentleman – the ultimate virile male in charge of all, efficient and powerful in dealing with public and private catastrophe. In this connection, the Maharani makes a significant observation. She speaks of her confidence in him to do the right thing in a crisis while the others (her fellow countrymen) had to be told what to do. He alone, according to her, knew instinctively what to do and how to do the right thing. Thus, this badge of natural leadership is bestowed by an Indian on an Englishman. It also shows the desire for continuing this relationship emanating from the colonised rather than the colonisers. Moreover, put in the mouth of a woman, it also determines wherein lay the 'true' masculinity.

The fact that the Maharani invokes the white man to come and take charge – an appeal which the white graciously accepts – also stresses the inadequacy of the colonised and lack of administrative ability. The Indians are shown as poorly suited to the task. They are also shown having no faith or confidence in their own people; even trained people are considered far below the untrained Europeans. The imperial power is accorded the final say in deciding on their readiness and capacity for self-rule; intervention is justified if things go wrong. In the face of rising nationalist demands seeking independence and the reluctance of the white colonisers to relinquish their hold on the colony, this portrayal not only denied the claim for independence but also demolished the basis of such a claim. Instead it posited moralistic paternalism.

In the face of utter devastation and anarchy the frail, helpless and defenceless Indians could not survive without the British help, male or female. But for the presence of the British and their unstinted generosity in reconstructing from scratch, India would face total ruin. In the context of World War II, the threat and apprehension of ruin, as voiced by Ransome, came from Germany. The essential vulnerability of India and the overpowering external German menace, together made the case for continuing the British connection with India.

Publicity: release of the film

In making a case for the continuation of British rule in India based on the legitimising twin aspects of development and partnership, the film offered a very complex representation of empire. It modified various hitherto popularly projected and accepted stereotypical images of both the master race as well as the colonised and their interpersonal relationship, highlighted by juxtaposing white femininity and coloured masculinity. Although the overwhelming message reinforced and did not negate the British racial and imperial domination, the ambiguity of the situation inherent in the use of a white woman as the chief protagonist involved in a cross-colour sexual alliance was not lost on the concerned British authorities. Consequently, despite a close control over production, as well as propaganda and advertisements, the immediate reaction of the BBFC was of doubt about the reception of this film – the first of its kind – especially by its white British audience. Unwilling to take a chance with them, they consequently insisted that the name of the film be changed from *The Rains Came* to *Rains in India* at the time of its release in England. This was in view of the objections of the India Office, which felt that an identification with the book of the same name might provoke protests in England because of the graphic description of interracial sexual immorality in the book.[65] The film in England was released eventually as *Rains over India*.[66]

However, true to the novel, the film used this pivotal interracial marriage question, a heretofore taboo subject in cinema
and one repugnant to the British, to reinforce the inherent differences between races and to underline Indian inferiority. In fact,
the film continues to see miscegenation as leading to personal and
social turmoil and views mixed marriages unsympathetically.
Ultimately, it served to accomplish the same end: the separation
of races.

The expected opposition born out of the book and its reading
did not really surface in Britain. In this, World War II made its
own contribution. In a war being fought for democracy, the principle of 'partnership' made sense to British cinema-goers and the
development of colonies could even be proudly accepted and
identified with. The multi-pronged propaganda adopted by
Britain before and during World War II to effect a change in the
imperial and colonial image was instrumental to this.[67] Yet,
objections did surface, born, as expected, out of racism, class
distinction and the consequent apprehensions regarding the
preservation of colonial domination. An alliance or contact
between a native male and European female, went against the
notions of male and superior European domination and created a
danger of loss of race, class and status. These status anxieties and
fears were certainly expressed, but remained largely ignored.

With regard to Indian audiences the apprehensions of the
British authorities were far less. It was widely believed that this
film would be well-received in India.[68] The novel was advertised
as follows: 'as fine a study of Indian life as E. M. Forster's *Passage
to India*'.[69] The publicity material of the film gave prominence to
the author's dedication to the novel: 'For all my Indian friends –
the princes, the teachers, the politicians, the hunters, the
boatmen, the sweepers.' In a widely-publicised quotation, Louis
Bromfield, the author of the novel, maintained, '*The Rains Came*
is a sympathetic picture on India' and 'the film is definitely pro-
India.' [70] His assertion that 'the public will see real and living
India for the first time' was given similar treatment. His 'affection
for India' and his being 'thunderstruck by the reality of the scenes
at the time of shooting' and the fact that while on location shooting he imagined himself in India because 'it was so real' were all
given great prominence by the film producers and distributors not
only in England and the USA but also in India.[71]

The huge publicity drive of *The Rains Came* also sought to secure greater authenticity for the film by specifying that claims to authenticity by earlier films were not creditworthy as most films about India had been banned from that country because of inaccuracies. Indeed, it was a great change from the earlier portrayals which had shown India as 'the land of mosques and minarets and temple bells', as 'a land of barbaric melodrama, strange pageantry and primitive taboos' or as 'a land – beautiful, bizarre and mystical – with its walled cities, its fakirs, its beggars, and muezzins, its veiled women and *nautch* dancers'. A large number of articles, advertisements, press handouts and publicity releases claimed that extensive research had gone into the making of the film. Claims were also made regarding the consultation of experts for picturing 'authentic social customs, life, home-decor, and music of India'.[72] Interestingly, these experts included British officials who had spent years in India and were considered to be 'well known for their knowledge of India'. Indian newspapers were flooded with advertisements claiming 'first foreign film presenting a true and sympathetic picture of modern India'.[73]

The Indian media, on the other hand, had started to condemn the film as 'anti-Indian' even when it was halfway through production.[74] Here, the advance comments and critiques in Indian media relating to *The Rains Came* were a part of the framework of knowledge available to Indian cinema-goers through their national dailies and cinema-related publications, which had been in the forefront of the opposition to empire cinema, especially in 1937–39. This was to colour the reception of this film – its acceptance and interpretation. The positive image of Rama with his 'white' attributes – with his zeal for serving the established law and order – was more pleasing to the white audience than to the coloured. Arguing for caution against the projection of 'positive images' of third-world countries and colonies by western cinema, Stam and Spence point out that, 'The positive image obscures the fact that at times such an image be as pernicious as overly degrading ones, providing a bourgeoisie facade for paternalism, a more pervasive racism'.[75] The Indian nationalists may well have seen the film's aborted individual attempt at racial integration as a 'particular discourse of power' used by white Europeans to justify their own privileged status.[76]

Moreover, a film hailing the princely states, which were recognised as the key supports for imperialism in its efforts to keep India divided and subjugated, could hardly be welcomed. A film posing for India an alternative well within the British empire was bound to meet with hostility. The princes were acknowledged not only as 'friends of the English', as Kipling had maintained, but as 'British lackeys'[77] who, as fellow conspirators with the British, were perceived to work against Indian interests.

The orientalist propaganda also boomeranged on the imperialists. The stereotypical image of licentious, slothful and inefficient oriental rulers were not only accepted by the nationalists but formed a major plank of their attack on Indian princes. Writers like Kanhaya Lal Gauba in his book, *H. H. or The Pathology of Princes* (1930), ridiculed the princes and took their pretensions apart with merciless wit, making fun of their extravagant and ostentatious life styles. Examples of princely misconduct were constantly hitting the headlines in the period between the wars. They included such scandals as the blackmailing of the young heir to the state of Jammu and Kashmir on his first visit to Europe; the sexual marauding of Maharaja Bhupinder Singh of Patiala, which forced the British authorities to ban him from Simla; the shoot-out in a Bombay street over a runaway mistress, which led to the abdication of Maharaja Tukoji Rao of Indore; the bankruptcy of the state of Bharatpur as a result of the widely extravagant Maharaja; the canine wedding fiestas of the dog-loving ruler of Junagadh; and the sadistic excesses of Maharaja Jay Singh of Alwar, finally deposed for what the British termed 'gross misrule'.

The 1930s were the years when the Indian nationalists leaders set about systematically propagating that princely India was an anachronism that had no place in the free India of the future.[78] The All Indian States' Peoples Conference produced a number of devastating reports under such titles as *The Indian Princes under British Protection* (1929) and *Indictment of Patiala* (1930), showing the princes to be parasitic, undemocratic and, above all, a creation of the British. Mahatma Gandhi, holding the British responsible for this state of affairs, claimed the states to be 'the greatest blot on British rule in India'. This concerted nationalist attack heightened during 1937–39, when the princes proved an impediment to federation. The release of *The Rains Came* at this historical juncture, when the socio-political consciousness against the princely states was at its height, could hardly expect to be favourably received.

However, the democratic space available for initiating and successfully carrying out popular protests, as in the case of *The Drum* and *Gunga Din*, no longer existed. The Congress ministries, which had formed popular governments in the provinces, had resigned in the wake of the viceroy unilaterally associating India with Britain's declaration of war on Germany on 3 September 1939. A Defence of India Ordinance restricting civil liberties came into force the day war was declared. Even before the war had been declared, an amendment to the 1935 act, which had installed popular governments in the provincial states, had been rushed through the British parliament giving the white-dominated central government and the bureaucracy emergency powers in respect of provincial subjects. By May 1940, the colonial masters had prepared a top-secret, draft Revolutionary Movements Ordinance aimed at a crippling pre-emptive strike at the Congress at the first opportunity.[79] In such a politically close social climate, it is not surprising that the film released after excision in 1940, was engulfed in the ensuing World War II, leaving hardly any tangible evidence of its impact on the Indian audience.[80]

Notes

1 The British had tried in the 1920s to project this image in which 'happy people living on the bounty of the constructive work of British rule' could be shown. However, the depiction was so complex that its explanation through film became a highly daunting task and the project had to be abandoned. See Milton Israel, *Communication and Power: Propaganda and Press in the Indian Nationalist Struggle, 1920–47* (Cambridge, Cambridge University Press, 1994), pp. 282–3.

2 IOR, L/P&J/8/128, Coll. no. 105-A, pt. XIII, Apr. 1936–1939. See minute paper, A. Dibdin of the, P&J department to under-secretary of state for India, 1 Dec. 1938.

3 BBFC, scenario reports, 1938. See comments of Col. J. C. Hanna and Mrs E. Crouzet on the scenario of *The Rains Came*, 22 Nov. 1938.

4 IOR, L/P&J/8/128, Coll. no. 105-A, pt. XIII, Apr. 1936–1939. P. J. Patrick of the India Office to political department in Simla, dated 25 May 1939: 'The British Film Censors have given us to understand that the story has been much modified in accordance with the suggestions and even the name altered'.

5 *Ibid.* See letter dated 4 Dec. 1939.

6 *Northamptonshire Evening Telegraph* (6 Jun. 1939).

7 In 1937 a proposal to film A. E. Mason's novel, *The Broken Road*, was rejected. The plot revolved around an Indian prince brought up and educated in England. Miss Shortt of the BBFC did not consider its central character to be a fitting theme for producing a film. In *The Rains Came*, the central character was similarly an enlightened western educated prince.

8 BBFC, scenario reports, 1938.

9 Allen J. Greenberger, *The British Image of India: A Study of Literature of Imperialism, 1880–1960* (London, Oxford University Press, 1969), p. 41.

10 These include Louis Tracy, *Heart's Delight* (1907), Flora Annie Steel, *A Prince of Dreamers* (1909), F. E. Penny, *The Rajah* (1911), Lawrence Clark, *A Prince of India* (1924), Frank Hatter, *The Marriage of Yusuf Khan* (1924), G. H. Bell, *The Foreigner* (1928), L. H. Myer, *The Near and the Far* (1929), L. H. Myer, *Prince Jali* (1931), J. R. Ackerley, *Hindoo Holiday* (1932), and Dennis Rincaid, *The Darbar* (1933). For details see Surender Singh, *Princely Life in Indian British Writing* (New Delhi, Reliance Publishing House, 1995), p. 19.

11 Ella Shohat and Robert Stam, *Unthinking Eurocentricism: Multiculturism and the Media* (London & New York, Routledge, 1994), pp. 161–3.

12 Some of the more important political personalities who advocated a counter-view were Thomas Mountstuart Elphinstone, John Malcolm, George Russel Clerk and the Duke of Wellington.

13 Maud Diver, *The Dream Prevails: A Story of India* (London, John Murray, 1938), p. 82.

14 Ian Copland, *The Princes of India in the Endgame of Empire, 1919–1947* (Cambridge, Cambridge University Press, 1997), p. 227.

15 For example, Lord Minto, in 1906, floated a plan for a Council of Princes to act as a counterbalance to the Congress. Under the Montegue–Chelmsford Reforms, this emerged as the Chamber of Princes in 1921.

16 Sir Louis Dane, foreign secretary's speech to the East India Association, cited in Copland, *The Princes of India*, p. 269.

17 William Barton, *The Princes of India* (London, Nisbet, 1934), p. 321.

18 Rosita Forbes, *India of the Princes* (London, The Right Book Club, 1939), pp. 30–2.

19 *Ibid.*, p. 48.

20 According to Gary R. Hess, this was the British propaganda in the USA. The British assumed a paternalistic attitude towards the Muslims, untouchables and other minority groups as well as the princes – all of whom, they claimed, needed their protection against domination by the high-caste 'fascist' Congress. See Gary R. Hess, *America Encounters India 1941–1947* (Baltimore & London, Johns Hopkins Press, 1971), pp. 120–1. Significantly, Maud Diver's *Royal India*, published in 1942, reinforced this argument. Based on a study of the fifteen principal states, Diver concluded that the princes provided the best government in India. See Maud Diver, *Royal India: A Descriptive and Historical Study of India's Fifteen Principal States and their Rulers* (New York, D. Appleton-Century, 1942), pp. 1–25.

21 Barbara N. Ramusack, *The Princes of India in the Twilight of Empire: Dissolution of a Patron–Client System, 1914–1939* (Columbus, University of Cincinnati, 1978), p. 240.

22 Charles Allen and Sharada Dwivedi, *Lives of the Indian Princes* (London, Century Publishing, 1984), pp. 287–8.

23 See Barton, *The Princes of India*, pp. 76, 321; Forbes, *India of the Princes*, p. 30.

24 Ramusack, *The Princes*, pp. 356–7.

25 Bharati Ray, *Hyderabad and British Paramountcy, 1858–1883* (Delhi, Oxford University Press, 1988), p. XIV.

26 For reformulation of British attitude towards imperial mission during this period, see Paul B. Rich, *Race and Empire in British Politics* (Cambridge, Cambridge University Press, 1986), pp. 50–91.

27 The awesome forces of destruction that the Europeans had unleashed on their own civilisation during World War I raised troubling questions about the assumptions on which their sense of racial superiority and commitment to the civilising mission had been based. For details see Michael Adas, *Machines as the Measure of Men: Science, Technology and Ideologies of Western Dominance* (Ithaca & London, Cornell University Press, 1989), pp. 380–401.

28 Frank Reeves, *British Racial Discourse: A Study of British Political Discourse about Race and Race-related Matters* (Cambridge, Cambridge University Press, 1983), pp. 112–27

29 *Motion Picture Herald*, 136:11 (1939), p. 46; *Los Angeles Examiner* (17 Aug. 1939); *Chicago Tribune* (7 Sep. 1939); *Variety* (7 Aug. 1939); *New Post* (Sep. 1939); *The Cinema* (15 Nov. 1939), p. 10; *Kinematograph Weekly* (12 Feb. 1943), p. 3.

30 IOR, L/P&J/6/1747, 1922–1930, p. 277.

31 Shohat and Stam, *Unthinking Eurocentrism*, pp. 158–60.

32 Edward Said, *Orientalism* (New York, Routledge & Kegan Paul, 1978), pp. 6, 207.

33 Jenny Sharpe, *Allegories of Empire: The Figure of Woman in the Colonial Text* (Minneapolis & London, University of Minnesota Press, 1993), pp. 61–154

34 Jenny Sharpe argues that in India the Mutiny of 1857 provided a powerful and enduring reference for the imagery of violence against European women and children by the subordinate groups and underlined the sexual fears of white women. At crucial moments, like the Ilbert Bill controversy (1883) and the Punjab Disturbances (1919), this racial memory of the Mutiny was revived and the crisis in British authority was managed through the circulation of the violated bodies of British women as a sign for the violation of colonialism. Sharpe, *Allegories of Empire*. See also Ann Stoler, 'Rethinking colonial categories: European communities and the boundaries of rule', *Comparative Studies in Society and History*, 13:1 (1989), pp. 134–61; and Richard Dyer, 'There's nothing I can do!: femininity, seriality and whiteness in the *Jewel in the Crown*', *Screen*, 37:3 (Autumn 1996), pp. 225–39.

35 Sharpe, *Allegories of Empire*, p. 137.

36 Personal communication from Patricia Uberoi, Apr. 1997.

37 D. G. Tendulkar, *Abdul Gaffar Khan: Faith is a Battle* (Bombay, Popular Prakashan, 1967), pp. 160, 172.

38 Some of the most notable were Margaret Noble (sister Nivedita), Mirra Richard (the mother) and Madeleine Slade (Mira Behan) who were the disciples, if not co-partners, of three of India's most revered figures, Swami Vivekanand, Sri Aurobindo and Mahatma Gandhi respectively. For those among the Indian and Sri Lankan nationalists who married foreign women in the 1930s see Kumari Jayawardena, *The White Woman's Other Burden: Western Women and South Asia during British Rule* (New York & London, Routledge, 1995), pp. 225–68.

39 Ann Stoler, 'Making empire respectable: the politics of race and sexual morality in 20th-century colonial cultures', in Jan Breman (ed.), *Imperial Monkey Business: Racial Supremacy in Social Darwinist Theory and Colonial Practice* (Amsterdam, V. U. University Press, 1990), pp. 35–70.

40 A shorthand typist, for example, recalled her love for Tyrone Power: 'When he kisses his leading lady a funny thrill runs up my spine to the heart. Sometimes in dreams which seem very real, I imagine, he is kissing me.' Cited in Jeffrey Richards, *The Age of the Dream Palace: Cinema and Society in Britain 1930–1939* (London, Routledge & Kegan Paul, 1984), p. 157.

41 Barbara N. Ramusack, 'Cultural missionaries, maternal imperialist, feminist allies: British women activists in India 1885–1945', in Nupur Chaudhuri and Margaret Strobel (eds), *Western Women and Imperialism: Complicity and Resistance* (Bloomington & Indianapolis, Indiana University Press, 1993), pp. 119–36.

42 Ella Shohat, 'Gender and culture of empire: towards a feminist ethnography of the cinema', in H. Naficy and T. H. Gabriel (eds), *Otherness and the Media: The Ethnography of the Imagined and the Imaged* (Langhorn, Harwood Academic Publishers, 1993), p. 64.

43 Partha Chatterjee, *The Nation and its Fragments: Colonial and Postcolonial Histories* (Delhi, Oxford University Press, 1993), pp. 121–8, 131–2.

44 For a feminist reading of *Mother India* see Mrinalini Sinha 'Reading *Mother India*: empire, nation and the female voice', *Journal of Women's History*, 6:2 (Summer 1994), pp. 6–44.

45 MSA, Home (special) F. no. 715, 1927, pp. 15–275.

46 *Ibid.* See *Kaiser-i-Hind* (8 Feb. 1925) and *Bombay Chronicle* (5 Dec. 1924 and 31 Jan. 1925).

47 ICC Evidence, vol. 1-IV.

48 IOR, L/P&J/6/1747, 1922–1930, pp. 430–2.

49 In some of the silent and early talkies the film-makers attempted to mould the middle-class woman in the privileged role of a companion to her husband, but set within the more traditional role of wifely devotion. One of the better known films on this theme was *Gun Sundari (Why Husband's Go Astray*, 1927), remade in 1934 in Hindi, Tamil, Telugu and Gujarati. In this, the heroine successfully acts modern in order to win her husband back from a dancing girl. Some of the other films on the same theme were: *Grhalakshmi (Educated Wife*, Homi Master, 1927) and *Typist Girl (Why I became a Christian*, Chandulal Shah, 1929). See Erik Barnouw and S. Krishnaswamy, *Indian Film* (New Delhi, Oxford University Press, 1980), pp. 33–6, 111.

50 Kathryn Hansen, '*Stri Bhumika*: female impersonators and actresses on the Parsi stage', *Economic and Political Weekly*, 33:35 (29 Aug. 1998), pp. 2291–300.

51 Ravi S. Vasudevan, '"You cannot live in society – and ignore it": nationhood and female modernity in *Andaz'*, in Patricia Uberoi (ed.), *Social Reform, Sexuality and the State* (New Delhi, Sage Publications, 1996), pp. 83–108.

52 For this, Hatem's analysis of three pioneering Egyptian female writers, Huda Sha'rawi (1879–1947), Malak Hijni Nasif (1886–1918) and Nabawiya Musa (1890–1951), is very useful. She

argues how a European woman who married an Egyptian man emerged as an Other in national, cultural and class terms. Such persons were considered very threatening since they robbed Egyptian women of bright men and eventually produced 'disloyal' young Egyptians. Interestingly, such a concept of nationalism came to be defined and used in sexual and cultural terms by Egyptian women to manipulate men and dissuade them from marrying foreign women. See Mervat Hatem, 'Through each other's eyes: the impact on the colonial encounter of the images of Egyptian, Levatine-Egyptian, and European women', in Chaudhuri and Strobel, *Western Women and Imperialism*, pp. 35–58.

53 IOR, L/P&J/8/128, Coll. no. 105-A, pt. XIV, Dec. 1938–Sep. 1939. See letter of A. G. Abbott from Surrey to the home secretary, dated 6 Apr. 1940. This was referred to the secretary of state for India.

54 Jayawardena, *The White Woman's Other Burden*, pp. 21–32.

55 G. Studdert-Kennedy, 'Gandhi and Christian imperialists', *History Today* (Oct. 1990), pp. 19–26.

56 Dea Birkett, 'The "white woman's burden" in the "white man's grave": an introduction of British nurses in colonial west Africa' in Chaudhuri and Strobel, *Western Women and Imperialism*, pp. 177–88.

57 Kathryn Hansen, *Grounds for Play: The Nautanki Theatre of North Indian* (New Delhi, Manohar Publications, 1992), pp. 188–9.

58 Margaret Strobel, *European Women and the Second British Empire* (Bloomington, Indiana University Press, 1991), p. 4.

59 *Ibid.* See also Gregory Martin, 'The influence of racial attitudes on British policy towards India during the First World War', *The Journal of Imperial and Commonwealth History*, 14:2 (Jan. 1986), pp. 91–113.

60 Partha Chatterjee points out that there was a clear demarcation between the 'world' (*bahir*) and the 'home' (*ghar*). The Indian venturing into the outside world and exposed to a dominant material culture could be westernised and acquire the latest in science, technology, economic organisation and political strategy, but only so long as the private space, the home – the sphere of women and family – was preserved as the centre not only of a superior culture but also of 'true' identity. Partha Chatterjee, 'The nationalist resolution of the women's question', in Kumkum Sangari and Sudesh Vaid (eds), *Recasting Women: Essays in Colonial History* (Delhi, Kali for Women, 1989), pp. 233–53.

61 Mrinalini Sinha, 'Gender and imperialism: colonial policy and the ideology of moral imperialism in late nineteenth-century Bengal', in

Michael S. Kimmel (ed.), *Changing Men: New Directions in Research on Men and Masculinity* (London, Sage, 1987), pp. 217–31.

62 Mrinalini Sinha, *Colonial Masculinities: The 'manly Englishman' and the 'effeminate Bengali' in the late nineteenth Century* (Manchester & New York, Manchester University Press, 1995), p. 16.

63 Ashis Nandy, *The Intimate Enemy: Loss and Recovery of Self Under Colonialism* (Delhi, Oxford University Press, 1983), pp. 4–11. Also see Sinha, *Colonial Masculinities*, pp. 2–12.

64 This change in the British perception still awaits scholarly investigation.

65 *The Rains Came*, a lengthy novel of 597 pages, shows Edwina to be a 'slut' and gives vivid descriptions of her sexual promiscuity and innumerable affairs with men of different nationalities and varied classes. It also shows how Edwina wants to be 'laid' by the Indian doctor. Apart from Edwina's sexual desires, there are descriptions of Miss MacDaid, the nurse, who also sexually covets the Indian doctor, accompanied by graphic descriptions of the passion she feels for his naked body. Another aged spinster imagines herself raped and made pregnant by the 'virile' Sikh who rescues her in the flood. See Louis Bromfield, *The Rains Came* (New York, Collier, 1976 [1937]).

66 A close parallel can be seen in the film, *Maisie's Marriage* (1923). Its original title was *Married Love* and was based upon Marie Stope's book of the same name. The book, associated with sex and birth control, had become highly controversial. Considered extremely objectionable by the British censors because of this association, the name of the film was changed. For details, see Annette Kuhn, *Cinema, Censorship and Sexuality, 1909–1925* (London, Routledge, 1988), pp. 77–96.

67 For an analysis of British propaganda during World War II, see Rosaleen Smyth, 'Britain's African colonies and British propaganda during the Second World War', *Journal of Imperial and Commonwealth History*, 141 (Oct. 1985), pp. 65–82.

68 *Film India* (Jun. 1939), p. 41.

69 *The Illustrated Weekly of India* (27 Nov. 1938), p. 20.

70 IOR, L/P&J/8/128, Coll. no. 105-A, pt. XIV, Dec. 1938–Apr. 1940. See *Northamptonshire Evening Telegraph* (6 Jun. 1939), and Louis Bromfield's article in *Photoplay*, 53:10 (Oct. 1939), pp. 26–7.

71 *Film India* (Jun. 1939).

72 IOR, L/P&J/8/128, Coll. no. 105-A, pt. XIV, Dec. 1938–Apr. 1939.

73 See, for example, *Bombay Chronicle* (6 May 1939), p. 28; and *Film India* (Jun. 1939).

74 *Bombay Chronicle* (16 Jun. 1939), p. 30.

75 Robert Stam and Louise Spence, 'Colonialism, racism and represen-tation: an introduction', in Bill Nicholas (ed.), *Movies and Methods*, vol. II (Berkeley & Los Angeles, University of California Press, 1985), pp. 639–60. A positive image begs the question: positive for whom? The positive image approach is intimately linked to status quo politics. Such images are generally integrationist and cooptive which obscure other realities of structural injustice, racial discrimi-nation, socio-political tensions and contradictions. Also see Shohat and Stam, *Unthinking Eurocentrism*, pp. 198–204.

76 Gary Peller, 'Race against integration', *Tikkun*, 6 (Jan–Feb. 1991), cited in Shohat and Stam, *Unthinking Eurocentrism*, p. 25.

77 Ramusack, *The Princes*, p. 238.

78 Copland, *The Princes of India*, p. 270.

79 Sumit Sarkar, *Modern India, 1885–1947* (Delhi, Macmillan), 1985, p. 376.

80 *Hindu* (2 Feb. 1940), p. 7, mentions S. Satyamurthy, president of the South Indian Films Chamber of Commerce, attending the premier of *The Rains Came* in Madras. However, his reactions and comments on a film marketed as 'the first pro-Indian picture from Hollywood' are not known.

5

Conclusion

As a social historian I have attempted to relate the empire cinema, its portrayal and ideological thrust, with wider social and historical forces. Such an analysis establishes cinema as effective historical evidence, which enriches our understanding of the period when it was made. The empire cinema emerges in this study as a major propaganda weapon used by the British government to sustain imperialism, subvert growing nationalism, establish relations of domination, lay claims to legitimacy, and undermine the demand for self-government and democracy in India. It played a significant ideological role in relation to its colonies at a time when colonial politics was under severe attack and the challenge to its authority was at its height, and when fascism was targeting British imperialism in a tense European situation, fast deteriorating towards a world-wide conflagration.

By the 1930s the legitimacy of the Raj had progressively diminished in India and there was a growing dissatisfaction with imperial rule. This diminution of credibility affected the dynamics of cinema projection resulting in the need for a more complex conceptualisation of imperial propaganda. The relations between the colonisers and the colonised, and the constantly changing political and strategic imperatives of colonial rule, particularly in this period of crisis, played a role in redefining imperial and colonial identities, conflicts and images.

This work identifies the processes of manipulation and control exercised by the colonial state in constructing cinematic images and ideological formations. The sharp division of opinion and interests among the ideologues and officials stationed in the colony or operating from the metropolis, and the white viewing

public, brought the contradictions of cinematic representations to
the forefront. Among the former were those belonging to the
BBFC, the India Office, the Indian censor authorities, the military
intelligence directorate, the administration in India and individual
army officers. Among the latter were British civilians and private
persons. These interest groups and individuals, with varying
political, commercial and moral standpoints, created conflicting
currents of opinion regarding the empire films, their content and
message, the construction of identities (both Indian and British)
and the responses and reaction of different sections of western
and Indian audiences. Film-makers, seeking to accommodate
these mutually contentious opinions, emerged with uneven and
contradictory offerings.

The reception of cinematic images and ideological formations,
mediated through categories of nation, race, class and gender in
relation to its vast and varied consumers, both white/western and
coloured/colonised, was diverse and contradictory. The latter
emerge as highly conscious consumers and meaning producers,
reflecting significant perceptual and political predilections. Their
political response to the empire films and direct intervention was
crucially connected with their class and community composition
and profoundly effected the politics and cultural policy of the
nationalists as well as the colonists.

In my conclusion, I wish to recapitulate some of the major
concerns and issues thrown up by this study and then go on to
offer a comment on post-colonial empire cinema and its counterpart, Indian cinema of the 1950s. In my opinion, the shape
assumed by cinema (both empire and Indian) in the immediate
post-colonial years reiterates the absolute necessity of historical
and contextual investigation highlighted in this study. The empire
films of the 1950s deserve a fuller investigation than has been
attempted here. Also my investigation, unlike that of the colonial
period, remains confined to the text. There is a severe paucity of
records through which to reconstruct the reception and possible
reactions of the post-colonial Indian audience particularly in relation to the empire films. Consequently, my concern is to indicate
the ways in which the post-colonial empire cinema differed from
or was similar in content, approach and ideological thrust to the
empire cinema of the colonial period, especially as the consolidation and projection of imperialism in a purely political sense was

no longer the major concern. How was imperialism portrayed in the new political context? How did the formerly colonised world and colonialism feature in the imperial imagery and cinematic vocabulary? Was there a shift – radical or nominal – or was only the context different?

Images and concerns: loyalism and nationalism

The three films undertaken for analysis show a running thread uniting them crucially in terms of images and ideological projections. However, there are significant differences among the three films informing the ways in which they represent imperialism and the colonised. The overall ideological structures of colonial domination inherent in the dominant discourse of the cinema are common to the three films. These films share a perspective that upholds British colonial enterprise as superior, civilising and modern. It also associates imperialism with order and rationality – qualities brought out by the contrast with disorder and irrationality – thus offering legitimation to colonial rule in India. In terms of modernisation and progress, the earlier backwardness of the colony signified in *The Drum* and *Gunga Din* was replaced in *The Rains Came* with the theme of development represented as a boon bestowed by the western civilisation. *The Rains Came* puts across this ideology of development to legitimate the forms of power exercised over the colonised people.

The progressively diminished legitimacy of the Raj was countered by projecting the unstinting support of the loyalist forces in India. All three films visualised an overarching category of 'loyalists' among the subject population in an attempt to strengthen the colonisers' hands as well as those of purported loyalists. These films, it was believed by some, worked towards creating loyalty in order to help India's regeneration. The films made use of varied categories of Indians from the aristocracy to the common man, the minorities and the Indian states subjects for their loyal fold. The projection of this vast reservoir of loyalty for the British rule suggested that India was ruled by consent.

The adventure genre films highlighted this consent through the Indian servicemen who laid down their lives in safeguarding this connection. The loyalty of these had been projected as legendary for more than a decade of film-making, beginning with *The Black*

Watch (1929), which was followed by more successful Hollywood films like the *Lives of a Bengal Lancer* (1935), *The Charge of the Light Brigade* (1936), *Wee Willie Winkie* (1937), *Storm over Bengal* (1938), *The Drum* (1938) and *Gunga Din* (1939). Several such adventure genre empire films were made during these years, which were set in colonies other than India. The two best known, among several other films of the same kind, were *Sanders of the River* (1935) and *The Four Feathers* (1939), produced in Britain by Alexander Korda, the maker of *The Drum*. These films similarly highlighted the role of the army or other loyalists in defeating rebels and in underlining the consent of the colonised to the British rule. The importance of these twin aspects of loyalty and consent, in relation to India, is located in the historical context of British rule in the late 1930s. In a situation of crisis of consent and loyalty faced by the British in India, these concepts assume importance not only in relation to the loyal servicemen but other categories of people projected in the films.

The Drum and *Gunga Din* went beyond all the earlier films by significantly widening the loyalist strata to include other categories of colonial society. *The Drum* appealed to the constituency of the Muslims and *Gunga Din* that of the untouchables of India; both categories had a tense relationship with Congress nationalist politics. In the former, the rags-to-riches story of Sabu was given great prominence in publicising the film. A lower-class Muslim boy working in the royal stables of Mysore State was chosen to become the toast of Hollywood. This transformation underlined the power of the superior white races to transport the loyalist from his humble origins to the heights of fame and riches. In the film, the loyalty of Sabu, playing Azim, saves the British from being massacred in Tokot, even though his advisers tell him that the massacre would undoubtedly lead to his restoration to the throne. Sabu symbolised the loyal Pathans and Muslims who were declared 'natural friends of the British'.

Gunga Din, similarly projected as the film's hero, was 'an untouchable with tremendous handicaps', who worked as a *bhishti* in the British Indian army. He was hailed as a loyalist who rose from his station in life to become 'a valiant fighting man' under the British. The film showed a metaphorical transformation of a half-naked Gunga Din wearing just a loin cloth, into a splendidly uniformed corporal in the British Indian army. These films held people like the actor, Sabu, and the character, Gunga Din, as symbols of hope in a society riven with caste hierarchy and problems of untouchability. By helping this sub-stratum of colonial society, the British appear to be offering an equal opportunity for upward mobility to its subject population without any distinctions of caste or creed.

Gunga Din also included in the loyal category the omnipresent common man of India. The very physicality of Gunga Din – his nakedness, extreme poverty, illiteracy, deprivation and pariah status – was posited as quintessentially those of a common man who suffered greatly at the hands of his own high-caste fellow citizens. In the film, it is this loyal common man who takes on his real oppressor, the high-caste Brahmin and nationalist, guru, who wants to oust this loyalist's real benefactors – the British – from India.

The Rains Came cast this loyal network farther to include Indian princes. Even more important than these princes, who were after all well known for their loyalty to their British masters, were the princes' state subjects. The film claimed political legitimacy in the colony based upon the immense reservoir of loyalty, respect and veneration which the Indian princes commanded among their state subjects as well as among many Indians in the British provinces. This claim meant legitimacy and acceptance of the British connection in at least two-fifths of India, inhabited by eighty-one million Indians, comprising a quarter of the total Indian population. These colonised subjects were shown to be recipients of some of the finest modern amenities of western life and civilisation in return for their loyalty to their British masters.

These three films collectively suggested that in the late 1930s the British had earned enormous good will among the people of India, who were loyal and did not want to break off the British connection. The earlier subtext of the adventure genre films implying that the British wanted to save India gave way in *The Rains Came* to the proposition that it was India itself that wanted the British to save her. This put the onus of retaining the British connection on the Indians themselves.

From the Indian nationalist point of view this loyal category symbolising a most unequal relationship between white masters and coloured residents was unacceptable. According to this, the rebel was a national and a loyal subject was a collaborator.

Consequently, the protest and agitation against *The Drum* occurred not only because the Pathans and Muslims were depicted as fundamentalists, communalists and backward but, above all, because they were depicted as loyal to the British connection. Their loyalty made them anti-national. The resultant agitation demonstrated their readiness to rise in defence of national claims and self-respect against their portrayal as loyal to the British. It was not only an outright rejection of the value put on such loyalty but also an assertion of their nationalism. Their regional identity and nationhood were conflated in their response to imperial hegemony.

The portrayal of loyalty and consent to the British connection in the empire cinema accommodated its dramatic counterpart, the nationalist challenge. However, empire films treated nationalism as a minor development, confined to a lunatic fringe and religious fanatics who represented no significant social force. The concept of nationalism in *The Drum* and *Gunga Din* was shown as essentially religious and fundamentalist. The Muslim fanatic of *The Drum* and the Hindu fundamentalist of the *Gunga Din* were cast in the same stereotypical mould. In the former, the attempt was to establish a Muslim Raj and in the latter, the professedly saintly and pacifist figure of the Hindu villain, modelled on Mahatma Gandhi espousing Hindu nationalism, had a hidden agenda to violently overthrow the British and impose Hindu rule. The films reinforced communal ideology by playing up blatantly the danger of the Muslims reclaiming their lost empire or the Hindus attempting to dominate India, to construct a threat from the inside rather than from the outside.

The arch villains in both these films represented a reversion to fundamentalist ideology in order ostensibly to challenge the ideological tenets of the modern age as projected by the colonial government. The film depicted their revolts against the legitimate authority as anti-western and, therefore, anti-modern and fundamentalist – all of which militated against the notion of nationhood. Significantly, religion in the British discourse on India had been projected as essentially anti-national, conducive more to division than unity.

The challenge of nationalism to British hegemony was shown to be further weakened by forceful propaganda projecting a socially fragmented India divided into watertight compartments of hierarchical caste clusters in both *The Drum* and *Gunga Din*. Religion and caste divisions challenged the ability of the colony to come together as a nation. Ultimately, the primary contradiction in India was not shown between nationalism and imperialism but within nationalism itself; a feature which was to prove useful in portraying Indian nationalists in the post-colonial period.

The Rains Came additionally limited the claims of nationhood. It delineated vast territorial areas of India inhabited by millions of Indians who were loyal and firmly committed to the imperial connection. In other words, vast regions and populations were signified to exist within this so-called nation state, for whom the very concept of India as a nation was alien and non-existent. For these millions of state subjects the territorial and ideological boundaries of nation coincided with their own states and its rulers. *The Rains Came* added significantly to the notion of a divided India, as represented in *The Drum* and *Gunga Din*, on religious and caste bases, by projecting two Indias: British India and Princely India. In a very forceful way, *The Rains Came* completed the fragmentation of India and rendered the nationalist claims to unity as unfeasible, redundant and unwarranted.

In positing the dialectics of colonialism and nationalism, the relations of power appear both to differ and resemble each other in the three films. For example, the absence of villain and revolt in *The Rains Came* posited an eloquent commentary on the ubiquitous acceptance of the British paternalistic connection with India, as well as negating the Indian nationalist challenge to and interrogation of this connection. Simultaneously, this film also offered a damaging comment on the concept of nationalism and its aspiration to democratic nationhood. It added substantial weight to the theory of several Indias co-existing side by side and the near impossibility of these coming together as a democratic national state, which was the demand of the nationalists.

The Rains Came abandoned the well-established, popular, market-tested high military adventure genre of *The Drum* and *Gunga Din*, which had characterised a decade of British and Hollywood film-making of empire cinema. This genre had not only demonstrated the physical mastering of the colonisers over the colonised, its violence and coercive dominance, but also made prominent the superior–inferior racial relationship between British officers and Indian sepoys – a significant microcosm of the wider colonial order. This change suggested the possibilities of fresh ideological negotiations, projections and image-making. The shedding of some of the stereotypical representations and images, leading to the reworking of Otherness in *The Rains Came*, opened up an ambivalent space to enable the old colonial modalities to be translated to a new terrain of colonial relationship.

In this reworking certain examples stand out: that of the oriental prince, the white woman in a colonial setting, and hitherto unattempted gender relations. All of these are intimately connected with the working of racism in a colonial situation. The portrayal of an oriental ruler underwent a dramatic shift. From a negatively-etched, stereotypical, lecherous, indolent, decadent, violent savage of the adventure genre films, he was more positively drawn, transformed into a western-educated, urbane, civilised, 'near white' colonial subject. The biologically based pseudo-scientific racism, so blatant in the adventure genre films, which identified the natives by their racial characterisation, was modified in favour of new eugenics, which envisaged the possibility of changing inherited qualities. In *The Rains Came*, the black and white binarism was diluted to hold out the possibility that the colonised can learn 'white' values. This 'enlightened' prince, however, was not without his 'inherent racial' weaknesses, and socio-caste bindings which set him apart from his white male counterpart and inferiorised him. Although loyal to the colonial masters he was without the more patent obsequiousness of the earlier depictions of the loyal oriental prince. His loyalty was not flaunted openly or asserted publicly like that of Prince Azim in *The Drum* or that of Gunga Din. Shown to be a product of his class and western education, his loyalty was made out to be a conscious and rational decision, coming naturally to him. The British accepted it as a matter of course. The recast Indian prince was the kind of person with whom the British could deal with ease and with an apparent, though not real, equality.

The reworking of the Other was accompanied by changes in the representation of the white woman. Although certain stereotypical traits characterise the white woman's portrayal in all three films, it was only in *The Rains Came* that she was brought to the centre stage from the extreme periphery of the narrative in all preceding films. In the adventure genre films, the colonial army service, an all-out male domain of intimate relationship and comradeship, accommodated the white female as a symbol of heterosexual monogamous patriarchy. Her presence in the film brought racism to the surface, marking out racially exclusive spaces reserved for the white, and exclusive interaction among the white in a world teeming with coloured inhabitants. In her role as a wife, the white woman in *The Drum* played a subsidiary, marginal and supportive role to her husband. The film concentrated on the image of the white woman as a chaste wife, whose only agenda was to further her husband's mission and work. In *Gunga Din* this white woman, an aspirant to wifehood, is shown as a disruptive force, rather than an asset, to the male bonding and their successful collective imperial endeavour. In this film her presence was exploited essentially for comic relief. She is ousted from the scene half way through the film without evoking any reactions.

In *The Rains Came* the white representation is made far more complicated, symbolised in and associated with the defiance of its white female protagonist. The licence given to the white woman to touch a native, a mere boy, in *The Drum,* evoking contradictory images of sexual and nurturing relationship, climaxes in a miscegenous alliance in *The Rains Came.* In a significant display of sexuality, Edwina takes the initiative in her relationship with Rama Safti – the Indian prince – signifying the western attraction for the Other. The film explores the possibilities of this transgression before the closure of the narrative with the death of Edwina. A resolution which, interpreted as a 'punishment', defines the situation now achieved as normative order, but only after establishing its positive fallout for the Other.

This subversion of the hitherto reigning images and ideology concerning white womanhood, sexuality and morality is resolved in the film through the transcendence of the white woman from a sexual, desiring, desirable subject to the position of a colonial representative in her asexual role of a nurturing, giving 'mother'. As the mother figure she is allowed a wider range of action and a larger moral space within which she acts. Her virtue is linked explicitly to self-sacrifice. 'White male honour' is finally redeemed through the destruction of the white female body and the triumph of an extremely benevolent nurturing imperialism. Also significant is the use of marginalised groups or individuals – the Scottish boy in *The Drum*, for example – to dissolve race categories.

The Rains Came marked a change from films dependent on the construction of active flamboyant masculinity expressed in military aggression and violence in *The Drum* and *Gunga Din*. Instead, it moved to a more complicated characterisation of white and coloured masculinity. The coloured man was made the hero, though bereft of 'hero-like qualities'. Rama completely lacks such stereotypical masculine attributes as leadership, self-confidence, dominating presence and, above all, a towering physicality. Even in his miscegenous relationship, it is the white woman who is the dominating and assertive partner. Rama is depicted neither as an initiator of this relationship nor a giver in it. He is a mere recipient and hence inferior. The superior role of the giver is reserved for the white woman.

Muted reference to certain contexts lying beyond the films' tacit representations crucially highlight the films' emerging potentials. One such field is the heteronormative context of power and identity. In *The Drum* and *Gunga Din*, despite projecting the heterosexual couple and heterosexuality as the ideal, what emerges forcefully on the surface is male bonding, evoking the homosexuality associated with an all-male army. Gunga Din, for example, with his dog-like devotion, which happily tolerates all the indignities and abuses inflicted upon him, is shown emotionally bound to the British sergeants. Similarly, in *The Rains Came*, the Indian prince, despite leaning towards miscegenation, has stronger bonds with the white male protagonist, and is shown to be chided and guided simultaneously by him, even in personal matters.

Yet, contradictorily, the masculinity of the colonised becomes equated in all three films with loyalty. This attribute characterised not only the highly masculine loyal Indian soldiers but also common people like Gunga Din, as well as the princes. Those who opposed the British were characterised by subterfuge, deceit, cruelty and deception – like the villains in *The Drum* and *Gunga Din*. Although *The Rains Came* does not have a conventional villain, the film portrays middle-class, educated Indians, the well-known torchbearers of nationalism, symbolised in the character of Banerjee, as essentially orthodox, fickle, disloyal, unstable and inferior. All these are stereotypical feminine characteristics associated with effeminate men. The masculinisation of loyalty rendered all anti-British elements effeminate and inferior.

The female counterpart of the colonised male in the empire film is not accorded a direct cinematic representation. Her presence is marked more by her absence. In the all-male adventure genre films she is characterised by a few fleeting images and conversational pieces. In *The Drum* and *Gunga Din*, references to *purdah*, polygamy, the harem and *nautch* girls conjured images of oriental women that accent negative impressions and cast reflections upon colonial society and its Other, the white western society. These characterisations reduce the colonised female to a sexualised, inferiorised Other and set her up in binary opposition to the chaste pure white woman. On the one hand, they worked to stress the liberated, western woman who enjoyed equality with men, and, on the other, they denigrated the oriental male, his culture and his civilisation. Even a western-educated male, like Rama Safti in *The Rains Came*, with a progressive modern public front, remains backward in his private social domain. In heading, ultimately, towards an arranged marriage within his caste and community he is shown to be located in a social structure of feudal gender relations, signified in the unvoiced but familiar images of *purdah*, polygamy, the harem and *nautch* girls.

The Rains Came, however, does mark a change from the near absence of a colonised female by creating a significant though small role for the Indian Maharani. In a comparatively positive characterisation, this Maharani is endowed with a great deal of agency. Concerned about the welfare of her state and its people, she is shown to be an efficient organiser. However, she is not cast in the role of a female regent – a role historically well-known in India and also celebrated in folklore and folk theatre – but as a mere shadow of her deceased husband, assuming limited agency only to fulfil his dictates. She does not emerge as an individual. The authority with which she speaks is a sign of her class standing, not of her race. Racially she is shown as savage, uncivilised, violent and inferior, bound by orthodox social and caste ways, which severely compromise the initiative she shows in safeguarding her state and its male succession. She is also shown to be well aware of the racial superiority of the colonisers and their bounties. Her 'wisdom' lies in this knowledge and its deployment.

Gender identities clearly emerge as an important function in colonial and nationalist dialectics in all three films. They highlight how the politics of gender and loyalism were complicated by their intersection with other categories and ideologies of race, ethnicity, class, religion and sexuality, especially as these categories were used in the films to fragment the colonised into individuals, groups and communities that otherwise might be capable of mounting a challenge to the imperialists.

Post-colonial cinema: insecurities and justifications

In a world recast and refashioned after World War II and the independence of large parts of it, there was a greater need for white people in both the US and Britain to feel secure about their superiority and hegemonic supremacy over the Other. Empire had played a powerful part, imagined and directly experienced, in the construction of their identity that was intimately linked to what it meant to be 'white'.[1] Empire had reinforced a hierarchical view of the world in which the white races had occupied a permanent place, with the colonised ranged in varying degrees of supposed inferiority. This confidence in their superiority was severely eroded by the two world wars where effective challenges had been mounted by colonial nationalisms against white prestige and hegemony leading to the loss of empire. This challenge questioned the alleged inferiority of the colonised.

In the 1950s, the west direly needed reassurance as well as justification of their colonial past in order to come to terms with the loss of empire. In Britain the rapid pace of decolonisation by the 1950s, leading to the independence of Jordan in 1946, India and Pakistan in 1947, Sri Lanka and Burma in 1948 and Israel in 1949 was received in various ways. For many it was a moral victory to be celebrated; for others it was a disaster to be deplored. Popular writing tended to show just a hint of concern at colonialist misdeeds but with the complacent belief that all had turned out well in the end. On the whole the dominant academic and popular perception of the imperial past and that of the Raj in particular was far from negative.[2] It was and remains difficult for the average British or white European citizen to take a negative view of the imperial position.

This predominant viewpoint, long nurtured in Britain through a rich diet of imperial propaganda, stood in the way of the British accepting the dismemberment of their colonial empire. Despite the loss of empire, the British policy-makers did not expect decolonisation to spell the end of imperialism. When Mountbatten, the last viceroy of colonial India, with the prerogative to rule autocratically if he so wished, became governor general of independent India, retaining influence but no effective power in a smooth change-over, this historical juncture threw light on the likely relationship of the two countries. There was a strong belief in the continuing reality of imperial links in some form or other until at least the late 1960s.[3] The long years of 'living together' (roughly 200 years in the case of India) could not be written off and it was assumed that ex-imperial territories would continue to align themselves with Britain.

In this the notion of a new Commonwealth of Nations with Britain at its head was expected to sustain the latter's influence though not power in world affairs. This replacement of the concept of trusteeship with a Commonwealth based upon British ideals helped to cushion the shock of loss of empire for many British people and enabled them to see the granting of independence as the fulfilment of mission – described by P. J. Marshal as 'the last stage of imperialism of ideals'[4] and not as a collapse of power.

Placed in this context, the empire films of the 1950s with an Anglocentric point of view skilfully emphasised an intimate relationship between Britain and India, suggesting the desire on the part of both countries to remain together in a Britain-centred world system. This was a system in which the British political hegemony over its vast colonial empire had led to modernisation, development, the transfer of technology and science with a consequent transformation of societies. This transformation was based upon western liberal concepts of parliamentary democracy and the rule of law as a particular gift of Britain and a triumph of a western ideology. For many British people it was axiomatic that their colonial record was much superior to that of any other power.[5] This aspect of imperialism turned the granting of freedom to India – the propagated destiny of India – into a moral victory to be celebrated rather than a disaster to be deplored. Consequently, the decolonisation shown in the films as abnegation turned out to be its most powerful justification of imperialism. The view that the British gave up its colonies rather than being forced to do so minimised the admission of losing an empire.

The rethinking of issues relating to empire and imperialism had not meant a reconceptulisation of imperial ideology. The need for reassurance and justification meant that the world continued to be looked at through colonial spectacles, so that white European and North American viewers and readers' hegemonic position remained intact. The imperial film continued to display a lack of historically specific understanding of the colonial contexts, central to which was the exploitation and repression of the colonised.

Reassurance found its chief anchor in the adventure genre films with colonial empire as their theme. As there remained a keen voyeuristic interest in the British empire, these films were made in the same old pattern. The decade of the 1950s saw a spate of these colonial adventure films, with India as its central locale, which had been dropped from the film-makers' agenda in the late 1930s in the face of severe objections raised in India and the issuing of new guidelines to the film-makers by the BBFC. The objections of the Indian provincial ministeries in 1937–39 had led to a banning of such films from exhibition in India. The contradiction inherent in the empire cinema directed to two different audiences – white/western and coloured/colonised – was finally resolved in favour of the former. The post-colonial films targeted the white/western audience more pointedly. The western film makers were aware that the adventure genre films, which had earlier proved inflammable in India and had been banned for their anti-Indian projections, could still be received enthusiastically by western audiences, conveying, as they did, the pleasures and benefits of pursuing high-adventure in the pioneering days of empire-building. The post-colonial films reassumed the successful formulae of those empire films, which attracted huge audiences in the west. These films allowed the white European and US populace to bask in the reflected glow of past glories imparting to them a sense of superiority – racial, ideological and civilisational.

It is interesting to note that the adventure genre that saw a revival in the west faced a retreat in post-colonial Indian cinema after its immense popularity in the colonial period. In the colonial days, these films played a prominent anti-British role and had affected the popularity of western films. Drawing upon both the Hollywood and indigenous traditions, this genre of films with its nationalist warrior hero/heroine fighting against imperialism had acted as an effective counterfoil to the empire cinema. It had provided a severe indictment of the British presence and its political order. Post-colonial India, with her accent on nation building, laid emphasis upon 'quality' production of films, socially relevant themes, educational and communication aspects, and production of better types of films to serve 'better instincts of humanity rather than the base standards of taste'.[6] The adventure genre was considered to provide an escape into the unreal world. Other genres, like the 'social', were considered better for portraying the aspirations of the infant nation.[7] The decline of the adventure genre, however, meant that action, thrills, magic and stunt content, considered extremely attractive to the masses, were reinforced in other genres.

The western audience, on the other hand, needed this unreal world. In 1951, Metro-Goldwyn-Mayer adapted two films, *The Soldiers Three* and *Kim*, from Kipling's stories. The former portrays the ambitions of Malik Rao, a fanatic who believes in violence to achieve his ends, and his crushing defeat at the hands of British Indian army. *Kim* portrays a white in the garb of an Indian who, after his adventures in mystic India, seeks out his true destiny as an Englishman with the British Indian army involved in the great game to defend the British Raj. *The King of the Khyber Rifles* (1954), made by Twentieth-Century Fox, adopted the well-known title from Talbot Mundy's novel that had been filmed in 1929. It shows Kuran Khan, a Muslim fanatic, seeking the extermination of the white masters and the establishment of his personal power. He is defeated by the British Indian army. The same year saw the release of *Bengal Rifles* (US title: *Bengal Brigade*) by Universal-International Films. It brought back the theme of the Indian Mutiny to the screen that had been banned in the empire days. This film was denied a licence for exhibition in India.[8] The British view of the uprising was likely to prove offensive to the Indian viewership. Moreover, India was now free to go public with its interpretation of the Mutiny. Indeed, in 1953, Sohrab Modi made *Jhansi Ki Rani* (*The Tiger and the Flame*), celebrating the legendary role of Laxmi Bai of Jhansi. It was a vehement condemnation of the British policy of ruthless annexation leading to the 1857 revolt, openly termed as the first war of independence.[9]

The last two films of this decade were British productions from the Rank studio: *Harry Black* (US title: *Harry Black and the Tiger*) in 1958 and *North West Frontier* (US title: *Flame Over India*) in 1959. The former shows a famous tiger hunter in India who allows his best friend to prove himself a hero and falls in love with his friend's wife. I. S. Johar, playing the comic-faithful native bearer of Harry Black in the film, is reminiscent of Gunga Din, and shares a special relationship with his master that involves emotional bonding on both sides. The *North West Frontier*, as with *The Drum*, portrays a Muslim conspiracy, aided by an outside power, to create a Muslim state by murdering its Hindu prince. A British colonel escorts the boy prince to safety, averting the impending anarchy and civil war.

Significantly, the portrayal of these themes had evoked an inflammable reaction in the colonial period. It would be highly instructive to study the reception of these themes and images in post-colonial India. However, there are no records available to indicate whether these films were screened at all (except in the case of *Bengal Rifles*) and, if screened, how they were received by the post-colonial audience. There is some evidence to suggest that the Indian government was not satisfied with these films and their portrayal of India.[10] After independence the Indian government started to discourage the shooting of western films in India, by imposing excessive taxation and high import duties on equipment. When the western motion picture companies submitted their scripts to the Indian Board of Film Censors for approval, it indicated that it did not want those films made in India.

These films followed closely the pattern set by earlier adventure genre films set in India. The greatly changed political context, however, either muted certain aspects of these films or found a new justification for those projections that had proved inflammable earlier to colonised subjects. For example, the projection of Hindu–Muslim antagonism and the emphasis on religious divisions of India in the empire films of 1950s, had the substantive contemporary reality of the Indian sub-continent now divided on religious grounds into two nation states: India and Pakistan. The former states of the NWFP and Punjab (the location of all adventure genre films), along with Sindh and Bengal were the areas subject to division. This partition of the territory caused a large-scale migration of population and attendant sectarian rioting involving Hindus, Muslims and Sikhs. The infant state, deeply scarred from its birth, took a long time to heal. The impact of partition was reflected in various facets of the nation's life, including cinema, especially in relation to intercommunity relationships.

The Indian film industry in the post-colonial period trod warily around the subject for fear of embroiling itself in sectarian controversy. The noticeable decline of Hindu mythological films,[11] which had played a very significant role in the colonial days in encoding messages of nationalist patriotism, may well be related to the young nation determining to remain secular in keeping with the Nehruvian national image. It may be remembered that recently the genre of the mythological film and TV serial has been constructing an imaginary glorious past in order to legitimise Hindu right-wing definitions of the nation, as witness Ramanand Sagar's television sagas, *Ramayana* (1986–88) and *Shri Krishna* (1998), and B. R Chopra's *Mahabharat* (1988–90).

It is not unlikely that the unease and denunciation of mythological films in the immediate aftermath of independence by noted political personalities and the national leadership[12] were connected with their sensitivity towards and concern with perils of growing sectarian identification in a communally tense situation. In fact, a proposal made to the Film Enquiry Committee, appointed in 1949, had sought to prohibit film actors and actresses from playing the roles of gods and goddesses.[13] The two films, *Ayodhaya Pati* (1950) and *Bhakta Prahlad* (1958), show 'the decay of this genre'.[14]

The trauma of partition, nevertheless, registered its effects in the emergence of dislocation and loss as a significant theme in the Indian cinema of the 1950s. In this, Ravi Vasudevan argues, the post-colonial social genre of the Hindi commercial cinema made a concerted effort to bind wounds and project Hindu–Muslim amity and communal harmony and constitute a new order of 'Hindu identity' simultaneously.[15] Social films of the colonial period had made a substantial contribution to popularising the social aspects of Indian society, which were an important concern of the nationalist leadership. One of the problems they had focused on had been religious sectarianism. Both social genre as well as historical genre films are important in this respect.

The historical genre films continued the earlier tradition

adopted in the colonial period in portraying the Mughals, well known for religious tolerance, syncretism, intercommunity marriages, and the flourishing of Hindu artists and craftsmen, to convey the message of Hindu–Muslim brotherhood. In the post-colonial period, this tradition was maintained and certain well-known legends associated with the reign of Akbar (1556–1605) became popular with the Bombay film-makers for conveying these sentiments. The three notable films in this respect were: *Baiju Bawara* (1952), dealing with the rivalry between two musicians in Akbar's court; *Anarkali* (1953), dealing with the legendary love between Prince Salim, the heir apparent to the emperor Akbar, and Anarkali, the slave girl; and Sohrab Modi's *Mirza Ghalib* (1954), dealing with the life of the best known poet in the Urdu language under the last Mughal king, Bahadur Shah Zafar.

Along with the portrayal of amity and good will, there existed other historical films that dealt with Chhatrapati Shivaji. Made in Marathi by Bhalji Pendharkar, these reiterated community identities, as they had done in the colonial period. The portrayal of Shivaji, as the founder of India's first Hindu kingdom based upon his *Dev-Desh-Dharm* (god, country and religion) ethics and war against Muslim kings tended to create 'allegories for communal and regional differences'.[16] Nationalism was evoked, but it was nationalism overwhelmingly identified, in certain regional pockets, with a single community.

Nationalism in the empire films, both colonial and post-colonial, on the other hand, remained a minor development, confined to villains shown as religious fanatics, shown to be motivated by no more than personal greed and ambition. Consequently, these films hardly demanded credibility from the western viewers regarding colonial nationalism. Yet, the stark reality of colonial nationalism and decolonisation remained, as also the fact that Indian cinema was making a direct comment upon colonialism and nationalism. The Indian film industry, which in the colonial period was not allowed to portray nationalism directly, felt free to do so after independence. A number of films were made that dealt directly with Indian nationalism countering British imperialism, showing nationalists as heroes, British loyalists as traitors to their country, and the colonisers as villains out to exploit and oppress the Indians. The first memorable film of this kind was

Shaheed made in 1948 by Ramesh Saigal in Hindi. He followed this with *Samadhi* in 1950. Both these films follow a similar nationalist trajectory in which two brothers belonging to affluent families are on different sides. In *Shaheed*, the villainous brother is in the British police helping them to wipe out nationalists and the hero is a nationalist revolutionary determined to set his nation free of foreign domination. In *Samadhi*, the villainous brother is an officer in the British Indian army and the hero joins the Indian National army. The latter is helping his countrymen in their fight against the British. In the ensuing confrontation the nationalist heroes die, but they triumph even in death, having successfully foiled the evil designs of the British and their toadies.[17] Toadies in the Indian cinema were the former loyalists in the empire films who had upheld British imperialism and had been hailed as heroes.

The two other notable films made in 1952 were *Anandmath* and *Rahi*, directed by K. A. Abbas. The former, based on Bankimchandra Chatterjee's novel, depicted the Sanyasi uprising against the British in the eighteenth century; and the latter, adapted from Mulk Raj Anand's novel, *Two Leaves and a Bud*, was set in pre-independence Assam. It shows the humbling of the British manager of a tea plantation and the Indian toadies at the hands of Indian workers.

The western film-makers were aware that nationalism and decolonisation, which made this mirror reversal of British collaborators possible, had to be accommodated within the structure and concept of imperialism as portrayed in the cinema. Imperialism, in this respect, needed to be explained and justified afresh in the post-colonial empire films. This justification can be gleaned from two empire romances, *The Rains of Ranchipur*, made by Twentieth-Century Fox in 1955, and *Bhowani Junction*, made in 1956 by Metro-Goldwyn-Mayer. Both these films deal more directly with Indian nationalism and the British imperialist relationship with their former colony. In many ways these Raj romances may really be called precursors to the Raj nostalgia, which hit Britain in a big way in the late 1970s and 1980s in the form of a series of films and television programmes about India.[18]

The Rains of Ranchipur, directed by Jean Negulesco, was a remake of Twentieth-Century Fox's earlier 1939 film *The Rains Came*. The film was updated to include Britain's recent colonial past, which necessitated certain changes. The film eliminated the gross caricature of the Indian educated middle class, the torch bearers of Indian nationalism, signified in the person of Banerjee. Prince Rama, the western-educated hero, played by Richard Burton, is transformed into a nationalist who is imprisoned by the British for his activities. By transforming Rama from a British loyalist to a nationalist the film also gave up the notion of two Indias, the British India and the princely India, as also its claim to the loyalty of princely India. This assumes significance in view of historical fact – the complete and relatively easy amalgamation of the princely states with the rest of India at the time of independence.[19]

Lana Turner, playing Edwina Esketh, falls for Rama but gives him up in the end. The film eschews the tragic ending. Edwina returns with her husband, Lord Esketh, who is transformed from a despicable *nouveau riche* upstart into a former war-hero fallen on hard times, who had married Edwina for her money. Miscegenation is negated – it is neither condoned nor condemned. It does, however, assume a more direct political colouring than in the earlier film. Yet, in both the versions, miscegenation remains a gift – voluntarily and lovingly given by the mother country, signified by Edwina in her nurturing mother role, suggestive of 'maternal imperialism'.

In the post-colonial context of India having achieved independence, the film represented Britain far more positively than its earlier version. It showed a moral victory for the British and the identification of their imperial identity as the 'giver of freedom' in a cordial atmosphere of love and friendship. In other words, an 'imperialism of ideals' finds its logical destination in their willing bestowal of freedom to its subject population. It also suggested that the British were not imperial-minded people and the ending of the empire was no tragedy. Instead, there was the immense satisfaction in making a gift of freedom to its people. Until the end, India remained a beneficiary of the empire. This love affair between colonial India and imperial Britain was carried much further in *Bhowani Junction*.

Various British writers, from E. M. Forster to William Buchan, have perceived 'Britain's long, intimate and passionate relationship' with the Indian subcontinent as a love affair, even a marriage.[20] A highly successful film based on this love theme was

Bhowani Junction, adapted from John Masters' novel of the same name and directed by George Cukor. It deals more directly with British aspirations and insecurities involved in the process of decolonisation by making comment on the nature of challenge from the nationalists during the last days of the Raj. It extends a unique defence of imperialism for its role towards an India that had gained independence.

There are close parallels between *The Rains* and *Bhowani Junction*. The central character in *Bhowani Junction*, as in *The Rains*, is a woman. Both films also use gender and race to redefine imperialism in the changed post-colonial context to offer a justification for British imperialism. Unlike Edwina, however, Victoria Jones (Ava Gardner) is not racially pure. She is an Eurasian. By focusing on the Eurasian community in India and their crisis of identity – represented by Victoria's search for her 'true' identity, racial, sexual, material and territorial – *Bhowani Junction* represents the trauma of the loss of empire and the identity crisis, which it triggered for the British. This identification was in no small way responsible for the extremely sympathetic treatment of the 'half-caste' female protagonist.

Victoria, like Edwina, is treated as an object of male desire. Her relationship with her three racially different men is used to comment upon Indian nationalists and the ambivalent placement of the British in an imperial world that was falling apart. Desperately seeking her identity, Victoria first reaches out to Patrick Taylor (Bill Travers), an Eurasian railway superintendent, who is contemptuous of Indians and refuses to accept the impending future and end of the Raj. Victoria rejects him. Eventually he dies a heroic death. Victoria is next courted by Taylor's Indian assistant, Ranjit Kasel (Francis Matthews), who looks forward to the independence of India. She goes so far as to wear a sari and consents to marry him according to Sikh religious rites. In a tense scene that takes place in a Sikh temple, Victoria flees, unable to go through a complete change of identity. Finally, she falls in love with Col. Rodney Savage (Stewart Granger). Victoria, however, refuses to go with him to England and live an English life. She wishes to stay where she belongs in India.

In view of the large-scale migration of Eurasians and others from ex-colonies to Britain, the USA and Australia, and the attendant heightening of tension in the 1950s, this stand assumes a political significance and makes an unequivocal statement. Britain in the 1950s was involved in an intense and acrimonious debate regarding immigration from its ex-colonies.

Savage is cast in the stereotypical image of the white army officer of the earlier empire films and shown from the British point of view as the fair-minded, honest, efficient and courageous Englishman, much loved by his subordinate Indians. The Indian viewpoint may well have differed and rejected these qualities of the colonel. He is shown to break the passive and peaceful resistance of followers of Gandhi, who were lying on the railway tracks to stop the train, by ordering his men to throw buckets of filthy sewage over them. The breaking up of passive resistance by such means is not only revolting in itself but an insult to caste. The colonel comments that because the passive resistors are high-caste men they will not be able to hold out. It would take them six months to purify themselves. Victoria's discomfort with Savage's action is perceptible in the film.

This plot is worked out against the backdrop of India in 1946, seething with discontent and unrest prior to the departure of the British. It portrays effectively the western understanding of Indian nationalism. The film fights shy of making a frontal attack on the nationalists, but uses a series of negative images and ideology to discredit them. Disunity among Indian nationalists is shown in various ways. In this, the old ploy of good Indian–evil Indian is adopted but with finer nuances indicative of the changed political scenario. The category of the good Indian of the empire films is reworked, personified by Ranjit Kasel and district collector Govindswamy. This characterisation comes close to that of Rama in *The Rains of Ranchipur*. He is no longer loyal and servile to the British. Well-educated and trained in handling complex administrative matters, he belongs to the Indian civil service (touted by the British as the finest civil service in the world and the greatest gift of the British to India). Although he works for the British, he is loyal to India and to the cause of India. In working towards the improvement of his country, pending its independence, he collaborates with the British, rather than against them.

The concept of loyalty in the post-colonial empire films had shifted. The earlier emphasis on the widespread loyalist support that the British could command in India, as shown in the colonial empire films, could hardly be evoked in the context of the total marginalisation of collaborators in India on the eve of independence. The primary identification of loyal Indians is shown to be with India. Their collaboration with Britain stands redeemed as Britain's role is in harmony with that of India's aspirations to independence rather than against it.

This shift renders even the British Indian army loyal to India. These loyal Indians are intelligent and sensitive not only to the British presence and the benefits of their presence in India but also to the threat posed to their country by their fellow country men – the Indian communists, who take their orders from Russia. These loyalists share with the British their grave concern regarding communist designs on their country. The Congress party organiser, Surabhai, is shown to abhor violence. Yet, he remains blind to the real threat of communists and revolutionaries to his country. His anti-British moves and attempts at strikes, passive resistance and disruption of communications are all shown to feed into the hands of communists who have infiltrated the Congress movement and are attempting to assume power in India after the British departure. He is shown to be short-sighted and even foolish as, ultimately, the film suggests, the Congress would be sidelined by the communist power games. In this, the film projects an interesting convergence of interest between colonial rulers and the Congress, the would-be rulers.

Posing the real threat is the communist leader, Ghanshyam, an out-and-out villain. He is a ruthless revolutionary willing to kill his people to achieve his aim of taking over from the British. The train smash caused by him, leaving several dead and injured Indians, signifies not merely physical violence but also a total collapse of morality and values in India, and condemns communism as a wholly destructive force.

Throughout the 1930s Jawaharlal Nehru, who would become India's first prime minister, popularised the vision of a socialist India. He stressed the need to inculcate a new socialist ideology within the national movement. India emerged after independence not only as a republic, but as a secular, socialist, democratic and sovereign republic. India under Nehru also publicly embraced a policy of non-alignment and friendship with socialist countries and the emerging Third World, and refused to align itself against communism. This Nehruvian vision of India, which economically included an industrialised modern India along with the Gandhian political philosophy and moral legacy, determined to a large extent the images and ideologies thrown up by Indian cinema in the 1950s. A fine example of socialist ideas and the value of labour in post-colonial India is the Hindi commercial film *Naya Daur* (1957), which argues for collectivisation as the proletarian way of managing new technology. Another film, which achieved outstanding artistic acclaim, was Satyajit Ray's debut film, *Pather Panchali* (*Song of the Road*, 1955), which evoked 'the classic symbols of a newly independent nation, the aftermath of the war and the shift towards Nehruite industrialism.' [21]

Here one needs to remember that the post-World War II situation showed a preoccupation of the west with communist subversion. Analysing this concern in relation to the colonial world, Frank Furedi argues that in the Cold War situation, with the very real advance made by forces linked to the Soviet Union and China, the British increasingly perceived communism as the potential future beneficiary of the growth of militant nationalism.[22] They felt that nationalist grievances could be exploited or manipulated by communists. Such a linkage in his opinion helped discredit the nationalist claims of the participants and was harmonious with imperial self-esteem. In this the USA, pursuing an anti-Soviet line, also encouraged the representation of mass anti-colonial movements as communist conspiracies.

The US anxiety about communist subversion had its impact even on film-making. In the 1950s Hollywood came to be targeted for harbouring communists. The House Un-American Activities Committee of the US Congress put Hollywood on trial in 1947. It openly alleged communist infiltration of the motion picture industry and declared it 'the greatest hotbed of subversive activity in the US'.[23] Hollywood was put on the defensive and felt pressurised enough to produce anti-communist films. *Bhowani Junction*, billed as a UK/USA production, based on a popular novel with a predominant anti-communist thrust, was a film which used this bogey of communism most effectively to deride both communism as well as colonial nationalism.[24]

In *Bhowani Junction*, the images of Indian nationalists of various hues had the cumulative effect of projecting a politically fractured India heading towards chaos – torn asunder by a multiplicity of voices and different interest groups – all going under the name of nationalism. The irreconcilable divisions of caste, class and religion posed in the empire films to deny the possibility of nationalism in India, became in the post-colonial films irreconcilable contradictions among Indian nationalists themselves. Nationalism could not be denied but it could certainly be belittled and derided. By contrast, India's teeming millions are shown to be helpless victims of the machinations of these national groups. The film implied that the absolute control of India in the hands of such representatives of nationalism was destructive. It helped to pose the unvoiced question of whether India was not better off under the British. This was the view that had publicly and repeatedly surfaced in Britain and had its private echoes in India, especially after the assassination of Mahatma Gandhi.[25]

The British, on the other hand, are shown to be humanitarian and concerned about this violence. About to quit India voluntarily, they are still capable and willing to help India. The diabolic plot of the communists to blow up the train passing through Bhowani Junction carrying a retinue of Congress leaders, including Gandhi, is foiled by Col. Savage, with the help of Taylor, who dies in this attempt. The capable handling of this anti-national activity provides its own defence of imperialism. The film suggests a post-colonial imperialism of dependency, showing the British in the role of supervisors of a world they had created – a liberal world – that needed to be defended against its opponents. The constant paternalistic supervision depicted in the earlier empire films was no longer considered necessary. Instead, fraternal assistance against subversion within and guarding against enemies without was all that was required.

The film concludes with Rodney Savage deciding to marry Victoria and remain in India. This ending is a significant departure from that of the novel. In the novel Victoria decides to remain true to her Eurasian origin and opts for fellow Eurasian, Taylor, although he is the least likeable of her trio of suitors. The novel had maintained the ground rule that like must go with like, negating the possibilities of miscegenation along two separate axes.

The substitution of the Eurasian Taylor by the Englishman Savage as the partner of Victoria is significant. Victoria's choice of Savage for a heterosexual relationship posits the 'true masculinity' of the British rather than of the Eurasian or the Indian. This three-way racial projection emphasises the difference between races and underlines overwhelming racial consciousness. Its final resolution in favour of the 'pure white' race helps establish its superiority.

Out of the three male suitors, the Indian alone lacks personality. Physically delicate, thin and short in comparison with his British and Eurasian counterparts, he is shown to lack self-confidence. Ranjit does not even have the courage to express his feelings for Victoria. In one scene his mother tells Victoria, 'You are stronger than he is and you will be able to make him into whatever you wish.' Although an atheist, like his mother, Ranjit desires to return to the fold of religion. Such an attempt suggests the hold of religion even among the educated Indians and the possibility of reversion into fundamentalism, with its innate, attendant evils. Significantly, religion could no longer be played up as anti-national, as in the colonial period, but it could certainly be played up as anti-western and anti-modern.

Ranjit is not only overawed and overshadowed by Victoria but also by his mother who calls him a weakling. In fact, the mother is held responsible for the sorry plight of her son. Cast in shades reminiscent of the Maharani of *The Rains*, the mother in *Bhowani Junction* is endowed with even more ruthless agency; she is shown to be aggressive, manipulative and domineering. This all-powerful mother, harbouring communists in her house, is denounced as an emasculating force and not a liberating one, as shown in the Indian adventure films, which had adopted the concept of *virangana* (warrior woman) most fruitfully in the colonial days. An important aspect of the adventure genre had been the female counterpart of the nationalist adventure hero in the form of the 'warrior woman'. Fearless Nadia, associated most strongly with the concept of the warrior woman, attempted a comeback, but the two films, *Carnival Queen* (1955) and *Diler Daku* (1957), met with indifferent results.

The warrior woman was replaced in the post-colonial Indian cinema with an essentially house-bound woman, happy under patriarchal domination without virulent aggressiveness. Such characteristics came to be associated with the westernisation and modernisation of a woman and a rejection of traditional values, and was therefore condemned.[26] An active agency, however, was not lacking for the woman in her mother role. Associated popularly with the female goddess, Durga or Kali, this mother was aggressive and warlike as well as nurturing. The concept of India associated with the female mother goddess was already popular in the colonial period. It emerged most forcefully in Mehboob Khan's *Aurat* (1940). This film consolidated the powerful dual imagery of the mother as both destructive and nurturing. Remade in 1957 by Mehboob Khan as *Mother India*, this blockbuster was a national epic and became the model for all later films.[27]

Bhowani Junction played upon this imagery of the Indian mother/nation as aggressive and destructive towards her sons/ nationalists. In the Indian situation, the positing of this unusual agency for Indian women was also grounded in their overwhelming participation in the national movement, frowned upon by the British.[28] In a way the film transplants the possible western fears evoked in the wake of the women's liberation movement in the west, on to India, by generating fears regarding emasculation at the hands of strident women. The film's unequivocal denunciation of such an agency shifts the coloniser's responsibility and the role it played in the inferiorising and emasculation of the Indian male to the Indians themselves. The ideological underpinning remains close to that of empire cinema of the colonial period. An emasculated Indian male could hardly match the expectations of a highly eroticised female like Victoria. Only a racially superior and virile man like Savage could be her fitting mate.

In uniting the half-Indian Victoria and her total identification with India with the English colonel, Savage, the film sought to contain not only the well-known contempt of Eurasians but also the overt racism of the British in India, which had contributed so powerfully to the growth of nationalist sentiments. This relationship also helped to present the British with their liberal, democratic and egalitarian ideals and challenged the charge that the Empire had been racist and iniquitous.

In making Rodney Savage opt for India, despite having the option to go home, the film introduces a fresh dimension to British imperialism. The colonisers' isolation from Britain and the constant reiteration that Britain was 'home' was turned on its head by making India home for the British. Savage's willingness to remain in the new India, suggested that India was and remained a much loved 'home' for the British. The concept of home justified British presence in India in a novel way. It may be remembered that in the 1950s there was a large British community in India. The India-as-home theme was taken up in the Raj nostalgia film *Staying On* (1980).

The long association of Britain with India is presented in a scene where Savage visits the grave of his female ancestor, who died during the Mutiny, to underline the generations of British men and women who had lived and died in India. Significantly, the author of this novel, just as the hero of the film, belonged to a family that had served in India for five generations. The heroine, Victoria, stands as a symbol and proof of this intimate relationship between Britain and India. The acceptance of Victoria (and her desire to stay in India) by Savage is an acceptance of British responsibility towards India. In the reigning political climate the film suggested a continuation of this relationship rather than a complete separation or drastic break. This film more than any other film represented Britain's hopes regarding its links with India and an attempt at the moral rehabilitation of imperialism and its colonial past.

In making this attempt, the post-colonial empire cinema carried forward what, indeed, had begun earlier in the colonial period itself: the reworking of major concerns like imperialism, nationalism, racism, and gender identities and relationships. This reworking sought to accommodate the changed realities without denying or negating the earlier portrayals in any way. This irreconcilable position merely confirmed the earlier images, ideologies and identities in new ways by subtly shifting the emphasis, without accommodating the point of view of the colonized. With the basic thrust remaining the same, the cinematic projections remained as remote from the former colonised peoples' perceptions and experiences as before.

Notes

1 A large number of scholars have commented on this. For a brief account of a body of historical writing that explicitly links empire and Britain's sense of national identity especially from the late nineteenth century to World War II, see P. J. Marshall, 'Imperial Britain', *The Journal of Imperial and Commonwealth History*, 23:3 (1995), pp. 379–94.

2 P. J. Marshal, *The Cambridge Illustrated History of the British Empire* (Cambridge, Cambridge University Press, 1996). See also

Lance E. Davis and Robert A. Huttenback, *Mammon and the Pursuit of Empire: The Political Economy of British Imperialism, 1860–1912* (Cambridge, Cambridge University Press, 1986). For a refutation of this view see Avner Offer, 'The British empire, 1870–1919: a waste of money?', *Economic History Review*, 47:2 (1993), pp. 215–38.

3 John Darwin, *The End of the British Empire: The Historical Debate* (Oxford, Basil Blackwell, 1991), pp. 1–9.

4 Marshall, 'Imperial Britain', p. 391.

5 In projecting this idea, the British were also concerned about distinguishing the British empire from its European equivalents: the fact that it was 'defensive rather than offensive', 'uniquely moral', 'less brutal' and the 'last rather than the first resort'. Other European countries 'oppressed their fellow citizens overseas' and 'drove them to revolt'. In the tropics, the Spanish and Portuguese imperial regimes were considered 'sleazy and corrupt', the Dutch 'nakedly mercenary', the Germans and the Russians 'brutally militaristic' and the French 'overbearingly chauvinistic' in imposing their own cultural values. The British alone, according to this viewpoint, ruled with a 'high-minded concern for the good of the ruled'. See Marshall, *The Cambridge Illustrated History*, pp. 371–2.

6 See *Report of the Film Enquiry Committee, 1951* (New Delhi, government of India, 1951), p. 49. After independence, this unfavourable reception of 'magic and fighting scenes' came to be officially incorporated in the censor policy of the government of Bombay. See *Indian Talkies, 1931–56*, Silver Jubilee Souvenir (Bombay, Film Federation of India, 1956), p. 81.

7 It is in the 'social' films of the 1950s that most scholars locate the articulation of an independent nation and its development. In this a major source of tension affecting the social and national consciousness was the problem of holding on to established norms and value systems while the nation made the challenging transition from a colonial backward economy and polity to industrialism and democracy. This genre, therefore, came to articulate the ambivalence of social attitudes to change and modernity.

8 Dorothy B. Jones, 'The portrayal of China and India on the American screen, 1896–1955', unpublished dissertation (Massachusetts, Center for International Studies, Massachusetts Institute of Technology, 1955), p. 75–6.

9 In works of fiction and drama by Britishmen in colonial and post colonial periods, Laxmi Bai emerges as the 'Jezebel of India' or 'Indian Boadicea', licentious and cruel. These depictions are used as

rationalisation for having killed her. For details of these works see, Joyce Lebra-Chapman, *The Rani of Jhansi: A Study in Female Heroism in India* (Bombay, Jaico Publishing House, 1988), pp. 135–3, 151–4.

10 Jones, 'The portrayal of China and India', p. 69. In some instances, even when, as in the case of *Bhowani Junction*, the script had been cleared by the motion picture advisor of India, it was not always possible to get clearance for shooting when this involved the active co-operation of the Indian government *Bhowani Junction* was eventually filmed in Pakistan.

11 After independence, with modernisation and industrialisation placing a premium on a more secular-scientific outlook, the overtly mythological film retreated into the background. Instead, as Chidananda Das Gupta argues, the popular cinema began to mythologise the present, creating new models of divine power invested in humans destined to protect traditional values. See Chidananda Das Gupta, *The Painted Face: Studies in India's Popular Cinema* (New Delhi, Roli Books, 1991), p. 166.

12 The members of Parliament in India condemned the mythologicals for 'trying to distort Hindu gods and goddesses and to depict them in such a manner as to bring them into contempt'. See Aruna Vasudev, *Liberty and Licence in the Indian Cinema* (Delhi, Vikas Publishing House, 1978), p. 108. In the colonial period C. Rajagopalachari had similarly condemned the filimic representations of Hindu gods and goddesses. See his interview in *Film India* (Nov. 1942), pp. 155–7.

13 Cited in Vasudev, *Liberty and Licence*, p. 87. The Madras government seriously considered this proposal. It favoured instituting a ban on mythologicals.

14 *Encyclopaedia of Indian Cinema*, compiled by Ashis Rajadhyaksha and Paul Willemen (New Delhi, Oxford University Press, 1995), p. 372.

15 See Ravi S. Vasudevan's insightful work, 'Dislocations: the cinematic imagining of a new society in 1950s India', NMML, Research-in-Progress Papers, second series, no. 89.

16 *Encyclopaedia*, p. 100.

17 This split, shown in the films of the 1950s, between pro-British and anti-British forces coexisting within a family had its resonance in the north Indian colonial situation. Similar splits were noticeable in a number of affluent families, especially those that had been recipients of British honours, titles and lands or those who were serving the British in professions such as the army and police. In the films of the 1970s this rebel hero became a cult figure in the person of

Amitabh Bachchan as the angry young man defying a corrupt law and state system upheld by his alter ego/brother.

18 According to the information provided by the British Film Institute more than ten films and several TV programmes on India under British rule were produced in Britain during this period.

19 The incorporation of the Indian states took place in two phases: just before independence and immediately after. Sardar Vallabhbhai Patel, who took charge of the new states department in Jul. 1947, together with P. M. Menon, as his secretary, used a skilful combination of baits and threats of mass pressure to make the states sign an Instrument of Accession with India (or, in a few cases, with Pakistan).

20 Denis Judd, *Empire: The British Imperial Experience from 1765 to the Present* (London, Harper Collins, 1996), p. 338. Commenting on the relationship of Edwina Mountbatten with Jawaharlal Nehru, Judd observes that 'it was perhaps entirely appropriate that the climax of the entanglement should be marked by an affair between the wife of the last viceroy and the incoming prime minister of an independent India.'

21 *Encyclopaedia*, p. 370.

22 Frank Furedi, *Colonial Wars and the Politics of Third World Nationalism* (London, I. B. Tauris Publishers, 1994), pp. 100–5.

23 *One Hundred Years of Magic, 1887–1987* (California, The Motion Picture and Television Fund, Hollywood, 1987), pp. 145–6.

24 This shared concern of Britain and the USA was reinforced by Britain retaining its importance as chief overseas market for Hollywood films. In the 1950s the television ownership in USA dramatically increased from nine per cent to eighty per cent. This reduced its domestic market for films by half, adding to the value of the overseas market. *Ibid.*, pp. 145–6.

25 The educated, middle-class, newspaper-reading public in India remembers how the British media had played up the assassination of the Mahatma and claimed that India had lost a precious life, which they had taken such care to protect for so many years. Many Indians felt the same. Communication from Vidya Vati, 9 Apr. 1997.

26 See Ravi S. Vasudevan, '"You cannot live in society – and ignore it": nationhood and female modernity in *Andaz*', in Patricia Uberoi (ed.), *Social Reform, Sexuality and the State* (New Delhi, Sage Publications, 1996), pp. 83–108.

27 The mother emerges as a central catalytic figure in a male world, shown to have a strong mother-fixation. The films of the seventies, like *Deewar* (1975) and *Trishul* (1978), both directed by Yash Chopra, portray a mother who both makes and unmakes her sons.

28 Women constituted ten per cent of those jailed for anti-British activities in the nationalist movement. See Hem Lata Swarup, Niroj Sinha, Chitra Ghosh and Pam Rajput, 'Women's political engagement in India: some critical issues', in Barbara Nelson and Najma Chowdhury (eds), *Women and Politics World Wide* (Delhi, Oxford University Press, 1997), pp. 361–79.

Bibliography

The author has made use of the following archives: British Film Institute, London; Film and Television Institute of India, Pune; India Office Library and Records, London; Maharashtra State Archives, Mumbai; National Archives of India, New Delhi; National Film Archives of India, Pune; and the Nehru Memorial Museum and Library, New Delhi. She has also made use of numerous additional resources including newspaper and film journal articles from India, the UK and the USA: Bombay Legislative Assembly Debates, 1934–1940; Central Legislative Assembly Debates, New Delhi, 1934–1940; Council of State Debates, New Delhi, 1927–1935; House of Commons Debates, 1932–1940; Indian Cinematograph Committee, Report and Evidence, vols I–IV, 1927–1928; and the Report of the film enquiry committee, 1951, New Delhi.

Books and articles (published and unpublished)

Adas, Michael, *Machines as the Measure of Men: Science, Technology and Ideologies of Western Dominance*, Ithaca & London, Cornell University Press, 1989.

Ahmed, Akbar S., *Millennium and Charisma Among Pathans: A Critical Essay in Social Anthropology*, London, Routledge & Kegan Paul, 1976.

——, *Pukhtun Economy and Society: Traditional Structure and Economic Development in a Tribal Society*, London, Routledge & Kegan Paul, 1980.

Allen, Charles, and Sharada Dwivedi, *Lives of the Indian Princes*, London, Century Publishing, 1984.

Allen, Robert C., 'From exhibition to reception: reflections on the audience in film history', *Screen*, 31:4 (Winter 1990), pp. 347–56.

Alter, Joseph S., 'Celibacy, sexuality and the transformation of gender into nationalism in north India', *Journal of Asian Studies*, 53:1 (1994), pp. 45–66.

——,'Celibate wrestler: sexual chaos, embodied balance and competitive politics in north India', in Patricia Uberoi (ed.), *Social Reform, Sexuality and the State*, New Delhi, Sage Publications, 1996, pp. 109–31.

Amin, Shahid, 'Gandhi as Mahatma: Gorakhpur district, eastern UP, 1921–22', in Ranajit Guha (ed.), *Subaltern Studies III: Writings on South Asian History and Society*, Delhi, Oxford University Press, 1984, pp. 1–55.

Anderson, Benedict, *Imagined Communities: Reflections on the Origin and Spread of Nationalism*, London, Verso, 1983.

Appadurai, Arjun, 'Number in the colonial imagination', in Carol A. Breckenridge and P. van der Veer (eds), *Orientalism and the Post-Colonial Predicament*, Delhi, Oxford University Press, 1994, pp. 314–40.

——, 'Putting hierarchy in its place', *Current Anthropology*, 3:1 (Feb. 1988), pp. 36–49.

Armes, Roy, *A Critical History of the British Cinema*, London, Secker and Warburg, 1978.

Babur-Nama (Memoirs of Babur), translated from the original text of Zahirud-din Mohammed Babur Padshah Ghazi by Annette Susannah Beveridge, New Delhi, Orient Books Reprint Corporation, 1970 [1922].

Bacchetta, Paola, 'The *sangh*, the *samiti* and the differential concepts of the Hindu nation', in Kumari Jayawardena and Malathi de Alwis (eds), *Embodied Violence: Communalising Women's Sexuality in South Asia*, New Delhi, Kali for Women, 1996, pp. 126–67.

Ballhatchet, Kenneth, *Race, Sex and Class under the Raj: Imperial Attitudes and Policies and their Critics, 1793–1905*, London, Weidenfeld and Nicholson, 1980.

Barnet, Correlli, *Britain and Her Army, 1509–1970: A Military, Political and Social Survey*, London, Helen Lane, Penguin Press, 1970.

Barnouw, Erik, and S. Krishnaswamy, *Indian Film*, New Delhi, Oxford University Press, 1980.

Barton, William, *The Princes of India*, London, Nisbet, 1934.

Baskaran, S. Theodore, *The Message Bearers: The Nationalist Politics and the Entertainment Media in South India, 1880–1945*, Madras, Cre-A: 268 Roypettah High Road, 1981.

Bhattacharya, Sabyasachi, 'Capital and labour in Bombay city, 1928–29', in D. N. Panigrahi (ed.), *Economy, Society and Politics in Modern India*, New Delhi, Vikas Publishing House, 1985, pp. 42–60.

Birkett, Dea, 'The "white woman's burden" in the "white man's grave":
an introduction of British nurses in colonial west Africa', in Nupur
Chaudhury and Margaret Strobel (eds), *Western Women and
Imperialism: Complicity and Resistance,* Bloomington &
Indianapolis, Indiana University Press, 1993, pp. 177–88.

Bond, Brian, *British Military Policy between the two World Wars,*
Oxford, Clarendon Press, 1980.

Bove, Paul A., 'Discourse', in Frank Lentricchia and Thomas
McLaughlin (eds), *Critical Terms for Literary Study,* Chicago,
Chicago University Press, 1990, pp. 50–65.

Brasted, Howard, 'The politics of stereotyping: western images of Islam',
Manushi, 98 (Jan.–Feb. 1997), pp. 6–16.

Breman, Jan (ed.), *Monkey Business: Racial Supremacy in Social
Darwinist Theory and Colonial Practice,* Amsterdam, V. U.
University Press, 1990.

Bromfield, Louis, *The Rains Came,* New York, Collier, 1976 [1937].

Callan, Hilary and Shirley Ardener (eds), *The Incorporated Wife,*
London, Croom Helm, 1984.

Callaway, Helen, *Gender, Culture and Empire: European Women in
Colonial Nigeria,* London, Macmillan Press, 1987.

Caplan, Lionel, 'Bravest of the brave: representations of "the Gurkha" in
British military writings', *Modern Asian Studies,* 25:3 (1991), pp.
571–97.

Caplan, Pat (ed.), *The Cultural Construction of Sexuality,* London &
New York, Tavistock Publications, 1987.

Chakravarti, Uma, 'What ever happened to the Vedic *Dasi*: orientalism,
nationalism and a script for the past', in Kumkum Sangari and Sudesh
Vaid (eds), *Recasting Women: Essays in Colonial History,* New Delhi,
Kali for Women, 1989, pp. 27–87.

Chakravarty, Suhash, *The Raj Syndrome: A Study in Imperial
Perceptions,* Delhi, Chanakya Publications, 1989.

Chakravarty, Sumita S., *National Identity in Indian Popular Cinema,
1947–1987,* Delhi, Oxford University Press, 1996.

Chandavarkar, Rajnarayan, 'Workers' politics and the mill districts in
Bombay between the wars', *Modern Asian Studies,* 15:3 (1981), pp.
603–47.

Chandra, Sudhir, *The Oppressive Present: Literature and Social
Consciousness in Colonial India,* Delhi, Oxford University Press,
1992.

Chartier, Roger, 'Intellectual history or sociocultural history: the French
trajectories', in Roger Chartier, *Cultural History: Between Practice
and Representations,* Cambridge, Polity Press, 1988, pp. 19–52.

Chatterjee, Partha, 'The nationalist resolution of the women's question' in Kumkum Sangari and Sudesh Vaid (eds), *Recasting Women: Essays in Colonial History*, Delhi, Kali for Women, 1989, pp. 233–53.

Chatterjee, Partha, *The Nation and its Fragments: Colonial and Postcolonial Histories*, Delhi, Oxford University Press, 1993.

Chattopadhyay, Ratnabali 'Nationalism and form in Indian painting: a study of the Bengal school', *Journal of Arts and Ideas*, 14–15 (Jul.–Dec. 1987), pp. 5–45.

Chaudhury, Nupur, 'Shawls, jewels, curry and rice in Victorian Britain', in Nupur Chaudhury and Margaret Strobel (eds), *Western Women and Imperialism: Complicity and Resistance*, Bloomington & Indianapolis, Indiana University Press, 1993, pp. 231–46.

Cohen, Bernard S., *Colonialism and its Forms of Knowledge: The British in India*, Princeton, Princeton University Press, 1996.

Cohen, Steven P., *The Indian Army: Its Contribution to the Development of a Nation*, Delhi, Oxford University Press, 1990.

Copland, Ian, *The Princes of India in the Endgame of Empire, 1919–1947*, Cambridge, Cambridge University Press, 1997.

Coultass, Clive, 'British feature films and the Second World War', *Journal of Contemporary History*, 19:1 (Jan. 1984), pp. 7–22.

Darwin, John, *The End of the British Empire: The Historical Debate*, Oxford, Basil Blackwell, 1991.

Das Gupta, Chidananda, *The Painted Face: Studies in India's Popular Cinema*, New Delhi, Roli Books, 1991.

Das, Sisir Kumar, *An Artist in Chains*, New Delhi, The New Statesman, 1984.

Davis, Lance E., and Robert A. Huttenback, *Mammon and the Pursuit of Empire: The Political Economy of British Imperialism, 1860–1912*, Cambridge, Cambridge University Press, 1986.

Dayal, Jai, *Go South with Prithvi Raj and his Prithvi Theater*, Bombay, Prithvi Theater Publication, 1950.

Diawara, Manthia, 'Black spectatorship: problems of identification and resistance', *Screen*, 29:4 (Autumn 1988), pp. 66–76.

Dickey, Sara, *Cinema and the Urban Poor in South India*, Cambridge, Cambridge University Press, 1993.

Dirks, Nicholas, 'Caste of mind', *Representations*, 37 (Winter 1992), pp. 56–78.

Diver, Maud, *The Dream Prevails: A Story of India*, London, John Murray, 1938.

——, *Royal India: A Descriptive and Historical Study of India's Fifteen Principal States and their Rulers*, New York, D. Appleton–Century 1942.

Dupree, Louis, *Afghanistan*, Princeton, New Jersey, Princeton University Press, 1973.

Dwivedi, Sharada, and Rahul Mehrotra, *Bombay: The Cities Within*, Bombay, India Book House, 1995.

Dyer, Richard, 'White', *Screen*, 29:4 (Autumn 1988), pp. 44–64.

——, 'There's nothing I can do!: femininity, seriality and whiteness in the *Jewel in the Crown*', *Screen*, 37:3 (Autumn 1996), pp. 225–39.

Eliot, T. S. (ed.), *A Choice of Kipling's Verse*, Suffolk, Methuen & Macmillan, 1983 [1941].

Elliot, J. G., *The Frontier, 1939–47*, London, Cassell, 1968.

Encyclopaedia of Indian Cinema, compiled by Ashish Rajadhyaksha and Paul Willemen, New Delhi, Oxford University Press, 1995.

Erdman, Joan L., with Zohra Segal, *Stages: The Art and Adventures of Zohra Segal*, New Delhi, Kali for Women, 1997.

Fanon, Frantz, *Black Skin, White Masks*, New York, Grove Press, 1967.

Farwell, Byron, *Armies of the Raj: From the Mutiny to Independence, 1858–1947*, London, Viking Press, 1990.

Fiske, John, 'Movements of television: neither the text nor the audience', in Ellen Seiter, Hans Borchers, Gabriele Kreutzner and Eva-Maria Warth (eds), *Remote Control: Television, Audience and Cultural Power*, London & New York, Routledge, 1989, pp. 56–78.

Forbes, Rosita, *India of the Princes*, London, The Right Book Club, 1939.

Fuller, C. J. (ed.), *Caste Today*, Delhi, Oxford University Press, 1996.

Furedi, Frank, *Colonial Wars and the Politics of Third World Nationalism*, London, I. B. Tauris Publishers, 1994.

Ginsburg, Carlo, *The Cheese and the Worm*, London, Routledge & Kegan Paul, 1980.

Greenberger, Allen J., *The British Image of India: A Study of Literature of Imperialism, 1880–1960*, London, Oxford University Press, 1969.

Greenhut, Jeffrey, 'The imperial reserve: the Indian corps on the Western Front, 1914–15', *The Journal of Imperial and Commonwealth History*, 12:1 (Oct. 1983), pp. 53–74.

Grossberg, Lawrence, 'Strategies of Marxist cultural interpretation', *Critical Studies in Mass Communication*, 1:4 (1984), pp. 392–421.

Guha-Thakurta, Tapati, *The Making of New 'Indian' Art: Artists, Aesthetics and Nationalism in Bengal, 1880–1920*, Cambridge, Cambridge University Press, 1992.

Gupta, Amit Kumar, *North-West Frontier Province Legislature and Freedom Struggle, 1932–47*, New Delhi, Indian Council of Historical Research, 1976.

Hansen, Kathryn, *Grounds for Play: The Nautanki Theatre of North India*, New Delhi, Manohar Publications, 1992.

——, '*Stri Bhumika*: female impersonators and actresses on the Parsi stage', *Economic and Political Weekly*, 33:35 (29 Aug. 1998), pp. 2291–3000.

Hatem, Mervat, 'Through each other's eyes: the impact on the colonial encounter of the images of Egyptian, Levatine-Egyptian, and European women', in Nupur Chaudhury and Margaret Strobel (eds), *Western Women and Imperialism: Complicity and Resistance*, Bloomington & Indianapolis, Indiana University Press, 1993, pp. 35–58.

Hauner, Milan, *India in Axis Strategy: Germany, Japan and Indian Nationalists in the Second World War*, London, German Historical Institute, 1981.

——, 'One man against the empire: the faqir of Ipi and the British in central Asia on the eve of and during the Second World War', *Journal of Contemporary History*, 16:1 (Jan. 1981), pp. 183–212.

Herbert, Charles, *Sexual Racism: The Emotional Barrier to an Integrated Society*, New York, Harper Colophon Books, 1976, pp. 57–144.

Hess, Gary R., *America Encounters India, 1941–1947*, Baltimore & London, Johns Hopkins Press, 1971.

Hughes, Stephen P., 'The pre-Phalke era in south India: reflections on the formation of film audiences in Madras', *South Indian Studies*, 2 (Jul.–Dec. 1996), pp. 161–204.

Hutchins, Francis, *The Illusion of Permanence*, Princeton, Princeton University Press, 1967.

Hyam, Ronald, 'Empire and sexual opportunity', *Journal of Imperial and Commonwealth History*, 14:2 (Jan. 1986), pp. 34–89.

Ibbetson, Denzil, *Punjab Castes: Races, Castes and Tribes of the Peoples of Punjab*, Delhi, Cosmos Publication, 1981 [1916].

Inden, Ronald, 'Orientalist construction of India', *Modern Asian Studies*, 20 (1986), pp. 401–46.

——, *Imagining India*, Massachusetts, Basil Blackwell, 1990.

Indian Talkies, 1931–56, Silver Jubilee Souvenir, Bombay, Film Federation of India, 1956.

Israel, Milton, *Communication and Power: Propaganda and Press in the Indian Nationalist Struggle, 1920–47*, Cambridge, Cambridge University Press, 1994.

Jackson, Martin A., 'Film and the historian', *Culture*, 11:1 (1974), pp. 223–40.

Jayawardena, Kumari, *The White Woman's Other Burden: Western Women and South Asia during British Rule*, New York & London, Routledge, 1995.

Jones, Dorothy B., 'The portrayal of China and India on the American screen, 1896–1955', unpublished dissertation, Massachusetts, Center for International Studies, Massachusetts Institute of Technology, 1955.

Judd, Denis, *Empire: The British Imperial Experience from 1765 to the*

Present, London, Harper Collins, 1996.

Kapur, Anuradha, 'The representation of gods and heroes: Parsi mythological arena of the early twentieth century', *Journal of Arts and Ideas*, 23–24 (Jan. 1993), pp. 85–107.

Kapur, Geeta, 'Mythic material in Indian Cinema', *Journal of Arts and Ideas*, 14–15 (Jul.–Dec. 1987), pp. 79–108.

——, 'Ravi Verma: Representational dilemmas of a nineteenth-century Indian painter', *Journal of Arts and Ideas*, 17–18 (Jun. 1989), pp. 59–80.

Kaura, Uma, *Muslims and Indian Nationalism: The Emergence of the Demand for India's Partition, 1928–40*, Delhi, Manohar Publications, 1977.

Klinger, Barbara, 'Film history terminable and interminable: recovering the past in reception studies', *Screen*, 38:2 (Summer 1997), pp. 107–28.

Kuhn, Annette, *Cinema, Censorship and Sexuality, 1909–1925*, London, Routledge, 1988.

Lebra-Chapman, Joyce, *The Rani of Jhansi: A Study in Female Heroism in India*, Bombay, Jaico Publishing House, 1988.

Lieten, Georges Kristoffel, *Colonialism, Class and Nation: The Confrontation in Bombay around 1930*, Calcutta, K. P. Bagchi & Co., 1984.

Low, Rachael, *The History of the British Film 1929–1939: Film Making in 1930 Britain*, London, George Allen & Unwin, 1985.

Ludden, David, 'Orientalist empiricism: transformation of colonial knowledge', in Carol A. Breckenridge and Peter van der Veer (eds), *Orientalism and the Postcolonial Predicament*, Delhi, Oxford University Press, 1994, pp. 250–78.

Mackenzie, John M., *Propaganda and Empire: The Manipulation of British Public Opinion, 1880–1960*, Manchester, Manchester University Press, 1984.

—— (ed.), *Imperialism and Popular Culture*, Manchester, Manchester University Press, 1986.

Markovits, Claude, 'Indian business and the Congress provincial governments, 1937–1939', *Modern Asian Studies*, 15:3 (1981), pp. 487–526.

Marris, Paul, and Sue Thornham (eds), *Media Studies: A Reader*, Edinburgh, Edinburgh University Press, 1996.

Marshall, P. J., 'Imperial Britain', *The Journal of Imperial and Commonwealth History*, 23:3 (1995), pp. 379–94.

——, *The Cambridge Illustrated History of the British Empire*, Cambridge, Cambridge University Press, 1996.

Martin, Gregory, 'The influence of racial attitudes on British policy towards India during the First World War', *The Journal of Imperial and Commonwealth History*, 14:2 (Jan. 1986), pp. 91–113.

Masselos, Jim, 'Bombay in the 1870: a study of changing patterns in urban politics', *South Asia*, 1 (Aug. 1971), pp. 29–35.

——, 'Power in the Bombay "Mohalla" 1905–1915: an initial exploration into the world of the Indian urban Muslim', *South Asia*, 6 (Dec. 1976), pp. 75–95.

Masters, John, *Bhowani Junction*, New York, Viking Press, 1954.

——, *Bugles and a Tiger*, New York, Viking Press, 1956.

——, *The Road Past Mandalay*, London, Michael Joseph, 1961.

Mayo, Katherine, *Mother India*, New York, Harcourt Brace, 1927.

Mechner, Joan P., 'On being an untouchable in India: a materialist perspective', in Eric B. Ross (ed.), *Beyond the Myth of Culture: Essays in Cultural Materialism*, New York & London, Academic Press, 1980, pp. 261–94.

Metcalf, Thomas R., *Ideologies of the Raj*, Cambridge, Cambridge University Press, 1995.

Moghadam, Valentine M., 'Revolution, Islam and women: sexual politics in Iran and Afghanistan', in Andrew Parker, Mary Russo, Doris Summer and Patricia Yaeger (eds), *Nationalisms and Sexualities*, New York & London, Routledge, 1992.

Morley, David, 'Changing paradigms in audience studies', in Ellen Seiter, Hans Borchers, Gabriele Kreutzner and Eva-Maria Warth (eds), *Remote Control: Television, Audience and Cultural Power*, London & New York, Routledge, 1989, pp. 16–43.

Mosse, George, *Nationalism and Sexuality: Middle Class Morality and Sexual Norms in Modern Europe*, Madison, University of Wisconsin Press, 1985.

Nandy, Ashis, 'Woman versus womanliness: an essay in cultural and political psychology', in Ashis Nandy, *At the Edge of Psychology: Essays in Politics and Culture*, Delhi, Oxford University Press, 1980, pp. 32–46.

——, *The Intimate Enemy: Loss and Recovery of Self Under Colonialism*, Delhi, Oxford University Press, 1983.

Nehru, Jawaharlal, *An Autobiography*, New Delhi, Jawaharlal Nehru Memorial Fund, 1982 [1936].

O'Hanlan, Rosalind, 'Imperial masculinities: gender and the construction of imperial service under Akbar', unpublished paper, 1996.

——, 'Warriors, gentlemen and eunuchs: maleness in Mughal north India', paper presented at the Department of History, Delhi University, 5 Feb. 1997.

Offer, Avner, 'The British empire, 1870–1919: a waste of money?', *Economic History Review*, 47:2 (1993), pp. 215–38.

Omissi, David, '"Martial race": ethnicity and security in colonial India, 1858–1939', *War and Society*, 9:1 (May 1991), pp. 1–27.

——, *The Sepoy and the Raj: The Indian Army, 1860–1940*, London, Macmillan Press, 1994.

Omvedt, Gail, *Cultural Revolt in Colonial Society: The Non-Brahmin Movement in Western India, 1873–1930*, Bombay, Scientific Socialist Education Trust, 1976.

One Hundred Years of Magic, 1887–1987, California, The Motion Picture and Television Fund, Hollywood, 1987.

Pandian, M. S. S., '*Parasakthi*: life and times of a DMK film', *Economic and Political Weekly*, 26:11–12 (Mar. 1991), pp. 759–70.

——, *The Image Trap: M. G. Ramachandran in Films and Politics*, New Delhi, Sage Publications, 1992.

Pant, Rashmi, 'The cognitive status of caste in colonial ethnography', *Indian Economic and Social History Review*, 24 (1987), pp. 145–62.

Pfleiderer, Beatrix, and Lothar Lutze (eds), *The Hindi Film: Agent and Reagent of Cultural Change*, New Delhi, Manohar Publications, 1985.

Prasad, Madhava M., *Ideology of the Hindi Film: A Historical Construction*, Delhi, Oxford University Press, 1998.

Pronay, Nicholas, and D. W. Spring (eds), *Propaganda, Politics and Films, 1918–45*, London, Macmillan, 1982.

——, and Jeremy Croft, 'British film censorship and propaganda policy during the Second World War', in James Curran and Vincent Porter (eds), *British Cinema History*, London, Weidenfeld & Nicholson, 1983, pp. 144–64.

Rajadhyaksha, Ashish, 'The Phalke era: conflict of traditional form and modern technology', *Journal of Arts and Ideas*, 14–15 (Jul.–Dec. 1987), pp. 44–77.

Ramasubban, Radhika, and Nigel Crook, 'Spatial patterns of health and morality', in Sujata Patel and Alice Thorner (eds), *Bombay: Metaphor for Modern India*, Bombay, Oxford University Press, 1995.

Ramusack, Barbara N., *The Princes of India in the Twilight of Empire: Dissolution of a Patron–Client System, 1914–1939*, Columbus, University of Cincinnati, 1978.

——, 'Cultural missionaries, maternal imperialist, feminist allies: British women activists in India 1885–1945', in Nupur Chaudhury and Margaret Strobel (eds), *Western Women and Imperialism: Complicity and Resistance*, Bloomington & Indianapolis, Indiana University Press, 1993, pp. 119–36.

Ray, Bharati, *Hyderabad and British Paramountcy, 1858–1883*, Delhi, Oxford University Press, 1988.

Reeves, Frank, *British Racial Discourse: A Study of British Political*

Discourse about Race and Race-related Matters, Cambridge, Cambridge University Press, 1983.

Reeves, Nicholas, 'Film propaganda and the audience: the example of Britain's official films during the First World War', *Journal of Contemporary History*, 18:13 (Jul. 1983), pp. 463–94.

Rich, Paul B., *Race and Empire in British Politics*, Cambridge, Cambridge University Press, 1986.

Richards, Jeffrey, 'Imperial images: the British empire and monarchy on films', *Cultures*, 2:1 (1974), pp. 79–114.

——, 'Korda's empire', *Australian Journal of Screen Theory*, 5–6 (1978), pp. 122–37.

——, and Anthony Aldgate, *Best of British Cinema and Society, 1930–1970*, London, Basil Blackwell, 1983.

——, *The Age of the Dream Palace: Cinema and Society in Britain 1930–1939*, London, Routledge & Kegan Paul, 1984.

——, *Visions of Yesterday*, London, Routledge & Kegan Paul, 1984.

——, 'Boys own Empire: feature films and imperialism in the 1930s', in John M. Mackenzie (ed.), *Imperialism and Popular Culture*, Manchester, Manchester University Press, 1986, pp. 140–64.

Rittenberg, Stephen Alan, 'The independent movement in India's North West Frontier Province, 1901–1947', Ph.D. thesis, Columbia University, 1977.

Rudolph, Susanne Hoeber, 'The new courage: an essay on Gandhi's psychology', in Thomas R. Metcalf (ed.), *Modern India: An Interpretive Anthology*, New Delhi, Sterling Publishers, 1990, pp. 323–41.

Said, Edward, *Orientalism*, New York, Routledge & Kegan Paul, 1978.

Sangari, Kumkum, 'Rethinking histories: definitions of literacy, literature, gender in nineteenth-century Calcutta and England', in Swati Joshi (ed.), *Rethinking English: Essays in Literature, Language, History*, New Delhi, Trianka, 1991, pp. 32–123.

Sarkar, Sumit, *Modern India, 1885–1947*, Delhi, Macmillan, 1985.

——, '*Kaliyuga, chakri and bhakti*: Ramakrishna and his times', *Economic and Political Weekly*, 27:29 (18 Jul. 1992), pp. 1543–66.

Sarkar, Tanika, 'Bengali middle class nationalism and literature: a study of Sarat Chandra's *Pather Dabi* and Rabindranath's *Char Adhay*', paper presented at NMML, 15–18 Dec. 1980.

Sarkar, Tanika, 'Bankim Chandra and the impossibility of a political agenda: a predicament for nineteenth-century Bengal', NMML, Occasional Papers series, no. 40.

Seiter, Ellen, Hans Borchers, Gabriele Kreutzner and Eva-Maria Warth (eds), *Remote Control: Television, Audience and Cultural Power*, London & New York, Routledge, 1989.

Sen, Indrani, 'Between power and *"purdah"*: the white women in British India, 1858–1900', *The Economic and Social History Review*, 34:3 (Jul.–Sep. 1997), pp. 355–76.

Seventy Five Glorious Years of Indian Cinema, 1913–88, Bombay, Screen World Publications, 1988.

Shah, Panna, *The Indian Film*, Bombay, Motion Picture Society of India, 1950.

Shah, Syed Waquar Ali, *Muslim League in North West Frontier Province*, Karachi, Royal Book Company, 1992.

Shankerdass, Rani Dhawan, *The First Congress Raj: Provincial Autonomy in Bombay*, Delhi, Macmillan, 1982.

Sharpe, Jenny, *Allegories of Empire: The Figure of Woman in the Colonial Text*, Minneapolis & London, University of Minnesota Press, 1993.

Shepard, Gill, 'Rank, gender and homosexuality: Mombassa as a key to understanding sexual practice', in Pat Caplan (ed.), *The Cultural Construction of Sexuality*, London & New York, Tavistock Publications, 1987, pp. 240–70.

Shohat, Ella, 'Gender and culture of empire: towards a feminist ethnography of the cinema', in H. Naficy and T. H. Gabriel (eds), *Otherness and the Media: The Ethnography of the Imagined and the Imaged*, Langhorn, Harwood Academic Publishers, 1993, pp. 45–84.

——, and Robert Stam, *Unthinking Eurocentrism: Multiculturalism and the Media*, London & New York, Routledge, 1994.

Singh, Surender, *Princely Life in Indian English Writing*, New Delhi, Reliance Publishing House, 1995.

Singha, Radhika, '"Providential" circumstances: the *Thuggee* campaign of the 1830s and legal innovations', *Modern Asian Studies*, 27:1 (1993), pp. 83–146.

Sinha, Mrinalini, 'Gender and imperialism: colonial policy and the ideology of moral imperialism in late nineteenth-century Bengal', in Michael S. Kimmel (ed.), *Changing Men: New Directions in Research on Men and Masculinity*, London, Sage, 1987, pp. 217–31.

——, '"Chathams, Pitts and Gladstones on petticoats": the politics of gender and race in the Ilbert Bill controversy, 1883–1884', in Nupur Chaudhury and Margaret Strobel (eds), *Western Women and Imperialism: Complicity and Resistance*, Bloomington & Indianapolis, Indiana University Press, 1993, pp. 98–116.

——, 'Reading *Mother India*: empire, nation and the female voice', *Journal of Women's History*, 6:2 (Summer 1994), pp. 6–44.

——, *Colonial Masculinities: The 'manly Englishman' and the 'effeminate Bengali' in the late nineteenth century*, Manchester & New York, Manchester University Press, 1995.

Smyth, Rosaleen, 'Britain's African colonies and British propaganda during the Second World War', *Journal of Imperial and Commonwealth History*, 141 (Oct. 1985), pp. 65–82.

Soila, Tytti, 'Valborgsmassoafton: melodrama and gender politics in Swedish cinema', in Richard Dyer and Ginette Vincendean (eds), *Popular European Cinema*, London & New York, Routledge, 1992, pp. 232–44.

Spain, James, W., *Peoples of the Khyber: The Pathans of Pakistan*, New York, Frederick A. Praeger, 1962.

Stacey, Jackie, *Star Gazing: Hollywood Cinema and Female Spectatorship*, London & New York, Routledge, 1994.

Staiger, Janet, 'The handmaiden of villainy: methods and problems in studying historical reception of films', *Wide Angle*, 8:1 (1986), pp. 19–28.

Stam, Robert and Louise Spence, 'Colonialism, racism and representation: an introduction', in Bill Nicholas (ed.), *Movies and Methods*, vol. II, Berkeley & Los Angeles, University of California Press, 1985, pp. 632–49.

Stead, Peter, 'The people and the picture: the British working class and film in the 1930s', in Nicholas Pronay and D. W. Spring (ed.), *Propaganda, Politics and Film, 1918–45,* London, Macmillan, 1982.

Stoler, Ann, 'Rethinking colonial categories: European communities and the boundaries of rule', *Comparative Studies in Society and History*, 13:1 (1989), pp. 134–61.

——, 'Making empire respectable: the politics of race and sexual morality in 20th-century colonial cultures', in Jan Breman (ed.), *Imperial Monkey Business: Racial Supremacy in Social Darwininist Theory and Colonial Practice*, Amsterdam, V. U. University Press, 1990, pp. 35–70.

Strobel, Margaret, *European Women and the Second British Empire*, Bloomington, Indiana University Press, 1991.

Studdert-Kennedy, G., 'Gandhi and Christian Imperialists', *History Today* (Oct. 1990), pp. 19–26.

Tendulkar, D. G., *Abdul Gaffar Khan: Faith is a Battle*, Bombay, Popular Prakashan, 1967.

Thomas, Rosie, 'Sanctity and scandal: the mythologisation of *Mother India*', *Quarterly Review of Film and Video*, 2:3 (1989), pp. 11–30.

Thompson, Edward, *A Farewell to India*, London, Faber & Faber, 1931.

——, *A Letter from India*, London, Faber & Faber, 1932.

——, *An End of the Hour*, London, Macmillan, 1938.

Vasudev, Aruna, *Liberty and Licence in the Indian Cinema*, Delhi, Vikas Publishing House, 1978.

Vasudevan, Ravi S., '"You cannot live in society – and ignore it": nationhood and female modernity in *Andaz*', in Patricia Uberoi (ed.), *Social Reform, Sexuality and the State*, New Delhi, Sage Publications, 1996, pp. 83–108.

——, 'Addressing the spectator of a "third world" national cinema: the Bombay "social" film of the 1940s and 1950s', *Screen*, 35:4 (Winter 1995), pp. 305–24.

——, 'Shifting codes, dissolving identities: the Hindi social film of the 1950s as popular culture', NMML, Research-in-Progress Papers, second series, no. 74.

——, 'Dislocations: the cinematic imagining of a new society in 1950s India', NMML, Research-in-Progress Papers, second series, no. 89.

——, 'Film studies: the new cultural history and the experience of modernity', NMML, Research-in-Progress Papers, second series, no. 105.

Woods, Philip, 'Film propaganda in India, 1914–1923', *Historical Journal of Films, Radio and Television*, 15:4 (1995), pp. 543–53.

Zutshi, Somnath, 'Women, nation and the outsider in contemporary Hindi cinema', in Tejaswini Niranjana, P. Sudhir and Vivek Dhareshwar (eds), *Interrogating Modernity: Culture and Colonialism in India*, Calcutta, Seagull, 1993, pp. 83–142.

Index

Note: 'n.' after a page reference indicates a note on that page.